NOURISHING THE NATION

11/6/22

For dear

Hugh &

Julie

Bon Profit!

Love

Veretin

New Directions in Anthropology
GENERAL EDITOR:
Jacqueline Waldren, Research Associate at the Institute of Social and Cultural Anthropology,
Oxford University and Director, Deia Archaeological Museum and Research Centre,
Mallorca

Migration, modernisation, technology, tourism and global communication have had
dynamic effects on group identities, social values and conceptions of space, place and
politics. This series features new and innovative ethnographic studies concerned with
these processes of change.

Recent volumes:

For a full volume listing, please see the series page on our website:
https://www.berghahnbooks.com/series/new-directions-in-anthropology

NOURISHING THE NATION

Food as National Identity in Catalonia

Venetia Johannes

berghahn
NEW YORK · OXFORD
www.berghahnbooks.com

First published in 2020 by
Berghahn Books
www.berghahnbooks.com

© 2020, 2022 Venetia Johannes
First paperback edition published in 2022

Library of Congress Cataloging-in-Publication Data
A C.I.P. cataloging record is available from the Library of Congress
Library of Congress Cataloging in Publication Control Number: 2019037819

British Library Cataloguing in Publication Data
A catalogue record for this book is available from the British Library

ISBN 978-1-78920-437-7 hardback
ISBN 978-1-80073-203-2 paperback
ISBN 978-1-78920-438-4 ebook

This paperback edition is dedicated to my grandfather,
Percy Preston-Lowe
(1918–2014)

and

My doctoral examiner,
Professor Marcus Banks
(1960–2020)

Contents

ഐം‍ളം

ILLUSTRATIONS

ACKNOWLEDGEMENTS

There are many individuals who were instrumental in the preparation of this book. In particular, I would like to thank my parents for supporting me throughout my doctorate, and encouraging me to pursue my research in Catalonia. I would also like to thank my husband, for being an irreplaceable presence at my side in the final months of writing. Thanks are also due to Prof. Emeritus Bob Parkin without whose invaluable advice, guidance and wisdom this work would never have come to fruition. Thank you also to the members of the University of Oxford's School of Anthropology and Museum Ethnography, including faculty, administration staff and fellow former students, who have contributed in some way to the development of this work. Finally, thank you to the anonymous peer reviewers for your time and invaluable comments on the early drafts.

Finally, I would like to thank the Catalan people themselves, whose creativity, tenacity and ways of life I celebrate in this work. I must extend a special thanks to my Catalan 'grandparents' Pere and Adelina, Noemi and the much missed Santi, Roger and Mercé, Berta and Jordi, Mon and Bernat, Marta, Cristina, the late Joan and their son Adrià, Josep, Jaume, my Catalan teacher Josep, Sat, her late mother Montserrat, Conxita and Irene, Pep and Rosa-Maria, Ramon of the Fonda Europa, Catalina, Carles and Ignasi, Jordi and Angels, Marina, Carmen, Jacinta and Juan, Pep, Magda, all the members of the Sardanistes Riallera and Boira, and the Gegants and Grallers del Carrer de la Riera of Vic. I would also like to thank the members of the Assemblea and Omnium Cultural, Toni Massanés and his team at the Fundació Alicia, the FICCG, the librarians of the Biblioteca Francesca Bonnemaison, and the many chefs and food industry professionals, who took the time to speak with me and contribute to my research.

NOTE ON LANGUAGE AND TRANSLATION

I will regularly include words in the original Catalan in this book, particularly where these words or concepts would be unwieldy to translate directly into English. Such words will be explained when introduced, and explanations can be found in the Glossary.

When using words in the plural, this is normally demonstrated by the simple addition of an 's'. However, where the word ends with 'a', this letter is removed and 'es' is added, e.g. 'escudella' to 'escudelles'. If the word ends in 'ca', then this is substituted to 'ques', e.g. 'coca' – 'coques'.

All quotes from informants and foreign language literature are my translations into English from Catalan or Castilian, unless otherwise stated.

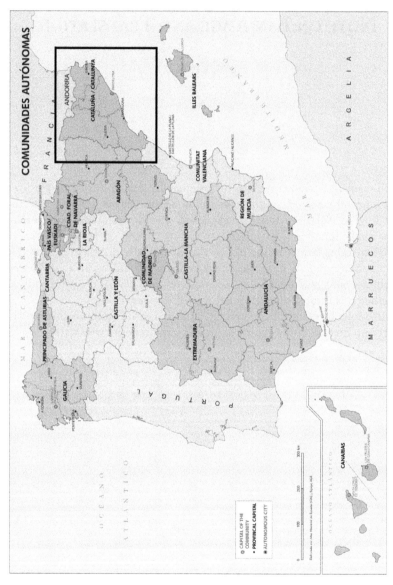

Catalonia within Spain. Instituto Geográfico Nacional de España, published under CC BY 4.0 licence.

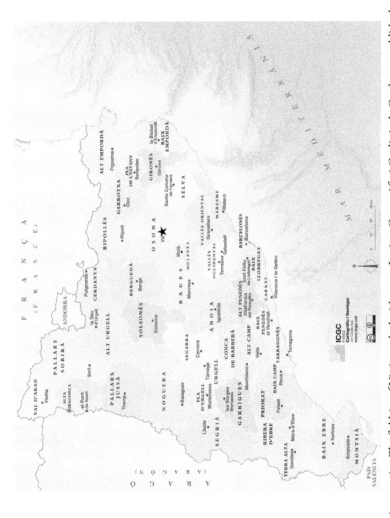

Catalonia and its counties. The fieldsite of Vic is marked with a star. Institut Cartogràfic i Geològic de Catalunya, published under CC BY 4.0 licence.

xiii

Introduction
Nourishing Catalan Nationalism

When I first arrived in Catalonia, in the summer of 2008, I was like most of the 32 million tourists who visit Barcelona every year. I expected a typically 'Spanish' holiday experience, to practice Castilian Spanish, and eat *tapas*. Yet it soon became clear that another language and identity was very visibly and audibly present, called 'Catalan'. Later, when my family and I travelled to Empordà, in the northeast, Catalan became even more prominent. In a small restaurant, we could find menus in Catalan, English and several other European languages – but not in Castilian. The food was clearly not the *paella* or *tapas* I had expected, but rich stews, combinations of meat and seafood, and fruit mixed with savoury dishes. This presence of a clear, strong,

Figure 0.1 'The Yolk of the Egg': Vic's Plaça Major (Central Square) in January 2018. Note the 'Free Political Prisoners' banner, and the pro-independence *estelada* flag on the town hall in corner of the square to the right. Photograph by the author.

Catalan identity intrigued me. Years later, as I studied nationalism during a masters in social anthropology at Oxford University, I was continually brought back to memories of a summer in Catalonia. My curiosity piqued, I delved further into Catalan nationalism for a doctorate in anthropology, to see how national identity is expressed in everyday life.

My aim here is to consider how food is used to express Catalan national identity in the Catalan Autonomous Community (CAC) of Spain. I seek to improve understanding of the lived realities (Llobera, 2004) of nationalisms and to do so through an ethnography of 'national' foods in Catalonia. I argue that, due to its quotidian and essential nature, food is an excellent means of studying the mundane, everyday, lived aspects of such movements. In doing so, I also aim to elucidate the ways in which food can be used to study nationalist movements more generally.

Ernest Gellner described nationalism as 'a theory of political legitimacy, which requires that ethnic boundaries should not cut across political ones' (Gellner, 1983: 1). While I believe this is a useful definition, the use of the term 'ethnic' begs a number of questions. I shall therefore draw on the anthropological sensibility of Benedict Anderson (1983: 6) that a nation is 'an imagined political community – and imagined as both inherently limited and sovereign', with cultural roots as the source of its power. His concept of this 'imagined community' is the most useful theory of nationalism when dealing with Catalan nationalism, especially in the arena of food.

The Catalan political theorist Montserrat Guibernau provides the most accurate definition of nationalism for the Catalan case, as 'a human group conscious of forming a community, sharing a common culture, attached to a clearly demarcated territory, having a common past and a common project for the future, and claiming the right to rule itself' (Guibernau, 2002: 3). Guibernau believes that nationalism itself is the 'sentiment of belonging to a community whose members identify with a set of symbols, beliefs and ways of life, and have the will to decide upon their common political destiny' (ibid.). Anthony Smith's notion of a 'common, mass public culture' and a 'common economy' (Smith, 1991: 14) as part of his definition of nationalism is also instructive in the Catalan case, because these are two fundamental parts of the Catalan national identity today, a fact that shall become apparent throughout this ethnography.

Now is an interesting time to study Catalan nationalism, due to recent political events, including the contested independence referendum of 1 October 2017. This event was the culmination of a rise in support for the Catalan independence movement within the Catalan Autonomous Community (henceforth, I will call it by its most common moniker 'Catalonia', or the '*Principat*'), which has gained force since approximately 2005 (Crameri, 2014). Nationalism has perhaps been one of the most enduring ideologies of modern times, rather than an example of false consciousness that will simply go away. Indeed, national identities have gained an almost untouchable reverence, and have 'acquired a privileged status as a resource or bargaining chip, a card which is difficult to trump, the defence of which does not have to be justified' (Jenkins, 2000: 159). Whilst globalisation produces weak states it does not accordingly weaken nationalism, and can even have the opposite effect as nations seek to reassert a political or cultural identity they feel to be at threat, perhaps due to globalisation itself (Pratt, 2003; Castells, 2004). Simultaneously, globalisation has also produced a renewed interest in local food cultures and traditional foodways (Freedman, 2007), which has ramifications for the construction of national cuisines (Ichijo and Ranta, 2016).

Despite the continuing power of nationalism and national identity in the twenty-first century, we are still lacking a consideration of their lived aspects (Llobera, 2004; Edensor 2003; MacClancy, 2007), although promising steps have been taken with the consideration of banal nationalism (Billig, 1995) and everyday nationalism (Skey, 2011). Michael Billig's theories are useful in relating to Catalonia, although Catalan nationalism is a cultural, civic nationalism, as opposed to a state-based nationalism (Llobera, 2004), which is the focus of Billig's approach. For Billig, we need to understand 'why people in the contemporary world do not forget their nationality' (Billig, 1995: 7) outside of crisis moments, and how national identity becomes commonplace and routine. This is done by more subtle means, such as the hanging of national flags in prominent places, the language by which people think about nationhood and their situatedness in a homeland.

The shying away from studying the lived realities of nationalism may be thanks to Gellner's view that 'their precise doctrines are hardly worth analysing' (Gellner, 1983: 124), because nationalism springs not from a particular set of circumstances but from a common social condition. He did modify his position somewhat in later life, but still denied the importance of culture to nationalism (MacClancy, 2007). In cultural nationalisms, identity is borne by institutions and practices in civil society and the shared values inherent in such a society (Keating, 1996), thus it is important to gain an 'emic' understanding of why nationalisms occur (Pi-Sunyer, 1983). To do so, one must consider cultural dynamics, as purely economic and political arguments do not suffice. Jeremy MacClancy recommends that to study nationalism we must look at the 'everyday, unofficial nationalism' (MacClancy, 2007: 14), based not on politics, but on everyday interaction.

I am inspired by the late anthropologist Josep Llobera's (2004) call for a better understanding of nationalisms through the anthropological study of their 'subjective feelings or sentiments' and 'concomitant elements of consciousness' (Llobera, 2004: 188). As he bluntly states, 'We cannot make a scientific inventory of the social facts of nationalism, for the simple reason that we lack the basic building blocks: good monographic studies of nations' (ibid.: 184). He attempts to examine these cultural aspects of nationalist movements in his work *Foundations of National Identity*, a seminal work on Catalonia. With this ethnography I hope to contribute to these 'building blocks' by considering Catalan national identity (Catalanism) through the perspective of food. I do so against the backdrop of a fraught relationship with the Spanish state that has given rise to the pro-independence movement in Catalonia, a movement that has gained strength over the last decade and brought questions of Catalan national identity into sharp focus for the area's population.

In this introduction I will detail why I believe food is a beneficial means for studying nationalisms, including some useful practical case studies that provide pointers for Catalonia. I then give a brief history of Catalonia and the nationalist movement, which is essential for understanding the contemporary situation, which I will also describe. As a further introduction to Catalan nationalism, I will introduce some of its key components and symbols, which are useful for understanding the rest of this ethnography. Next, I will outline my methods for data collection, including an introduction to my fieldsite of Vic. Before outlining the rest of this book, I define my approach to questions of identity, performance and power, as well as the scope and limitations of this work.

Food as National Identity

Food might at first not seem an obvious choice for studying a politicised ideology such as nationalism. Yet, food is one of the fundamental ways that particular human societies have differentiated themselves from others and asserted a separate identity. The act of eating 'lies at the point of intersection of a whole series of intricate, physiological, psychological, ecological, economic, political, social and cultural processes' (Beardsworth and Keil, 1996: 6). Food is central to our sense of identity, a means of expressing in-group affiliation and delineating boundaries, demarcating insiders from outsiders (Fischler, 1988; Bell and Valentine, 1997; Ohnuki-Tierney, 1993). Food helps to reveal the 'rich and messy textures of our attempts at self-understanding' (Narayan, 1995: 64).

In seeking to study the lived reality of nationalisms, food as an everyday point of reference is a useful lens through which to consider such movements. Catherine Palmer (1998), inspired by Billig (1995), considers food to be one of three 'flags' or cultural objects with which national sentiments are associated in everyday practice (the others are the related concepts of the body and landscape). Jeremy MacClancy, based on his experiences in the Basque country, suggests that 'turning foodstuffs and dishes into bearers of national identity is a down-to-earth way to make an otherwise abstract ideology more familiar, domestic, even palatable' (MacClancy 2007: 68). This approach also applies to Catalonia, where questions of national identity permeate every aspect of life. More recently, Atsuko Ichijo and Ronald Ranta, on focusing on the specific topic of food and national identity, have claimed that:

> Practising and asserting national identity through food means making choices and decisions that provide direct links to, among others, the nation's perceived or imagined history, social traditions, culture and geography. Through these decisions and choices people get to 'perform the nation'. (Ichijo and Ranta, 2016: 8)

This performative aspect is beneficial for understanding modern nationalisms, which are increasingly viewed as continually evolving, changing processes, rather than as static objects (Raviv, 2015). On a practical level, food is also useful for entering informant discourses in national arenas as a more 'palatable' subject than controversial issues such as language or politics, which may alienate potential informants (a factor also recognised by Avieli, 2018). Choosing food as a subject of study is therefore both a research strategy and a research focus. I do not wish to argue that food is the most important delineator of Catalan identity. This role falls to the Catalan language, the most prominent means by which Catalans differentiate themselves from the 'Other', namely Castilian-speaking Spain. Still, like language, food is a thread that runs through all manifestations of Catalan identity, due to its ability to carry 'powerful meanings and structures under the cloak of the mundane and the quotidian' (Sutton, 2001: 3).

Useful terms of reference for this phenomenon (and which will be used throughout this work) are 'gastronationalism' (DeSoucey, 2010) and 'culinary nationalism' (Ferguson, 1998). Sociologist Michaela DeSoucey (2010), defines 'gastronationalism' thus:

> The use of food production, distribution, and consumption to demarcate and sustain the emotive power of national attachment, as well as the use of nationalist sentiments to produce and market food ... It presumes that attacks (symbolic or otherwise) against a nation's food practices are assaults on heritage and culture, not just on the food item itself. (DeSoucey, 2010: 433)

DeSoucey recognises that gastronationalism often acts as a tool for state intervention, something that has also been recognised by Ichijo and Ranta (2016) and Di Giovine and Brulotte (2014). The protection of certain foods as carriers of national identity, even in the face of international criticism (or *because* of it, as in the case of *foie gras*), is a means of protecting the nation. As Ferguson (1998) has demonstrated when considering the development of French cuisine in the nineteenth century, this process can work both externally and internally. As French cuisine developed its international reputation for excellence, so too did the cuisine of the centre (as well as language and norms) become imposed on the periphery to create a unified French nation that subsumed regional products and dishes into the whole (Ferguson, 1988).

On regional cuisines, there is some debate about when the regional becomes national, and vice-versa. Sidney Mintz (1996) categorically stated that national cuisines cannot exist, because cuisines belong to a region, never a country. So-called national cuisine can only exist in contrast to some other national cuisine, 'a holistic artifice based on the foods of the people who live inside some political system, such as France or Spain' (Mintz, 1996: 104). The illusion of national cuisines remains because regions contribute chefs and ideas. While perceptive (one can draws parallels to the raising of folk culture to national culture – Gellner, 1983), Mintz is arguably too keen to oversimplify reality by presuming the existence of a nation-state, while forgetting that states may contain more than one nation (like Spain). Despite his shortcomings, Mintz's concept of 'signature foods' (1996: 7) is a useful one for this work. These are foods positioned within the histories of those who have eaten them, through which they become 'conditioned with meaning'. Through regular consumption, a population comes to consider themselves experts on this cuisine.

Rachel Laudan (2013) agrees with Mintz that familiarity is a basic element of cuisines in the milieu where they are eaten, but she also accepts the existence of national cuisines. I will adopt her definition of national cuisine henceforth:

> A national cuisine is usually thought to be one which is familiar to all citizens, eaten by all of them, at least on occasion, and found across the entire national territory, perhaps with regional variations. It is assumed to have a long continuous history, and to reflect and contribute to the national character. (Laudan, 2013: 324)

While accepting the existence of national cuisines (as an example of 'invented tradition', Hobsbawm, 1983) she highlights that these cuisines are recent, nineteenth-century constructions. The modern concept of national cuisines came into being with the arrival of nation-states. In this period, the centralisation of the nation-state, industrialisation, internationalisation and urbanisation were all intertwined, leading to the rise of 'middling cuisines' and homogenous eating habits and diets. By the early-twentieth century, national cuisines were a useful tool for citizens to understand the abstract concept of their own or others' national identities.

Ichijo and Ranta (2016) have systematically addressed the relationship between national identity, nationalism and food. Like MacClancy, they argue that the study of food and nationalism 'sheds light on a variety of dimensions of politics and the way it matters to us' (Ichijo and Ranta, 2016: 1), as a form of 'everyday nationalism'. They approach the topic from three areas: unofficial/bottom up (phenomena that are not controlled by the nation-state), official/top-down (mediated by the nation-state, i.e. 'gastronationalism' *sensu strictu*) and at the global level (how the nation-state interacts with global actors via food). While I believe their approach somewhat dichotomises social reality, (it may not be possible to neatly categorise every instance of the interaction between food and nationalism), and I take a broader interpretation of gastronationalism than either theirs or DeSoucey's (that it can be used to describe sentiments from the bottom up), some of their conclusions are highly relevant for this work.

Gastronationalism in Action

There have been few in-depth, direct studies of the intersection of food and national identity, and such literature has often been a by-product of other research. That said, this situation has begun to change in recent years. Wilk's work (1999) on Belizean cuisine is a key text in understanding national cuisine and identity. Belizean nationalism is comparatively young (they achieved independence in 1981), and in cross-national encounters it became clear that a cohesive national cuisine was necessary to present Belize as a nation on a global scale. Thus, interactions with globalisation were essential for developing Belizean national cuisine. Often, national foods were former festival foods, or 'poor' dishes that were converted into national cuisine – a similar process to that of international Italian cuisine (Helstosky, 2004). Goody (1982) recognised a comparable process amongst Ghanaian elites, who showed a preference for local as opposed to European foods to oppose colonial rule.

Two contributions from José Sobral and Maria Yotova in Domingos, Sobral and West's *Food Between the Country and the City: Ethnographies of a Changing Global Foodscape* (2014) raise the questions of both the idealisation of rurality (and, by implication, the past) as well as the importance of social changes, and global trends, in the industrialisation of food. Sobral demonstrates that in the nineteenth century the countryside was defended as a cradle of authentic Portuguese national cuisine. As in the rest of Europe, this occurred against a background of cultural and political nationalism that gained pace with urbanisation. The rural linked both past and present as the only place to grow proper Portuguese products for use in 'traditional' cuisine. More recently, Portugal saw a rejection of fast food and demand for so-called traditional foods and 'authentic' cuisine towards the end of the twentieth century, part of a global criticism of the agro-food industry (Belasco, 2007; Pratt, 2007).

The rural ideal also plays a part in Yotova's account of Bulgarian yoghurt in national identity construction. The rural is made manifest in the figure of the grandmother and of old-fashioned 'grandmother's yoghurt' (DeSoucey, 2010, noted a similar role of grandmother's in *foie gras* production). The village is seen as the cradle of Bulgarian national identity, and as in Portugal it is these places that are regarded as keeping culinary traditions alive. Despite this official discourse, modernity is crucial to the development of this narrative. The industrialisation of food in the Communist era was essential for creating this 'traditional' food, when a formerly regional, seasonal product could finally become an everyday 'source of national essence' (Yotova, 2014: 177). Bulgaria and Portugal also show well how food and cuisine becomes intimately connected with notions of landscape and territory, artefacts that feature frequently in nationalist ideologies.

Sobral recognises the important role of cookbooks in national cuisine and places them in parallel with B. Anderson's concept of imagined communities, by their 'establishing boundaries and identifying certain dishes and recipes as national; hence, they are a powerful instrument for the reification of national cuisines' (Sobral, 2014: 150). Arjun Appadurai (1988) has contributed substantially to the discussion of cookbooks as creators and disseminators of national cuisine (his work is discussed in more detail in the next chapter). MacClancy (2007) also dedicates an entire chapter in his ethnography of Basque nationalism to this subject.

Like DeSoucey (2010), MacClancy also considers the political dimension of the promotion of cuisine by politicians. As a key part of European identities, food and drink has been central to many of the policies of the EEC and CAP (Delamont, 1995), and the decision to protect certain products can become a means of self-promotion and national identity assertion, for example, feta cheese in Greece when opposed to Danish 'feta' (Sutton, 2001; DeSoucey 2010). In this case, foods express national identities in the context of the European Union, a phenomenon also noted by Klumbyte (2009) with the 'Euro' versus 'Soviet' brand sausage in Lithuania. As Leitch (2003: 442) has pointed out, 'food and identity are becoming like the 'Euro,' a single common discursive currency through which to debate Europeaness and the implications of economic globalization'. National foods can appear in cases of 'gastrodiplomacy', a top-down gastronationalism strategy considered by Ichijo and Ranta (2016) in the case of Global Thai initiative.

Clearly, a connection with the past is a common feature in discussions about national cuisine. David Sutton (2001) considers the relationship between the senses and memory on the Greek island of Kalymnos, where food plays a leading role. He briefly discusses B. Anderson's theory of an imagined community, but finds it too limiting in a practical, emotional, lived sense. Inspired by Billig (1995) Sutton believes that something more embodied (i.e. food) is required to prevent people forgetting their national identity alongside many other shifting identities. Food creates memories that can be significant on an individual and regional level, which become national with travel, migration and interaction with non-Greek communities. His work is part of a corpus of 'anthropology of the senses', which has much relevance to the anthropological study of food. However, I have found it less useful for the study of Catalan gastronationalism. Based on the experiences of fieldwork, it appeared that shared senses, while important for the individual and familial experience of food, were less relevant in creating national identity affiliation.

Roland Barthes sees food advertising in France as showing clearly that 'food permits a person ... to partake each day of the national past' (Barthes, 1961: 27). This fact has come into sharp relief with the development of heritage cuisines, particularly as intangible heritage for humanity in recent UNESCO designations. According to Michael Di Giovine and Ronda Brulotte (2014), in the introduction to their *Edible Identities: Food as Cultural Heritage*, food becomes heritage when it has the capacity to bind groups together in commensal spaces that may stretch across space and time, allowing groups to feel a connectedness with their ancestral past. The same could also be said of national foods. The commercial interests at stake in these designations should not be ignored, nor their ramifications at a governmental level. At the same time, most of these 'local foodways' (French, Mexican, Mediterranean) have international recognition and a tourist industry (downplayed during the nominations). Kim (2016) on Korean Kimchi, recognised as a UNESCO intangible heritage in 2013, has demonstrated that the food's association with Korea was a result of concerted efforts by the Korean government to 'establish *kimchi* as the embodiment of Korean culture and identity' (Kim, 2016: 40). Despite the application presenting *kimchi* as an ancestral, authentic product, the industrialisation of *kimchi*, and international competition with Japan and China, were crucial in *kimchi*'s development as a national food. Ichijo and Ranta (2016) have considered the role of national entrepreneurs in developing culinary imagined communities in regard to the British catering industry. Yet more interesting is their conclusion that these applications may be symptomatic of an underlying identity crisis.

Several contributions from Hanna Garth's (2013) *Food and Identity in the Caribbean* are also instructive. Schacht (2013) describes how the hardy cassava plant and its fruit have come to symbolise the Makushi people of Guyana, as a 'we food'. Cassava consumption differentiates Makushi from other Guyanese groups, indicating how foods can come to represent peoples symbolically. Considering Guyana more generally, Richards-Greaves (2013) describes how the Guyanese in turn claim difference from other Caribbean cuisines through their combination of spices and culinary procedures, the flavour of their food and the insistence on homegrown produce. This is also seen in Cuba (Garth, 2013b), where the emphasis is also placed on food grown in a particular region associated with its history (though ironically Cuba imports most of its food). Cuba has its own dish that represents national identity, the *ajiaco*, a stew that contains a variety of different ingredients that symbolise the Cuban people. In both Cuba and Guyana, the culinary *combinations* of food give dishes a unique, national character, even if their ingredients are foreign (a similar process occurs in Catalonia, which shares its ingredients with much of the Mediterranean, but has unusual food combinations – Vackimes, 2013).

Also in South America, Jane Fajans' (2012) ethnography *Brazilian Food: Race, Class and Identity in Regional Cuisines*, considers how the regional interacts with the national, and the global, through cuisine. She describes the processes some foods have undergone to change from regional to national or global foods, or how others symbolically represent the nation itself (e.g. rice and beans as symbol of racial mixing). Inspired by B. Anderson, she underlines the importance of everyday foods as national foods, but also of foods eaten regularly on special occasions, e.g. *feijoada* for Saturday lunch: '*feijoada* is eaten by "everyone" at the same time on the same day, thus allowing everyone to embody and share its essence and identity' (Fajans, 2012: 96).

Feijoada's history as a poor dish, associated with slaves, also helped its status. However, the more complex class relations implicit in the historical consumption and preparation of this dish are de-emphasised, another common theme in the development of national foods. Fajans also considers the role of the restaurant industry in the preservation of regional cuisines, which has implications of class, self-consciousness and culinary evolution. Finally, she emphasises the important role that migration, internationalism and tourism have on the creation of different perceptions of the 'national'.

Steffan Igor Ayora-Diaz's (2012) work on cuisine and identity in the Yucatan provides a parallel with Catalonia. Both regions have a unique identity, the result of historical developments, and both see the imposition of a central Mexican or Spanish national identity as a homogenising, threatening and even neo-colonialist force, which attempted to silence regional differences, or co-opt aspects of regional cuisines to become national. In both regions, the regional elite in the nineteenth century had enough power and resources to resist this force and assert their own heterogeneity, although support for separatism in the Yucatan withered, unlike in Catalonia. In the Yucatan, two forms of cuisine have resulted from this situation: the culinary and the gastronomic fields. In the first, there is an emphasis on cosmopolitanism, openness and the adaption of different cultural traditions to local tastes, and this implies an inclusivity and progressiveness – a situation that is likewise idealised in Catalonia (which I discuss further in Chapter Three). The second is the gastronomic field, which was inspired by the dishes of local communities using local ingredients, creating a more restrictive, exclusive cuisine unique and one specific to the Yucatan, with specific rules, techniques and aesthetics. In this context, Yucatan identity and gastronomy served two purposes: 'on the one hand, they underline the specificities of local culture and society and local–cosmopolitan relations, on the other, they affirm the Yucatecans' opposition and resistance to central Mexican culture and power structures' (Ayora-Diaz, 2012: 26).

Emiko Ohnuki-Tierney's *Rice as Self* (1993) follows the history of rice in Japan and its centrality in Japanese identity. Of particular significance is the image of the rice paddy and its landscape. Rice cultivation represents not just 'our food', but also 'our land', as well as the common theme of a glorification of rural life. Land and seasonality become connected with national identity through food and agriculture.

Finally, there has been an increased focus in recent years on gastronationalism in Israel. Yael Raviv's *Falafel Nation* (2015) and Nir Avieli's (2018) ethnography *Food and Power* both provide contrasting insights into the role of food in the development of an Israeli national identity over the last century. Raviv's approach to both food and national culture as a process that is continually reforming and evolving is beneficial to understanding the intersection of food and national identity. Liora Gvion's *Beyond Hummus and Falafel* (2012) focuses on how the Palestinian community in Israel uses food to assert their identity in contrast to the dominant, Zionist state narrative, a situation that in some ways (though not others) parallels that of Catalonia within Spain.

The presence of this newly emergent body of literature is a sign that the intersection of food and national identity is an increasingly relevant one in studies of food in society, identity politics and nationalism, particularly the everyday realities of nationalist movements. In all these examples, food provides a mirror through which to study national identities and surrounding issues. The relationship between the regional and national, urban–rural relations, the role of history and the idealisation of the past, the influence of governmental structures, the influence of globalisation and the creation of identity through difference are all factors that play into this topic, and will be relevant to the discussion in later chapters.

A Brief History of Catalonia

There is a massive literature on Catalan history, and much work on Catalan identity has had a strong historical element to it. As a shared history is so central to contemporary Catalanism, it is sometimes difficult to separate objective history from nationalistic narratives (Bray, 2011). In the words of the anthropologist Gary W. McDonogh, 'the development of historiography in modern Catalonia has reflected that of economic and political life' (McDonogh, 1986: 33). The earliest document to refer to the Catalan people by name dates from 1117. The oldest written text to be written entirely in a recognisable form of Catalan dates from 1131. There is still uncertainty over the origin of the name 'Catalonia', but a popular view holds that it originates from 'Gothalonia', a reference to the pre-Islamic Visigothic period (Chaytor, 1933).

In 1137 Aragon was united with Catalonia through a dynastic union. Thanks to a flourishing empire that included at various times Sicily, Sardinia, Naples, Malta and parts of Greece, Catalonia–Aragon became prosperous through its principle port of Barcelona. In 1283, Pere III (who has the epithet of 'the Great' in Catalonia) officially instituted the Catalan Corts (or Court), by which his descendants would be bound. The Corts convened once a year, and in the mid-fourteenth century the Corts created a new governing body to act outside of usual sessions, the Generalitat, or Parliament.

Despite its position as one of the wealthiest countries in Europe at the time, this did not make it immune to the crisis of the late Middle Ages. In 1410, Martin I, the last King of Aragon of Catalan extraction, died without an heir. Many pro-Catalan historians have blamed Catalonia's decline on the subsequent Compromise of Caspe, whereby the Castilian Ferdinand of Trastamara was elected to take the throne. The uneasy relationship between the Corts and their new rulers often led to outright revolt.

With the marriage of Ferdinand's grandson, Ferdinand of Aragon, to Isabella of Castile (becoming the Catholic monarchs), the creation of a unified Spain began. In 1486, the year in which Columbus reached the New World, Catalan merchants were expelled from the Casa de Contratación in Seville, the commercial heart of the city that was soon to have exclusive rights over trade with the New World. This was to set the tone for the treatment of the Catalans where trade with America was concerned. Elliott (1963) takes the view that this exclusion was key to the continued presence of separate Catalan identity, as it officially encouraged a continued sense of difference.

As Catalonia's splendour waned, so Castile's grew, along with Catalan resentment. Catalans 'felt themselves being gradually and irrevocably elbowed out of the many lucrative offices in the Monarchy' (Elliott, 1963: 13). Still, towards the end of the fifteenth century, Catalonia saw some stability after the turmoil of the previous hundred years, even if this came with a sense of dissatisfaction that increased as the decades continued. This eventually manifested in the Catalan Revolt of 1640–1659, against the Count-Duke of Olivares' overuse of Catalan resources in the war with France, also called the Reapers War. This conflict is now celebrated in Catalonia's national anthem, *Els Segadors* (the Reapers). The war concluded with the Treaty of the Pyrenees (1659), ceding Perpignan (North Catalonia) to France.

In 1700, the last Spanish Habsburg monarch died without direct heirs, leaving the throne open to the French Bourbon Philip of Anjou (later Philip v). The Austrian Habsburgs and other European powers feared French dominance in Europe and challenged the Bourbon claim, precipitating the War of the Spanish Succession (1701–1714). Catalonia supported the losing Austrian faction, which accepted defeat in 1713. The Catalan armies continued to fight for another year, until 11 September 1714, when Barcelona surrendered after the gruelling Siege of Barcelona. The date is now celebrated as Catalonia's national day or *Diada*. The siege in 1714 has become a celebrated moment in contemporary Catalanism, and its tercentenary was commemorated in 2014. Today it provides an example of shared national myths that are 'common reference points which enable members of the nation to communicate more readily' (Hosking, 2016: 213).

As punishment for Catalonia's refusal to recognise him in 1713, Philip v abolished all Catalan institutions in the *Decreto de Nueva Planta* (1716), representing the end of a measure of independence from the absolute will of the Spanish monarch. The Catalan language was prohibited for official purposes, and later also in schools. Although these measures did have some effect, the process was hampered by the inherent weaknesses of the disorganised Spanish state, and many official documents were still written in Catalan into the nineteenth century. Catalan never stopped being spoken by the urban lower classes, or in the countryside (Keown, 2011b).

Following this defeat, Catalonia soon recovered and began a period of industrialisation that would reach its height in the next century. The end on the ban on trade with the Americas in 1778 lead to a massive increase in the markets for Catalan products, most of which were textile-based. The Napoleonic Wars briefly halted growth, but afterwards industrialisation continued at a faster pace. Underpinning all these changes was the emergence of a wealthy and powerful industrial–commercial bourgeoisie, who became the new power holders in the region (Gary W. McDonogh charts the rise and fall of this social group in his *Good Families of Barcelona* (1986)). Eager to flaunt their new social prestige through cultural works, and in common with similar industrial elites at that time, this group would be essential to the development of nineteenth-century Catalan nationalism. Another consequence of the rapid industrialisation was the development of a large working class composed of both native Catalans and immigrants (many from southern Spain), which mobilised rapidly (the first trade union appeared in 1840: McRoberts, 2001).

Catalanism was in no way a uniform phenomenon among the entire population. Catalan society during the nineteenth and early-twentieth centuries was heavily stratified, characterised by great social inequality between the bourgeoisie and the working classes, and differing political opinions to match. It was in the latter group that anarchist and communist doctrines found fertile support. The nineteenth and early-twentieth-centuries produced a litany of violent protests from this group, culminating in the Tragic Week of 1909, where forced conscription for one of Spain's colonial wars set off a week of violent anti-militarist, anti-clericist and anti-monarchist protests led by anarchist, republican and socialist groups.

It was the Catalan Renaissance (*Renaixença*), the nineteenth-century cultural movement that recovered Catalan as a literary language, which created the atmosphere in which Catalan nationalism was to flourish and provided the cultural foundation for a separate political existence (Balcells, 1996). As in other parts of Europe, the *Renaixença* was a literary movement, and the emergent Catalan literature implied dreams of independence, both political and linguistic. By the 1870s, everyday Catalan speech was acceptable in literature, but this highlighted the problems with a lack of standardisation and education in Catalan. Political autonomy appeared the best solution to achieve these goals. In brief, this concern over language was transformed into a distinct national and political identity in Catalonia.

However, there was a continued sense of political subservience in Catalonia at this time. Two of the main reasons why Catalan nationalism grew so rapidly were a slump in prosperity thanks to the loss of the Spanish colonies and markets, and anger at a political system that favoured Castilian speakers over Catalans (Crameri, 2000; McDonogh, 1986). While the Catalan Renaissance undoubtedly had a forceful effect, use of Catalan was heavily proscribed. For example, in 1862 Catalan was prohibited in documents drawn up by notaries, and in 1896 it was prohibited in telephone conversations (Hall, 2001).

1892 saw the founding of the first Catalan political party, the Lliga Catalana (Catalan League), which won an unexpected victory in 1901 (Brenan, 1990). In the wake of the break-up of the Spanish Empire, especially the loss of Cuba in 1898 (a key market for Catalan products), Catalanism seemed increasingly attractive to wealthier Catalans (Keown, 2011b). In the early-twentieth century, Catalanism found itself in a complex situation. Self-government (not actual independence) was at the top of the agenda, but Catalan politicians also had the dream of acting as role models for the modernisation of the rest of Spain (Keating, 1996). They attempted to promote

Catalonia as Spain's saviour – an idea that received short shrift in Madrid. In 1914 Catalonia was granted its own very limited self-government institution, the Mancommunitat.

Primo de Rivera's dictatorship (1923–1930) at first received strong support from the Catalan bourgeoisie. They hoped he would protect them from their own working class, who had made Barcelona a hotbed of left-wing factionalism (Brenan, 1990; McDonogh, 1986). It soon became obvious that Primo had no intention of honouring Catalonia's self-government, an embarrassment for conservative Lliga-based Catalanism that destroyed its credibility. The bourgeoisie realised too late that Primo would always have an ingrained mistrust of Catalans, even if they supported him.[1]

In April 1931, Francesc Macia (nicknamed '*l'Avi*', grandfather, in Catalan) of the left-wing Esquerra Republicana Catalana (ERC) proclaimed a Catalan republic. Three days later he arranged a deal with Spain's now republican government to settle for autonomy. In 1932, Catalonia gained its first statute of autonomy under the Second Spanish Republic, when the Generalitat was reinstated. This was not to last long, as the Spanish Civil War (1936–39) began five years later. The victorious Franco regime instituted a thorough repression of the Catalan language after the war, a fact that is essential to understanding the present-day importance of the Catalan language (Gore and McInnes, 1998; Llobera, 2004). Catalonia had aligned itself with the Republican side (the least centralist option), and in the eyes of many Francoists, to be Catalan was to be Republican.

Almost immediately, Franco's regime imposed linguistic restrictions on the use of Catalan, and by extension on Republican Catalan nationalism. All obvious linguistic manifestations of a separate Catalan identity, such as street signs, were removed and replaced (Gade, 2003). Public written and spoken use of Catalan was banned, books in Catalan were publicly burned and pulped, all Catalan publications suspended, and the Institute of Catalan Studies closed down. History books were rewritten to 'glorify centralism and devalue national minorities' (McDonogh, 1986: 35). Not only was Catalan completely banned in primary and secondary education, but Catalan schoolteachers were transferred from the region and replaced by Castilian speakers. The consequences of these measures were clearly felt in the early post-transition years when most Catalan speakers could not write the language (Crameri, 2000). Catalans were urged to 'speak Christian', and 'stop barking', after Franco called Catalan 'the language of dogs' (Wardhaugh, 1987).

The attitude of most of the population was passive resistance (Hargreaves, 2000; Guibernau, 2004; Llobera, 1989). It was within family circles that reading Catalan literature took place, and many middle-class families preserved small Catalan libraries. More generally, it was in the family that Catalan lore, attitudes and customs were passed down (Llobera 1996).

The Catalan language was deliberately preserved as a 'systematic resistance strategy' (Guibernau, 2004: 63). Ironically, one of the effects of Franco's repression was to make Catalan synonymous with freedom and rebellion. Some elements of Catalan culture were permitted in the later years of the regime but relegated to a folkloric curiosity. The term *folclórico* (folkloric) has a more loaded meaning in Spanish than its English translation, implying backwardness and irrelevance. Even today, there is still controversy about the UNESCO designation of *castells* (human towers) as folklore (Vaczi, 2016).

During the Franco years, another effective means of Castilianisation was to encourage the migration of Castilian-speaking workers to Catalonia in order to dilute the Catalan-speaking population. By the 1960s, Castilian-speaking migrants collected together in immigrant ghettos, where they had no need to speak Catalan or either linguistically or socially assimilate (Balcells, 1996). However, this had an unintended result: the speaking of Catalan took on an aspirational aspect; Castilian became associated with poorer, working class migrants, and Catalan with the wealthier, middle and upper classes, thus making it more attractive to second-generation immigrant families. An exception to this was amongst the very wealthy descendants of the industrial elite, who preferred Castilian in the home, in contrast to the Catalan of their recent ancestors, even while speaking Catalan in their workplaces (McDonogh, 1986).

In 1977, two years after Franco's death, a million Catalans demonstrated peacefully in Barcelona in favour of autonomy on 11 September, Catalonia's national day, proving that Catalan nationalism had not disappeared (contrary to the predictions of Hansen, 1977). Following the creation of the Spanish Constitution in 1978, Catalonia was given the status of an autonomous community, and the Generalitat was reinstated in 1979. Catalan was accepted as one of Spain's six official languages. The Generalitat (mostly lead by the conservative, Catalanist Convergència i Unió, (CiU)) began a cultural policy of promoting Catalan culture to ensure its preservation. Another, more covert, political goal for CiU was to differentiate Catalonia from Spain and allow the party to control Catalan culture and identity (Crameri, 2008).

Catalonia Today, and the Origins of the Current Crisis

Today, Catalonia is home to about 7 million of Spain's 47 million people. As one of Spain's wealthiest and most industrialised regions, at present it accounts for 19–20 per cent of Spain's GDP and a quarter of the country's exports (BBC, 2017a). Catalonia received 43.3 per cent of Spain's foreign investment in 2003–2017, the highest of any Spanish region (Stothard, 2017). 2017 however saw a 40 per cent fall in foreign investment, most noticeable in the latter part of the year (ACN, 2018a), no doubt due to the recent referendum. Economic disagreements, for instance the fiscal deficit between Catalonia and Spain (estimated at 8–10 per cent) have lent support to pro-independence sentiments. Catalonia owed about €72.2 billion (in 2016) to the Spanish government (Bosch, 2017), which would be problematic in the case of an independence vote.

The Centre d'Estudis d'Opinió (CEO) has monitored attitudes about Catalan identity and the political situation since 2005. These studies have shown a population where about half lean strongly towards a Catalan identity over a Spanish one. According to the most recent survey in 2016, 46.6 per cent consider themselves more Catalan than Spanish or just Catalan, 38.7 per cent equally Spanish and Catalan, and 10.9 per cent only Spanish or more Spanish than Catalan. This final figure has seen a dramatic increase since 2012, when it was just 5.8 per cent, suggesting a rise in pro-Spanish attitudes (Centre d'Estudis d'Opinió, 2016: 53), perhaps as a result of the polarising force of the pro-independence movement. Data from 2012 demonstrates that language has significant effects on self-identity, as the percentage of those identifying as only Catalan or more Catalan than Spanish rises to 75.5 per cent in respondents whose language of identity is Catalan (Centre d'Estudis d'Opinió, 2012: 38).

Since 2011, the CEO introduced questions on how respondents would vote in a referendum ('do you want Catalonia to become an independent State?'). The changing results over the last six years have shown subtle variations in support for the movement. In 2011, 43 per cent stated they would vote in favour, which rose to 56 per cent in 2013 (Crameri, 2014). October 2012 until December 2014 saw a peak in support for Catalonia as an independent state (Centre d'Estudis d'Opinió, 2018), and 2014 also saw the highest self-identification as either only Catalan, or just Catalan and Spanish (55.3 per cent. Centre d'Estudis d'Opinió, 2015: 56). By chance, this period coincided with my fieldwork, and may have been related to events in 2010, and the run up to the tercentenary in September 2014. Since 2014, the results on the independence question have been more mixed, suggesting a roughly even split between Yes and No. In October 2017, the CEO reported the highest support for independence since 2013 (48.7 per cent Yes versus 43.6 per cent No. Centre d'Estudis d'Opinió, 2018: 11). The most extreme divergence was in January 2018, which showed that 54 per cent did not want independence, as opposed to 41 per cent who did, the largest difference in four years (ibid.). This is probably the result of the uncertainty caused by the political crisis.

There are three main pro-independence political parties in Catalonia today, the Partit Demòcrata Europeu Català (PDeCAT), which platforms as Junts per Catalunya (JuntsxCat, Together for Catalonia), a centre-right, pro-independence political platform; Esquerra Republicana de Catalunya, (ERC or Esquerra), a left wing, pro-independence party; and Candidatura d'Unitat Popular (CUP, Popular Unity Candidacy), which is far-left and pro-independence. PDeCAT is a successor to the Democratic Convergence of Catalonia (CDC), which renamed in 2017 due to corruption scandals involving the founder, Jordi Pujol. CDC, in the form of Convergència i Unió (CiU, in coalition with the Democratic Union of Catalunya, UDC) was a force in its own right in Spanish politics, supporting state-wide ruling parties at national elections throughout the 1990s. Carles Puigdemont, who was President of the Generalitat during the 2017 crisis, came from JuntsxCat. Other parties primary in the political sphere include Ciudadanos (Citizens), a pro-unionist, centre-right Catalan party, as well as regional representatives of Spanish-wide political parties, the socialist PSC-PSOE, conservative Partido Popular (PP) and left-wing Podemos.

The main source of conflict between Catalonia and Spain today is the result of controversy over the Generalitat's 2006 Statute of Autonomy, which highlights most of the key areas of controversy in the relationship between Spain and Catalonia. It was intended to permit greater self-government, for example, greater control over judicial appointments, immigration and fiscal policy. Catalans were redefined as members of a nation, and Catalan given preference over Castilian.

The right wing Partido Popular and other bodies soon presented an appeal stating that 113 articles of the 221 in the Statute were unconstitutional. In June 2010, the Constitutional Court reached a decision in which fourteen articles were declared unconstitutional, and 20 altered. The alteration that caused the most anger in Catalonia concerned the court's decision that Catalonia's definition as a nation has no legal value, and it can only exist within 'the only and indissoluble unity of the Spanish *nation*' (Pericay, 2010; emphasis added).

Another important section the Court has removed refers to the money Catalonia transfers to other autonomous communities and the expenditure the Spanish Government makes in Catalonia. Conflict over financial issues has been a feature of Madrid–Autonomous region relations since 1979 (del Río Luelmo and Williams, 1999), and Catalonia has very little control over the funding it receives. Those seeking to change Catalonia's relationship with Spain, or end it altogether, have often brought up the economic argument. The 2008 economic crisis intensified these debates. Due to its comparative wealth in Spain (by GDP it is 22 per cent wealthier than Spain's average), Catalonia has a large fiscal deficit of 9.76 per cent (i.e. almost 10 per cent of earnings in Catalonia leave it and are not returned in public investment). This makes Catalonia one of the most heavily taxed regions in Europe (Gibson, 2010).

Following the ruling, a million and a half people joined a protest in Barcelona on 10 July 2010. Aside from fomenting independentist sentiments, the ruling had the effect of creating solidarity across political lines (Nationalia, 2010). All in all, the 2010 judgement only served to worsen a feeling of dissatisfaction with the central government, leading many to question the current model of autonomy. It should be said though that Catalonia has a high degree of autonomy, second only to Navarre and the Basque Country. The Generalitat controls environment, industry, agriculture, transport and commerce. Catalonia has its own police force, the Mossos d'Esquadra, which replaced the national police and Civil Guard in 2008. The Generalitat also performs a legislative function within Catalan Civil Law, which concerns mainly family and inheritance law (Mas i Solench, 1990).

In September 2012, Catalonia's national day (*Diada*) was the setting for a large-scale protest in favour of independence in Barcelona,[2] attended by about 1.5 million people, including myself. This event showed the clear shift towards pro-independence aims in contemporary Catalanism and emphasised raising international awareness. The Diadas of the following years played host to similar protests with inventive flair, such as a human chain across the Catalan coastline in 2013 (an act Vaczi (2016: 365) called 'ritual territorialisation'), or participants arranging themselves in a 'V' (for 'votar', to vote) across Barcelona in 2014.

As a reaction to the 2012 protest, the ruling President of the Generalitat, Artur Mas (CiU) announced a snap election on 25 November 2012 and platformed on an independence referendum. While CiU lost seats to the ERC, pro-independence parties made up half the Generalitat. Following a coalition between CiU and ERC, in January 2013 the Generalitat announced a 'Declaration of Sovereignty', stating that they would hold a vote on independence in 2014. The Spanish government rejected the proposal in April 2014, and Spain's constitutional court ruled the referendum to be unconstitutional in March.

In September 2014, Mas finally admitted that the referendum would be non-binding but would still symbolically take place. Once more, the Constitutional Court ruled this as unconstitutional, but an unofficial referendum went ahead. Results were 80 per cent in favour, although less than half of Catalonia's 5.4 million eligible voters participated. September 2015 saw new elections, with pro-independence parties platforming on a unilateral declaration of independence. This was to circumvent Spain's restriction on a binding vote, since it would represent a campaign promise. JuntsxCat (formerly CiU) and ERC (running jointly as Junts pel Si, 'Together for Yes') narrowly managed to gain a majority by forming an uneasy coalition with CUP, which has ended up pushing above its weight in terms of seats (CUP has 10 seats, versus JuntsxCat 31 and ERC 26). CUP's refusal to back Artur Mas lead to the election of Carles Puigdemont, former mayor of Girona, as President of Catalonia in January 2016.

The start of the current political crisis began in June 2017, when Puigdemont announced a referendum on Catalan independence for 1 October 2017, illegal according to the Spanish Constitution. Despite being blocked by the Spanish Constitutional Court, by late September it was clear that the referendum would go ahead anyway. In response, the Spanish Civil Guard initiated Operation Anubis, a series of raids on Catalan government institutions and arrests of Catalan politicians. 5000 members of the Civil Guard were dispatched to the region on 21 September in large ferries stationed at Catalan ports, a situation that seemed to many like an occupation.

The night before 1 October, to ensure polling stations opened, activists camped out in many overnight. The following day, as people attempted to vote, the Civil Guard tried to stop voters and forcibly closed polling stations, leading to violent clashes between protesters and police. This was in contrast to the Catalan police force, the Mossos d'Esquadra, who allowed polling stations to remain open, and which has led to investigations for disobedience, and charges of sedition against its leader, Josep Lluís Trapero Álvarez. 92 per cent voted in favour of independence, though turnout was only 43 per cent.[3] As a result of the referendum, the Catalan Parliament declared independence on 27 October 2017, with 70 votes in favour to 10 against (135 left the chamber before the vote). On the same day, the Spanish Senate invoked article 155 of the Spanish Constitution, which imposed direct rule over the region. The Catalan Parliament was dissolved, and Rajoy set new regional elections for 21 December. On 30 October, charges of rebellion, sedition and misuse of public funds were laid against Carles Puigdemont and other Catalan politicians. Puigdemont fled to Belgium with four colleagues on the same day. On the 2 November, fourteen former Catalan politicians were called to Spain's supreme court to testify on their role in the referendum. All except Oriol Junqueras (ex-vice-President) and Joaquim Forn (ex-interior minister) were granted bail. The internment of these politicians pending a full trial (they were deemed a flight risk) followed in the wake of the publicised arrest of two prominent pro-independence leaders, Jordi Sànchez, the president of the Catalan National Assembly (ANC), and Jordi Cuixart, the president of Òmnium Cultural, on 16 October. The plight of the four prisoners has engendered a popular support campaign, symbolised by the wearing of yellow ribbons.

The December political elections ended in a stalemate, despite a record turnout (80 per cent). Catalan pro-independence parties (JuntsxCat, CiU and CUP) had the joint parliamentary majority at 70 seats (47.5 per cent of the popular vote), although the largest party (36 seats) was pro-unionist

Ciutadans. Puigdemont technically remained President, however a Spanish court ruled that he could not take up his office without returning to Spain, where he faced arrest. Eight of the elected officials in the new government were also either in exile or imprisoned. Finally, on 1 March, Puigdemont agreed to step down in favour of detained activist Jordi Sànchez, head of the ERC. On 21 March, Sanchez likewise dropped his bid, after the Spanish Supreme Court rejected his request to be freed to attend the investiture ceremony. The role was passed to Jordi Turull (PDeCAT/JuntsxCatalunya), who was also under investigation for his role in the referendum. His leadership bid on 22 March failed thanks to lack of support from the CUP, who felt his manifesto was not radical enough. The following day, Mr Turull and four former members of the Catalan Parliament were arrested by order of the Supreme Court of Spain, before another vote could go ahead. Many of these politicians had earlier been freed in November, but it was decided that they were a flight risk and should be remanded in custody. This brought the number to 25 separatists who had been charged with sedition, rebellion, embezzlement and other crimes relating to the referendum. This number was reduced to twelve[4] when the trial began in February 2019. The trial closed in June 2019, and at the time of writing a judgement was expected in October.

Puigdemont refused to return to Spain, claiming that he would not receive a fair trial. The Spanish government sent out a European arrest warrant for Carles Puigdemont and other politicians, which lead to Puigdemont's arrest in March 2018 in Germany, where he was tried for rebellion and misuse of public funds. The former charge was dismissed; however, the latter was upheld, meaning he could be extradited. Eventually, Spain dropped the arrest warrant. A new President of the Generalitat, Quim Torra (also of JuntsxCat), took charge in May 2018, leading to the lifting of Article 155 in June. Torra is widely regarded as being even more separatist that Puigdemont. Meanwhile in Madrid, Mariano Rajoy's government lost power through a vote of no confidence from other parties, a result of his handling of the Catalan crisis, and political corruption. Socialist Pedro Sánchez, who took power in June, is more receptive to Catalan demands (support from regionalist and nationalist parties, including those of Catalonia, were instrumental to his power bid). Sánchez has even suggested a referendum on greater autonomy for the region (Stothard, 2018), although he gradually toughened his stance in 2019 (Hall, 2019).

The Catalan situation was one of the key issues in the Spanish general election on 28 April 2019. While Sánchez won the largest share of votes (29.6 per cent), at the time of writing he still needed to form a coalition government with other parties (including Catalan separatists) to form a majority and ensure his continued position as Prime Minister. Differences of opinion on political solutions for Catalonia have become a source of contention in these talks (Mount and Hall, 2019). The ongoing trial in Madrid of the twelve Catalan separatist politicians and public figures for rebellion, sedition and misappropriation of public funds has further complicated negotiations. The defendants include four recently-elected Catalan MPs, who were suspended by the Spanish parliament's governing body in May 2019 (Mount, 2019), a move which caused anger in Catalonia. At the time of writing, there still appeared to be no solution to the deadlock. What is certain is that while the political crisis of late-2017 has passed, the uneasy relationship between the Catalan and Spanish central governments seems set to continue.

Catalonia historically had strong support for the European Union, with its emphasis on 'A Europe of the Regions' (Llobera, 2004). In practice, within the EU, national Spanish initiatives easily overwhelmed those of the regions, and there have been arguments suggesting that the European Community has had a negative effect on regionalisation (del Río Luelmo and Williams, 1999). Many Catalans in recent years have felt that the EU has failed to protect them (Strubell, 2008). This sense of disillusionment has turned to outright anger following the events of the 2017 regional independence vote, with the European Commission's statement that the Catalan crisis is an 'internal matter' for Spain (European Commission, 2017). Recent protests in 2018 have seen a more anti-European sentiment (including slogans of 'This Europe is shameful', shouted during March 2018 protests outside the offices of the European Commission in Barcelona).

During my last visit in January 2018, anger directed at European inaction was a common point of discussion. During a fundraising dinner I attended, the teenage daughter of one of the imprisoned politicians gave a speech in which she described her bewilderment that these events could happen in Europe. This disillusionment has been compounded by treatment of Catalan MEPS following the May 2019 European Parliament Elections. Three exiled politicians, (former President Carles Puigdemont, Toni Comín and Clara Ponsatí), had originally been banned from running by the Spanish Electoral Commission, but were later permitted to do so by a Madrid court. Puigdemont, Comín and jailed Oriol Junqueras were elected as MEPs. Controversy arose after Puigdemont and Comín were refused entry to the European Parliament (EP), ostensibly because Spanish authorities had not sent complete lists of elected MEPs (in an attempt to resolve the situation, all new Spanish MEPs were later refused entry). Oriol Junqueras was also refused permission by the Spanish supreme court to leave jail and travel to Brussels to take up his seat. In response to the perceived inaction of the European Parliament, in June 2019 76 cross-party MEPs called for more action to protect the rights of the three Catalan MEPs. At the time of writing, the impasse remained unresolved.

Symbols of Catalan Nationalism

In this section, I will introduce and elaborate upon some of the crucial symbols of Catalan national identity. Being aware of these symbols is essential to understanding expressions of Catalan identity in everyday life, as they appear frequently in food-related discourse. This includes the Catalan language, national character, the Catalan flags (*senyera* and *estelada*), festivals and performances such as the *sardana* dance, *castells* and supporting Barcelona football club.

Language is a key symbol of Catalan identity. It is language that really separates Catalans from the rest of Spain (Crameri, 2000; Balcells, 1996, McRoberts, 2001). It therefore sets identity boundaries, provides a historical link and continuity with the past[5] and is the foundation on which Catalan culture is based. Due to its immediacy in everyday life, the association between language and identity occurs not only in political and intellectual discourses, but also in the popular mind. Catalans will not consider another person to be truly Catalan unless they can speak the language, and are comfortable using it regularly (Hargreaves, 2000; Woolard, 1986; DiGiacomo, 2001). Catalan politician and architect of modern Catalanism Jordi Pujol took the view that those who speak Catalan, and who live and work in Catalonia, are Catalan. Language has also been key to the claim of Catalonia as an open nationalism, willing to accept those who make the effort to learn the language and integrate. Considering the high levels of immigration to Catalonia in the last hundred years, and the fact that these groups generally have a higher birth rate than native Catalans, language-based identity has been far more successful than one based on race or birth.

In Spain, there are now about 4 million native Catalan speakers. Current statistics show a very high level of Catalan awareness amongst the Catalan population. In 2011, 95 per cent of the population understood the language, while 73 per cent could speak it and 79 per cent read it. Only 56 per cent of the Catalan population can write the language, but this is still an improvement on 1986, when only 31.5 per cent could write it (Idescat, 2013).

Learning and speaking Catalan are believed to bring out the characteristics of the Catalan character, or *seny*, in an individual. Language, and *seny*, are seen as making up the *fet diferencial* that differentiates Catalans from other Spaniards (Hargreaves, 2000). It is characterised by a sensible, rational, down-to-earth attitude, a business-like and hard-working approach to life. This is often contrasted with the supposed character of Castilian speakers, who at best are alleged to be more superficial and impatient than the reserved Catalans, and at worst lazy, profligate and irrational (Smith, 1996). Catalans also tend to see themselves as better educated and having more in common with the rest of Europe (Wardhaugh, 1987; Gade, 2003).

A Castilian-speaking immigrant who learns Catalan demonstrates the 'hard-working ambition and good sense that qualifies one as a genuine Catalan' (Woolard, 1986: 63).

The flip side of *seny* is *rauxa*, a propensity to seek relief from social constraints by excess and lack of control. It is said that this propensity has created the wild creative talent evidenced by Catalonia's many famous contemporary artists, such as Salvador Dalí, Joan Miró, or Antoni Tàpies, and in the food world vanguard chef Ferran Adrià and his acolytes (*Seny* means that these artists can profitably make use of these creative outbursts).

Seny is the positive side to the perception of Catalans as stingy, mean and money-grubbing in other parts of Spain (Catalonia's fiscal demands fit perfectly into this negative stereotype). So prevalent and widely accepted is *seny* in public discourse that a popular advertising campaign for the Catalan Banc Sabadell during fieldwork emphasised *seny* as a positive characteristic. More recently, the president of Banc Sabadell, Ana Botín, asked that *seny* should return to Catalonia in these 'difficult times' (El Nacional/Efe, 2018).

In contemporary Catalonia, there are two flags in use: the *senyera* and the *estelada*. The *senyera* is a simple design of four red bands across a yellow background. The *estelada* is a variation on the *senyera* with a blue triangle over the *senyera*, which bears a white five-pointed star (these two designs can be seen on the front cover). A variation of the *estelada* is a red triangle, instead of blue, which often represents left-wing political leanings. While the *senyera* represents Catalonia as a whole (it is part of Barcelona's coat of arms), and the *Països Catalans*, the *estelada* is unequivocally associated with pro-independence Catalanism. The origins of the *senyera* are hazy, but the four-barred standard as a symbol of the Catalan kings was in evidence by the tenth century, thus coinciding with the mythical beginnings of Catalonia. The *estelada* developed in the early-twentieth century with the move towards pro-independence attitudes in Catalan politics, probably inspired by the Cuban flag.

The *senyera* is a ubiquitous symbol in Catalan everyday life. It appears on balconies, graffiti, and is present on the huge selection of Catalan-themed memorabilia. However, since my research began, the independentist *estelada* noticeably gained in popularity over the *senyera*. This may be because the *senyera* is shared with several autonomous communities that are better integrated into Spain (e.g. Valencia), and is part of the Spanish coat of arms from the Crown of Aragon (Balcells, 2008). The *estelada* is a much clearer symbol of deeply felt Catalanism because it has not been used to promote any agenda unrelated to Catalan nationalism. Indeed, it is telling that when I tried to buy a *senyera* at the end of my fieldwork in Vic, I was unable to find one. Shopkeepers no longer bothered to stock them, as there was only demand for *estelades*. This 'war of flags' has been recognised in international news outlets (BBC, 2017b).

The *senyera* and *estelada* also take pride of place at popular festivals. These events are a 'culminating moment for the expression of national identity. Local events, celebrations, folkloric, religious and even pre-Christian festivals acted as a catalyst of nationalist expression' (Conversi, 1997: 155). Festivities in Catalonia can be divided into two types: national celebrations shared across Catalonia, and the more local or regional events and festivals. There are three national days throughout Catalonia. These are St. George's Day on 23 April, St. John's Eve on 23 June, and the September *Diada* on 11 September. Saint George is one of Catalonia's national saints, alongside the Virgin of Montserrat, and his celebration is associated with roses (Catalonia's national flower) and books. St. John's Eve is celebrated throughout Spain but has been Catalanised with the *Flama del Canigó* (Flame of Canigó) that is ceremoniously carried from the Canigó mountain to the rest of Catalonia to represent solidarity amongst Catalan-speaking areas. The September Diada remembers a traumatic moment in Catalan history, the end of the Siege of Barcelona in 1714. There is some interplay between the national and the local in these events, as national celebrations are celebrated with a local interpretation.

Catalonia's regional festivals, in particular the Patum of Berga, have been the focus of folklorist Dorothy Noyes. Her main work, *Fire in the Plaça* (2003), provides an account of the unique Patum ritual in Berga, held on Corpus Christi. She draws attention to the way in which regional and location-specific cultural acts are incorporated into wider Catalan culture, and how issues universal to Catalonia are manifested in localised acts. The festival has changed over time, following the changes in Catalan society and politics since the 1970s.

The presence of flags was also noted in John Hargreaves (2000) detailed account of the 1992 Olympic Games in Barcelona, a seminal event in modern Catalan history. His work emphasises the important role that Catalan identity played in the run up to the games and the event itself. He exposes the national and international politics at play, a scene dominated by simmering resentment between the Catalan and Spanish authorities, which never erupted thanks to careful diplomacy. Despite claims that the games would lead to cultural homogenisation, he believes that they represented a triumph of Catalan culture, and that they led to the stimulation of both cultural and economic development.

One way that the organisers of the 1992 Olympics marked the event out as Catalan was by the presence of the *sardana*, Catalonia's national dance, in the opening ceremony. This circular dance is particular to Catalonia, and is often seen at Catalonia's three national festivals, and at other events with a strong Catalanist focus. It is regarded as a manifestation of idealised aspects of Catalan character and *seny*, for its calm, measured and precise movements, concentration and diligence (Brandes, 1990). The dancer must count continually to remember which formula of steps to follow, which vary depending on each dance. As Noyes (2011a) remarks, the Catalans' stereotypical business aptitude carries on into perceptions of the *sardana*, as they count even while they dance. More recently, its form as a circular dance in which anyone can participate has made it a metaphor for inclusivity (Crameri, 2008). The *sardana* dates from about 1850, and the actual roots are unknown (Martí i Pérez, 1994), though it is reputed to originate from the staunchly pro-Catalan Empordà region in the north-east.

A further manifestation of Catalan identity are the *castells*, or human towers. Unlike *sardana* groups, which have seen reduced popularity amongst young people (ibid.), the *castells* have become increasingly popular in recent years. They originated in Valls, a town south of Barcelona, the point of origin of another now popular food event, the *calçotada* (spring onion eating). There are now many groups spread throughout Catalonia. Like the *sardana*, they too can be seen as symbolic of Catalan identity. Anthropologist Mariann Vaczi (2016), in her research on *castells*, described how the making of the tower, called *fer pinya* (making pinecone) is a metaphor for the resolution of political conflicts as participants come together in a shared enterprise. The construction of a tower requires mathematical precision and decision-making (again, manifestations of *seny*), and is open to anyone who is capable of forming part of the collective whole. Yet *rauxa* also plays a part in the creativity needed to construct truly difficult towers. The metaphor of *rauxa* is also appealing to *independentistes* who see too much *seny* and caution in Catalan politics. *Castell* building can 'condense the two faces of the Catalonian independence process' (Vaczi, 2016: 363). In 2010, the *castells* were also granted UNESCO intangible cultural heritage status, which has made them 'a desirable asset for a political movement that seeks to establish its authenticity' (ibid.: 356). *Castells* have also been used on food packaging to promote Catalan-made products.

When anthropologists have taken an interest in Catalonia, they have often focused on kinship. This has often been combined with studies of the home, which is unsurprising considering that the house is one of the most powerful symbols of Catalan kinship (Asano-Tamanoi, 1987; Bestard-Camps and Contreras Hernandez, 1997; Llobera, 1997). Joan Bestard (1990) is of the view that the emphasis placed upon the house is a result of the impartible inheritance practiced in Catalonia, an unusual practice within Spain. This distinctiveness led to the creation of a nationalist ideology called *pairalisme* in the nineteenth century, centred on the *casa pairal* (ancestral home), which was presented as the ideal for the foundation of the Catalan nation (Llobera, 1997, 2004).

It is therefore difficult to separate kinship studies by Catalan authors from nationalist texts. The Catalan case provides an interesting context for the discussion of kinship and the early development of nationalist sentiments. Due to the focus on the house, regular commensality is a central element of *pairalisme*, and expresses the intensity of family relations. Even today, to live in the same house over generations is a source of pride, and it is still important to ensure family continuity (Bestard-Camps and Contreras Hernandez, 1997; Asano-Tamanoi, 1987). The related ideal of a self-sufficient household with its own garden (*hort*) is deeply rooted in the Catalan house (Robertson, 2012), and has been used in Catalanist political discourse throughout the twentieth century (DiGiacomo, 1987). In the nineteenth century, the rural ideal of the Catalan family and *casa pairal* was a political concept amongst elite, industrialist families (McDonogh, 1986). The family, and the *masia* (farmhouse) was a symbol of a unified, homogenous bulwark against Spanish centrism. Factory owners utilised the ideal of kinship structures and the Catalan house to give themselves a paternalistic role for their workers in new colonies (living complexes built around factories), to better control them. Thus, 'the colony became the *casa pairal* writ large' (McDonogh, 1986: 57), appealing to the workers' emotional and familial ties. The elite responded to popular unrest in the lower classes by promoting this conservative, sentimental view of the Catalan collective family and disciplined household, thus implying that social disorder was antithetical to being Catalan.

Territory and land also appear regularly in nationalist ideologies. As Llobera (2004: 48) perceptively points out, 'territory is perhaps one of the most concrete and important phenomena that exists for human beings'. Just calls this connection between nation, state and territory 'geographical circumscription', suggesting that 'the existence of a state presupposes the existence of its territory' (Just, 1989: 75). Catalonia is no exception. Balcells (2008) recognises several such sites of memory, including: sites associated with Barcelona's defeat in 1714; the Canigó mountain in France, associated with the *Flama del Canigó* events held every St. John's Eve; Montserrat, (literally 'jagged mountain') an eye-catching natural landmark that contains the sanctuary of the Virgin of Montserrat; the six-hundred-year-old Generalitat's Palace; and finally Barça's Camp Nou stadium and museum in Barcelona. There is no denying the importance of the FC Barcelona football club as a sign of national identity (Beary, 2011). Under the Franco regime, supporting Barça was a way of covertly supporting Catalanism (Ranachan, 2008).

Food and Cuisine in Catalonia

Because food will be the focus of this book, it is useful to place a special focus on existing academic work on food and identity in the region, and the role of food in Catalan society. It is impossible to overemphasise the central position of Catalan food and its associations in Catalan culture. In the words of Robertson in his fieldsite of Mieres:

> Food is the essence of conviviality in Catalonia, and although its processes are so ephemeral, the sensual intensity of eating together has a binding power that is everywhere apparent in the social life of Mieres. (Robertson, 2010: 72)

Robertson sums up several features of the position of food in Catalonia here. Its association with conviviality and sharing is a powerful metaphor for togetherness. In a case of conflictual identity, it is the 'nostalgic enactment of identity through which the consumption of particular foods proves to be a powerful statement of identity and difference' (Roser i Puig, 2011: 231). MacClancy (2007) makes similar remarks about Basque cuisine, where food is mobilised to suggest a prestigious and distinctive culture. Cuisine becomes a national virtue, and eating in a local manner becomes a way of consuming history.

Following Franco's death, Catalans renewed their interest in gastronomy. Several writers, such as Robertson (2010), Noyes (2003) and Roser i Puig (2011), have found the experience of deprivation to be pertinent to the history of Catalan cuisine, thus linking food once again to memory. High levels of food awareness were maintained throughout the autochthonous Catalan population, and Catalonia prides itself as a country where locals know how to eat well. Visceral memories of past hunger sharpen the importance of food and create a connection with festivity, when food would be available. Noyes in particular draws attention to the importance of commensality in times of famine, when sharing food is a 'labour of love' (Noyes, 2003).

Robertson (2010) speaks of memories of the Civil War being mainly tied up with food. This time is known as the *misèria* (time of wretchedness), and some of his informants refused to speak of it because it was so painful. Post-war, the Franco government used hunger to control Spain's population, and the policy of autarky (self-sufficiency) to reward political loyalists (del Arco Blanco, 2010). According to Robertson, food was a constant subject of conversation amongst those who lived through this period. Indeed, food (or a lack of it) acted as a lens through which informants remember and interpret the past.[6]

The Catalan government also uses food to promote cultural nationalism, a common top-down strategy for government actors (Ichijo and Ranta, 2016). Actions of this kind go back to 1993, when cuisine was recognised as a part of popular and traditional culture to be protected under law (Llei 2,1993). The wording of the act recognises the importance of cuisine in Catalan culture, reasoning that 'Catalan society has been a protagonist of cultural evolution in the area of cuisine and gastronomy that has brought them to be considered as part of its immaterial heritage'.

According to Davidson (2007), food is a medium through which the Catalan government engages in a new relationship with the rural by officially denominating areas and the products linked to them. The government therefore acts as the protector of produce, place and by extension cultural patrimony. Taste has now been officially recognised to develop a government-sponsored identity, or as Davidson puts it, 'literally packaging a nation' (Davidson, 2007: 40). It is telling that Ferran Adrià, the head chef of former restaurant El Bulli, received the St George's Cross, the highest award for contributions to Catalan culture, in 2002. This illustrates the official recognition of cooking and cuisine as an important part of Catalan culture and expression (Roser i Puig, 2010). Chefs Carme Ruscalleda and Ada Parellada received the same awards in 2004 and 2016 respectively. From an economic perspective, the food and drink industry is also Catalonia's most important industry, employing 17.9 per cent of the region's workforce, and representing 19.8 per cent of industrial turnover (Generalitat de Catalunya, 2018). Catalonia was also European Region of Gastronomy in 2016.

Anthropologist Sophia Vackimes (2013) has considered the relationship between the Catalan *nova cuina* of molecular gastronomy, and national identity. She draws attention to the apparent contradiction between the hyper-modernity of the culinary techniques and the idealisation of tradition. She sees this as part of a clever marketing strategy on the part of the regional government and the chefs themselves. The ideal of the 'tradition of modernity', where the culinary creativity of Ferran Adrià and his fellow chefs are presented as part of a Catalan ideal for innovation stretching back into history, is simply part of this marketing appeal. This is part of a general trend globally to fetishise the local, one that began with the government promotion of *terroir* in France and is far from unique to Catalonia.

Like Davidson (2007), and DeSoucey (2010), Vackimes sees the Generalitat as one of the principal agents in this process, particularly 'by linking nature and the physical landscape with 'authentic products' and a creative 'native talent'' (Generalitat de Catalunya, 2012: 280 in Vackimes, 2013). Nonetheless, she concludes by criticising the Generalitat's implied hypocrisy in glorifying 'local foods' for political and touristic ends, while neglecting either agricultural producers, or those who experience food insecurity due to poverty.

However, despite these sentiments, she still focuses more on the world of Catalan *nova cuina* than on the everyday culinary reality of the average Catalan. The commonality of this approach is not surprising, considering the number of Michelin starred restaurants in the region (as of 2019, the region had 66 Michelin stars across 54 restaurants, about a quarter of Spain's total 284 stars in 209 restaurants), and the wealth of material on *nova cuina*. For instance, journalist Raphael Minder (2017), in *The Struggle for Catalonia*, one of several works to appear in the last decade explaining the Catalan crisis, chooses to focus primarily on *nova cuina* in his chapter on Catalan cuisine. He places particular emphasis on the conflict between Ferran Adrià (of restaurant El Bulli) and another highly influential chef, Santi Santamaria (of Restaurant Can Fabes), the first Catalan chef to receive three Michelin stars.

Once close friends and stars of the Catalan restaurant scene in the 1990s, their relationships cooled as their cooking styles diverged, Adrià moving away from Catalan cuisine to focus on experimentation and new cooking techniques, whilst Santamaria championed local ingredients, Catalan staples and pro-independence politics. Their relationship never recovered after the *New York Times* journalist Arthur Lubow recognised Adrià (not Santamaria) as a leader of the Spanish and global new food movement in 2003. In 2008, Santamaria published *La Cocina al Desnudo* ('Naked Cooking'), a diatribe against Adria's 'molecular gastronomy', which he implied poisoned diners. Their conflict became infamous in journalistic and culinary circles, and split Catalan restaurateurs into opposing camps. According to Minder, in the end Santamaria alienated even those chefs who supported his approach. Thanks to a more flexible approach, and training internships at El Bulli, Adrià has had a greater influence over the current generation of Catalan chefs. The controversy ended with Santamaria's death in 2011, although reverberations of their differing approaches still remain today.

A piece of recent work on food in Catalonia is a chapter in Di Giovine and Brulottes' edited volume *Edible Identities* (Garcia-Fuentes et al, 2014). The authors consider how the renovation of Barcelona's market halls is connected with the recovery of traditional Catalan cuisine. They also introduce several key concepts that are essential to understanding Catalan cuisine, such as the importance of regionality and landscape, and also claims of the loss of cuisine (even though recent trends suggest the reverse). The renewed interest in Catalan cuisine and culture from the 1980s onwards coincides with a gradual resurgence in interest in markets. The promotion of Mediterranean cuisine plays a part in this revival, as well as in tourism promotion strategies and immigration. What is most interesting for my research however is that Garcia-Fuentes et al recognise the importance of the market in Catalan social life, that despite their use in heritage promotion or tourism schemes and 'elite' cuisine, they are 'interwoven into the fabric of everyday life' (ibid.: 170). They are thus essential spaces of contemporary expressions of Catalan social and food identity.

A more recent take on Catalonia's position as a world centre of gastronomic excellence in restaurant cuisine comes from a 2016 study by the Universities of Barcelona and Girona into the concentration of Michelin starred restaurants in Catalonia. The report suggests that, amongst other reasons, Catalonia is at an advantage for the following reasons:

Catalan tradition and culture has always given a role of protagonist to cuisine, because the majority of celebrations are related to meals or with concrete dishes. Moreover, it must be highlighted that Catalan society is interested in gastronomy and that implies being mentally open to accepting dishes and new techniques that perhaps more conservative societies have not accepted in the same way. (Bernardo et al, 2016: 125)

Food is therefore a common subject of debate and conversation within the area. It is an important part of government policy, yet also a regular feature of the everyday discourse at the grassroots level, transcending the dichotomies of top-down/bottom-up view of food. Due to this widespread explicit recognition of the importance of food in Catalan social life, food is one of the most fruitful areas on which the researcher can focus to understand contemporary Catalan national identity.

Research Methods

As an anthropologist, my main research 'strategy' or 'methodology' was that of ethnography. Fundamentally, that is living and experiencing the social reality that the researcher wishes to study. I lived for approximately 15 months in Catalonia, from June 2012 to September 2013. The first two months I spent in Barcelona, perfecting my Catalan and Spanish language, and preparing for the move to my main fieldsite, the town of Vic. I also followed this year-long stay with shorter research visits in the intervening years, the most recent of which was in January 2018.

For placing myself in the field, my main strategy was to learn Catalan to a high standard before entering the field. Both Noyes (2003) and Waldren (1996) found that speaking Catalan in their field sites was enthusiastically received. This is not surprising considering the important role of language in Catalan identity. In doing so, a researcher positions themselves as someone who was willing to understand and appreciate Catalan culture, and also implied a measure of *seny*.

In terms of the data itself (i.e. the discourse on Catalan cuisine and identity) there were two main factors that needed to be present. Firstly, Catalan informants needed to have a developed and extensive discourse around the notion of 'their' foods, foods to which they have attached their own identity (or 'signature foods', in the words of Mintz, 1996). Secondly, there must be unities in this discourse amongst informants, to provide a set of shared symbols and worldview (Guibernau, 2002). That is not to say that opinions should be identical between informants, and indeed one of the characteristics of cultural nationalisms is their multivocality (MacClancy,

2007; Bray, 2011). Despite individual nuances, there must be an overall set of themes and agreed parameters that define what makes Catalan food, or a Catalan cuisine. This must both be clear to the outside observer (i.e. the field researcher) and recognised by Catalans themselves, being both an emic and an etic category.

I aimed for as wide a variety of informants as possible (following MacClancy, 2007). The only criterion was that they considered themselves as 'Catalans', from informants who saw themselves as members of a unjustly repressed 'nation' that deserved independence, to others who identified as Spaniards living in the Catalan 'region'. They can roughly be divided into three groups. Firstly, those who had careers or a strong interest in food (amateur and professional chefs, producers, restaurateurs, food writers, teachers etc.). Secondly, Catalan activists, be it in the pro-independence movement, pan-Catalan civil societies like the Assemblea Nacional Catalana (ANC) and Omnium Cultural, or in cultural activities such as *sardana* dancing, the *castells*, or *gegant* carriers (*geganters*). Finally, as in any fieldwork (Watson, 1999), the rest of my informants formed a nebulous group of friends and acquaintances that I came to know through the course of my stay. For the purposes of anonymity, I refer to most of my informants by first name only, making exception for well-known figures such as chefs or journalists (unless they requested anonymity for certain statements). Some informants saw the presence of an outside research as an opportunity to promote national rhetoric (both pro- and anti-Catalan), and such expressions may not reflect reality (especially in cases of claimed cultural distinctiveness – Harrison, 2003). But this is all the more reason to focus on such expressions, to better understand the national identity under study.

My main research method was the ethnographic interview. Ideally, I tried to carry out several interviews with each informant, and interact with them in everyday settings. I also used the technique of photo-elicitation in the latter half of fieldwork, normally in group interview settings, using images I had collected throughout fieldwork. These images were a springboard for discussion, or to clarify and probe attitudes about specific foodstuffs or aspects of culinary culture.

Outside of interactions with informants, written material on Catalan cuisine has also been essential. This includes cookbooks (which I discuss in detail in chapter one), newspaper and magazine articles, and occasionally blog posts. This selection of gastronomic literature has created a rich discourse on the subject, which many Catalans use to construct their own ideas about food.

A particularly useful source has been the magazine *Cuina*, Catalonia's foremost Catalan-language food-focused publication (the editor, Josep Sucarrats, became a crucial informant). Other useful publications were

Descobrir, a Catalan travel magazine limited to Catalan-speaking areas, and *Sàpiens*, a Catalan history magazine, which promotes a decidedly Catalanist message (all three are owned by the same publisher, Sàpiens). I also used articles on food and other national subjects from popular newspapers in Catalonia, such as *La Vanguardia*, *El Periódico*, *Ara.cat* and *El Punt Avui*.

Participant observation was also a crucial research method for this book. This included eating with Catalans (and hearing what they said about their food), and cooking with them. Other participant observation included the *busca-bolets* (mushroom hunting), a central part of Catalan food-based identity, and the *matançes de porc* (pig killings), where I helped with preparation of the carcass and participated in the meal afterwards. I also include experiences of festive days and events in participant observation. This included all of Catalonia's three major national days, experienced in both Barcelona and Vic, with a special focus on the role of food in these events. Other festive events that I observed were Catalan food festivals and specialist markets.

The Fieldsite: Vic

In August 2012, I moved to the city of Vic, in the county of Osona, province of Barcelona. Vic is a small city of about 40,000 people, 70 kilometers north of Barcelona. I selected Vic for a number of reasons. It was recommended to me as a fieldsite by Catalan acquaintances, as Vic is regarded as one of the 'most Catalan' towns, a symbolic centre and historical bastion of Catalanism. It is associated with several important Catalan figures, including Catalonia's national poet, Jacint Verdaguer, the philosopher and scholar Jaume Balmes, and Bishop Josep Torras i Bages, who wrote *La Tradició Catalana* ('The Catalan Tradition') in 1892, the basis for conservative, Catholic Catalanism.

Its geographic location in the centre of Catalonia may also have contributed to this symbolic status. This location had practical advantages, as I could easily travel to other parts of Catalonia. Vic is fairly unknown to non-Catalans, so I had less concern with the effects of a large tourist industry on my research. Vic is, however, popular with tourists from within Catalonia, particularly the weekly market on Saturday in the central square (Plaça Major). There is also a smaller weekly market in the Plaça Major on Tuesdays, and another weekly market on Sundays in the Remei quarter (a working-class district across the river from the old city, with a high immigrant population), as well as an active calendar of annual markets. Markets are a site of 'traditional' Catalan sociality, and Vic has advertised itself as a 'City of markets', further strengthening its Catalan credentials (Congdon, 2015).

This climate was also another factor that, indirectly, brought me to Vic. It is a city known for its fog (*la boira*), a result of its location in the bend of a river. This has created a unique climate that is ideal for cured sausage production, particularly the Protected Geographic Indication (PGI) *llonganissa de Vic*. Much of Catalonia is famous for sausages (*embotits*), and as I will discuss in this work, they are themselves Catalan symbols. Vic's identity as a centre of production for this archetypal Catalan product reaffirms its reputation as a truly Catalan place. The sausage industry is also a testament to the importance of pig-raising to Osona's economy. This industry has even left Vic with a sensory footprint, the so-called '*eau de Vic*': a farmyard smell of the pig farms surrounding the city, mixed with a metallic hint from the slaughterhouses, first evident on arrival.

Agriculture and agro-food industries accounted for 3.8 per cent and 10.8 per cent respectively of Osona's workforce in 2008 (more recent, post-crisis data is lacking). The percentage of the population employed in primary industries, 4.3 per cent, is particularly high when compared to the rest of Catalonia (1.3 per cent) (Generalitat de Catalunya, 2009). The importance of agriculture, and its rural ambience, means that Vic is often associated with the ideal of the *pagès* (tenant farmer), an ideal that is significant to Catalanism.

As Vic has such a reliance on the agro-alimentary industries and an international reputation for the PGI *llonganissa de Vic*, an initiative was also taking place during my fieldwork to recognise Vic as a UNESCO City of Gastronomy (it was ultimately unsuccessful). Vic University also was the first in Spain to offer a Masters in Communication and Gastronomy from 2006 (sadly, by my arrival it had closed due to low uptake numbers). Still, the candidature and the course showed an interest in food and 'gastronomic heritage' within Vic, another reason to locate within the city.

During my stay I lived in the Plaça Major (central square). I selected it for convenience, but soon realised that this was a highly emotive location in Catalan nationalism. I have already described the role of Vic as a symbolic hinterland, and to live in the very centre of that, in the Plaça Major, fortified my Catalan connections in the eyes of many informants. To use a popular food metaphor, it was said I was living in '*el rovell de l'ou*', the yolk of the egg, to describe how central this location was to contemporary Catalanism.

I also spent a few weeks (over several visits) in other parts of Catalonia, particularly the north-eastern region of Empordà (on the border with France), and the southern tip of Catalonia in the Ebro Delta (the so-called *Terres de l'Ebre*, Ebro Lands). This was on the advice of informants, to experience the contrast in Catalan regional food cultures. Empordà has also contributed disproportionately to Catalan cuisine itself and is the place where many of

Catalonia's food figures have chosen to open restaurants. This is probably due to the proximity to France and the popularity of tourism in the area.

Nationalism, Identity, Power: Definitions and Limitations

The focus of this book is clearly on nationalism, but I have also introduced words such as 'identity', 'ethnicity' and 'tradition'. I prefer the term national identity to ethnicity, because I believe that the latter is not an appropriate word to apply to the Catalan people, who very clearly refer to themselves as members of a 'nation', not an 'ethnic group'. However, the word 'nationalism' (*nacionalisme*) is also disliked for its political connotations in Spain as another term for Francoism or Spanish nationalism. The word '*Catalanisme*' (anglicised to 'Catalanism') is more acceptable, although its most accurate translation is 'Catalan nationalism', because the word describes the ideologies behind Catalan nationhood. For clarity I will use both Catalanism and Catalan nationalism.

It is worth elaborating on the approach to identity taken in this book. It is a truism to say that national identities cannot exist outside of the people who have created them, hence the need to focus on the developers and practitioners of nationalisms. Identity here is a sense of affiliation and belonging that is grounded within those individual practitioners and performers of the nation, that is also essential for their sense of being within the world, and their interactions with it. In the literature on the study of everyday life in national identity, the role of performance has been given special significance. The work of Tim Edensor (2002, 2006) is useful here, inspired by the Butler's theory of identity performance. He has focused on how national belonging is perpetuated in everyday life, a space where 'national identity is continually reproduced, sedimented and challenged' (Edensor, 2006: 526). As he explains, 'performance continually reconstitutes identity by rehearsing and transmitting meanings' (Edensor, 2002: 69).

This approach also ensures identity is viewed as a dynamic. As national identity relies on repeated acts, not on an original copy, by its nature it is impossible to replicate these acts perfectly (Lavi, 2003; Edensor, 2002). For this reason, national identities are never static, but continually evolving and adapting to contemporary realities within communities. They are dynamic, contested, negotiated, continually in a process of reinvention and flux (Edensor, 2006; MacClancy, 2007). This is a point emphasised by Zoe Bray in her ethnography on Basque nationalism, such that identity becomes 'the product of a fluid and changing application of markers and boundaries by individuals in a constant process of identification and self-identification' (Bray, 2011: 217). Her conclusions are unusual but perceptive, as they stress the individual experience of identity, whereas most work has so far stressed the collective element of nationalisms. Vaczi (2016) in her conclusions on the performative nature of *castells*, recognises the comforting role identity performance can play in times of geopolitical uncertainty. She also recognises that performing the nation can be a source of enjoyment. To view identity as dynamic and performative fits well with the ethnographic approach used in this book. This view of identity as continually changing may appear contradictory in light of the claims of many national ideologies to timelessness and permanence (Llobera, 2004). Hence the importance of questioning and examining such claims from a neutral perspective.

Identities are inherently relational. They are constructed in opposition to what they are not, even when cross-cultural similarities between opposing identities exist but are ignored or denied (Harrison, 2003). From the outside, it may seem as though there is one unified Catalan national identity. From the inside however, it becomes clear that there are many different shades of 'being Catalan' (revealing once more the usefulness of an ethnographic approach for understanding these movements). In other parts of Spain, Bray (2007) and MacClancy (1997) in the Basque country, and Medeiros (2013) in Galicia have recognised that there may be different versions of allegiance to a 'nation', from strong nationalists with political ambitions to 'non-nationalists' who show pride in symbols of Basque or Galician identity. There are rarely any illusions about local or political elites and their manipulation of these sentiments. In this regard Catalonia is not unique. During my fieldwork in 2012–2013, Catalans were aware that both the incumbent government and the opposition used Catalanist fervour to its own ends. There is a deep mistrust of the political class, even if they are Catalan (Crameri, 2014).[7] The result is that Catalanism is separated from politics in the minds of most informants. This may explain why Catalan nationalism has been such an enduring movement, because it has not been the exclusive preserve of a single political party or spectrum (Crameri, 2008). This is not a unique phenomenon to Catalanism however, as Billig (1995) has pointed out in examining other cases of banal nationalism.[8]

Catalan symbols are a source of pride, despite attempts to co-opt them for political gain. Vaczi (2016) has seen this trend in the *castell* groups, who avoid political affiliations, though they will perform for NGOs. Her research also demonstrates how Catalan symbols, such as the *castells*, can mean different things to different social groups or classes within the region, from conservative Catalans to lower classes and immigrants. By meaning many things to many people, national discourse can appear inherently contradictory. Edensor (2006) suggests that a problem with the continued focus on elite constructions of national identity means that it appears the masses are powerless to resist ideological messages given to them from above. However, running with the notion of identity as inherently contested, performative and flexible, in practice those who employ these symbols in their daily lives also supply their meaning, which might be very different from their original connotations (Guibernau, 1996, in Edensor, 2006).

This point has complex ramifications for understanding power structures and relations in Catalonia. A Foucauldian view of the power dynamics is relevant here, most obvious in the fact that the Generalitat controls popular media (it owns the Catalan Media Corporation, which controls radio and television in the region), and the education system. Providing funding to city and town councils for use in advertising or cultural events that promote Catalan-ness is another way to subconsciously encourage identification. The Generalitat's policies 'reaches into the very grain of individuals, touches their bodies, and inserts itself into their very actions and attitudes, their discourses, learning processes and everyday lives' (Foucault, in Lukes, 2005; 88–89), to promote pro-Catalan behaviour and sentiment. It is difficult to say how much of the current political crisis has been the result of this covert signalling of Catalan difference over almost two generations. This is a situation that has often irked the central government, especially in education. To further complicate the situation, centrists inside and outside Catalonia manipulate perceptions of the Catalan government's attitude in their own power plays, both within the region, and at state level politics. One could also argue that the cultural ideal of *seny* versus *rauxa* is a hidden means of social control, as it encourages non-violence and conformity to Catalan institutions (Vaczi, 2016),[9] just as the nineteenth-century elite used the same ideology to control their workers (McDonogh, 1986).

However, most Catalans are aware that the Catalan local government-controlled media is promoting pro-Catalan discourse. They are also aware of the competing discourses from centrist and pro-Spanish media. Neither has managed to hide their own mechanisms, as Foucault believed power structures did. The views of Steven Lukes (2005) and James C. Scott (1990) are more interesting in the Catalan case. They demonstrate a more flexible, pragmatic approach to power hierarchies, and reactions to exertions of power. One could argue that Lukes's three dimensions of power are active in Catalonia, in particular his third dimension or ideological power. That most members of Catalan society '*consent* to power and *resent* the mode of its exercise' (Lukes, 2005: 150) is a more accurate description of what happens in the minds of Catalans. The level of resentment varies depending on where an individual stands on the spectrum of Catalan identity, from *independentista* to 'more Spanish than Catalan'. From a purely rational perspective, supporting Catalan nationalism opposes the interests of many of the region's inhabitants, due to the uncertainty and economic downturn engendered by independence politics in autumn 2017. Based on my fieldwork in January

2018, this may have created a situation of 'latent conflict'[10] (ibid.: 28) within the region.

I should also make clear that I am focusing on how food is reflected in national identity. There are other identities on which I will not be able to focus due to the lack of space. One of these is gender, and the other is class. Both are themes that have been considered extensively in discussions of food (Counihan and Kaplans' edited volume (2013) has addressed the former, whilst Bourdieu's *Distinction* (1984, 2010) has examined the latter, and Pratt (2003) has also contrasted nationalisms with class-based movements). Issues of gender are present in discussions of Catalan food, but they are not especially relevant to the present discussion of food's relationship to nationalism. While I saw some examples of class-based attitudes perpetuated in Catalonia in a very few households, I cannot claim to have recognised a clear scheme of social classes into which my informants placed themselves. While a study of this situation in contemporary Catalonia may be interesting (updating the work of Giner, 1980 and Pi-Sunyer, 1974), I found it of little direct relevance to the two interlinked subjects under study, that of food and nationalism. Moreover, Llobera (2004) has suggested that an excessive focus on class and identity in Catalonia has clouded in-depth study of the region.

My intention has never been to create a description of Catalans' everyday diet. My research focuses on the *discourses* about foods, and what foods mean, rather than nutritional content, eating patterns etc. I also do not have scope here to discuss the Catalan industrial food system in depth, nor Catalonia's role in the global food system. I also focus little on the role of the Catholic Church in Catalonia. Llobera (2004: 17) considers a 'strong Catalan "national" Church' to have been essential to Catalanism. However, I did not find a strong connection between religious belief and a Catalan identity today, except in the secularised celebration of national saints' days. While I would also have liked to consider the question of recent immigration to Catalonia, and its effect on food, I believe such a topic would be worthy of its own research project (moreover, I was unable to place myself in such a way to gather relevant data).[11] Likewise, Catalonia's role as a very popular tourist destination is touched upon in the work, but is less of a focus here for reasons of time and scope.

I only focus on the Catalan Autonomous Community (CAC), an important delineation because this defines neither the borders of the Catalan language, nor of Catalan identity. Catalan is spoken in a larger group of areas called the *Països Catalans* (Catalan-speaking areas), which includes the CAC, the Balearic Isles, Valencia, Andorra, Roussillon (Northern Catalonia) and a small strip of Aragon (*La Franja*). According to the anthropologist Oonagh O'Brien (1994), who has extensively studied Catalan identity in French

Catalonia, the situation there is very different from the CAC. Abandoning Catalan and adopting French is essential for social mobility.

A current in Catalan nationalism has been the notion of a unified *Països Catalans*. The image of the *Països Catalans* is a popular motif on pro-Catalan and pro-independence memorabilia, much like Urla's (1993: 825) descriptions of the 'bounded visual image, detached and floating in space' in Basque nationalism, to both delineate a nation and act as a brand-like, personal logo. In Catalonia the discourse of the *Països Catalans* has often been used to show how these areas have been subjugated to the decisions of nation-state powers (Spain and France). Contemporary controversy has also revolved around whether 'Catalan' can be used to describe its dialects in Aragon and Valencia, heavily influenced by ruling political parties in those areas (CNA, 2015; Castelló and Castelló, 2009).

Structure of the Book

The first chapter provides an overview of Catalan culinary literature from the medieval era to the present day. This will provide a history of Catalan cuisine and introduce some of the texts and writers who will feature in this work. It is also useful to consider how some of these cookbooks are perceived by Catalans today, and how they are used to construct contemporary culinary identity. Chapter Two considers the culinary aspects that make Catalan cuisine, including the primary sauces, and attitudes to 'signature dishes' (Mintz, 1996). In doing so I introduce many of the key concepts present in Catalan food-based identity and relate them to general attitudes about Catalan national identity.

In Chapter Three, I consider Catalan cuisine in various contexts. I discuss the campaign to recognise Catalan cuisine as a UNESCO intangible cultural heritage, and the context of Catalonia's cuisine in the Mediterranean and *Països Catalans*. Within this chapter I will include an update on the role food has played in the current political crisis since October 2017.

Chapter Four provides an exploration of the gastronomic calendar, according to which each festive day has an associated food, and its connection with markets and seasonality in national identity. The discussion then progresses onto the place of landscape in Catalan gastronationalism, inspired by a Catalan saying that 'a cuisine is a country's landscape in a pot'. Finally, in Chapter Five I explore the controversies surrounding recently developed, explicitly Catalanist foods, which are associated with the three national days. I will conclude by summarising the main findings within Catalonia about intersections between food and nationalism, and also provide some more general methodological suggestions for studying the subject in other contexts.

Notes

1. History would repeat itself again under Franco, as wealthier Catalans who aligned themselves with Franco (nicknamed 'Catalans of the Eixample' – DiGiacomo, 2001), in the hopes of protecting Catalan industries, found an inherent mistrust of Catalans.
2. I attended the three Diadas from 2012 to 2014, so can describe them from personal experience.
3. By contrast, average voter turnout for the region in the last ten years approached 70 per cent (Statista, 2019).
4. The defendants are Dolores Bassa, Meritxell Borràs, Jordi Cuixart, Carme Forcadell, Joaquim Forn, Oriol Junqueras, Carles Mundó, Raül Romeva, Josep Rull, Jordi Sànchez, Jordi Turull and Santi Vila.
5. Catalans are fond of referring to *la nostra llengua mil.lenària* – our thousand-year-old language (DiGiacomo, 2001).
6. In my experience, this claim that food is a popular topic of conversation is certainly true, though this applied to all generations, not just the older ones. I also did twice hear some mention of the *misèria* amongst informants who had lived through it, and in one instance this had galvanized the attitudes of these informants against Spain.
7. This is no doubt due to corruption scandals. One recently implicated Jordi Pujol and his family, one of the architects of contemporary Catalanism. The political fallout was so great that his party (CiU) was renamed, to distance the party from his legacy.
8. 'If banal nationalism were only to be found in the words of politicians, it would hardly be embedded in the ordinary lives of those millions of people who treat the genus of politicians with cynical disdain' (Billig, 1995: 94).
9. 'Between the two polarities, one has to cultivate *seny* in order not to fall into *rauxa*, which makes *seny* popular instead of top-down repressive' (Vaczi, 2016: 361).
10. 'What one may have here is a *latent conflict*, which consists in a contradiction between the interests of those exercising power and the *real interests* of those they exclude' (Lukes, 2005: 28).
11. Vic's Remei quarter would provide an ideal site for this kind of study.

Chapter 1
CATALAN COOKBOOKS
CREATING CATALONIA THROUGH CULINARY LITERATURE

Why Consider Cookbooks?

When introducing Catalan cuisine, it is best to start with an overview of the cuisine through time, connecting its developments with the historical timeline of Catalonia. The ideal tools for this are cookbooks, manifestations of the eras that produced them. According to Appadurai (1988), cookbooks tell unusual cultural tales in complex civilisations. They can 'combine the sturdy pragmatic virtues of all manuals with the vicarious pleasures of the literature of the senses' (ibid.: 3). Hence, they serve the dual purpose of being both mundane guides to the everyday activity of cooking, and provide an ideal to which readers can aspire. Yet their nature as aspirational texts has meant that historians and social scientists have been wary of using cookbooks as a research tool, because they may not represent reality. While this may be true on occasion, cookbooks can be useful in other ways, because they are reflections of the societies that produce them. Cookbooks are 'a special category of texts' that 'tell us more about a people's collective imaginations, symbolic values, dreams and expectations, in so far as these are connected with the art of eating and drinking' (Fragner, 1994: 71).

It has been noted, albeit infrequently, that cookbooks too can play their role in constructing national identity. Nations are created through print capitalism (B. Anderson, 1983), founded in widespread literacy and the ability to disseminate printed material that creates 'imagined communities' of a nation of readers. Cookbooks also began to have a privileged position in middle class households at about the same time as the nation. Newspapers, the primary literary source of the imagined community, could also carry cooking advice and recipes (Goody, 1982). Cookbooks and other culinary literature are therefore in a privileged position to act as purveyors of nationalist discourse.

Priscilla Ferguson (1988) has recognised the essential role of texts in creating a French 'gastronomic field', and by extension, a culinary nationalism. Food no longer remains simply a base product, but becomes a form of cultural consumption and essential part of the social fabric. More recently, Lara Anderson (2013) has demonstrated how cookbooks were used in the creation of the Spanish nation-building project of the late nineteenth century. As she explains, 'all of the texts considered contain strategies and rhetoric typical of the nation-building projects' (L. Anderson, 2013: 4–5). Unlike France or Italy, which had already developed national and culinary identities, Spain's national cuisine in the mid-nineteenth century was largely non-existent. The elite consumed French cuisine, and popular cuisine was impoverished and regionalised. Spanish cookbook authors explicitly recognised the lack of a cuisine as symptomatic of the lack of national unity. One such writer was even commissioned by the dictator Primo de Rivera. Additionally, a national culinary repertoire was seen as a way of uniting Spain's regionally diverse regions at a cohesive, national level.

Hence, to better understand Catalan gastronationalism, it is necessary to study cookbooks, and gastronomic books (i.e. books on informed eating). Cookbooks become a means of standardising cuisine, and their texts show how food becomes a symbol or metaphor of the ideals of Catalan nationalism. Returning to Appadurai once more, cookbooks must be viewed as 'revealing artefacts of culture in the making' (ibid.: 22) in a contemporary setting. If we want to study the development of contemporary national identities, then we must study their cookbooks.

It would be impossible to analyse all the cookbooks in Catalonia, and my informants remarked that there seemed to have been more cookbooks published on Catalan cuisine than ever before. There are no clear statistics on the Catalan cookbook market, however according to an email from the secretary of the guild of Catalan booksellers, there has been a definite increase in the publication of cookbooks, inspired by the prestige of celebrity chefs and television shows (M. Marín i Torné 2018, personal communication, 8 February). In this chapter I will introduce the most essential cookbooks through Catalonia's history, starting with the medieval cookbooks *Llibre de Sent Soví* ('Book of Saint Soví') and *Libre de Coch* ('Book of Cooking'), going on to the increasingly nationalist cookbooks of the nineteenth and twentieth centuries. This will also double as a history of Catalan cuisine, showing how cookbooks on national cuisine are often published when Catalan nationalism is experiencing a high point. I will conclude by presenting the contemporary situation and introducing some of the writers and texts that I will draw upon over the rest of the book.

Medieval Cookbooks in Present Parlance

Catalonia has had a long history of cooking manuals, the earliest of which is the *Llibre de Sent Soví* in 1324 (also called *Libre de totes meneres de potatges de menjar*, 'Book of all recipes of dishes'), and later the famous *Libre de Coch* of 1520 by Robert de Nola, the first printed cookbook in the Catalan language, which became something of a bestseller of the era in both Catalan and Castilian, going through 10 editions in one century.

Catalans take pride in the fact that their cuisine was seen as a one of the best in Europe at the time, and was mentioned in other European cookbooks of the day (Grewe, 2009). Indeed, one sentiment I heard was that Catalonia had had two golden ages, in terms of political power and culinary influence throughout the known world: one in the medieval era and the courts of the Catalan–Aragonese empire, and one today with Ferran Adrià and the *nova cuina* movement. An appreciation of Catalonia's medieval history is often present in everyday discourse (Keown, 2011a), which is reflected in attitudes about cuisine.

For instance, one Barcelona chef, Fermí, considered the medieval era a golden age in Catalan politics, economy and gastronomy, and showed great pride in the *Llibre de Sent Soví*. He connected the later political ostracism with the decline in the culinary reputation of Catalan cuisine, which only experienced a resurgence in popularity in the 1980s. This too he connected to political movements, in this case the end of the Franco dictatorship and the establishment of democracy and the Catalan government. The current situation of Catalonia as a centre of culinary vanguardism is therefore presented as part of a historical trend. This combination of both idealising past cuisine, and simultaneously championing *nova cuina* styles is not seen as contradictory, merely part of a 'tradition of innovation' that encapsulates Catalan cuisine (Bernardo et al, 2016).

The most important edition of the *Llibre de Sent Soví in* recent times was the 1979 edition by Rudolf Grewe. Grewe's book included the original recipes, adapted to modern readers. He also inserted an in-depth introduction to the cuisine of the era, setting the scene for understanding the environment of the cuisine in the medieval court. It is significant that the edition was published just after the end of the Franco era, an example of the restatement of Catalan culture that occurred at this time.

Grewe claims that with Catalan cuisine 'we are sure that we can talk of a medieval Catalan cuisine with its own personality. Numerous "dishes *a la catalana*" that figure in the foreign recipe books prove that well enough' (Grewe, 2009: 30). He credits this situation to the economic success of the Catalan–Aragonese Empire. More recent editions emphasise this aspect

(Santanach, 2006). Even though this is historical research, there is a subtle pro-Catalanism present throughout the text.

The existence of dishes currently recognised as Catalan at the time of the writing of *Sent Soví* is a preoccupation of modern-day editors. Many informants see the book itself as a demonstration of the antiquity of Catalan cuisine, through the presence of an early form of some essential sauces in Catalan cuisine such as the *sofregit* and the *picada*. The view that Catalan cuisine has this unbroken tradition from the medieval golden age to the present day draws parallels to the notion that the Catalan nation has had an unbroken history and fully-formed sense of national identity since this time. This view has been especially promoted in the Generalitat-sponsored UNESCO intangible cultural heritage campaign, where these cookbooks have been essential in backing up claims to antiquity and uniqueness. Part of the original campaign aimed to have the *Llibre de Sent Soví* recognised in UNESCO's 'Memory of the World' programme.

While one should not be too hasty to dismiss this argument, and in the case of cuisine there are almost certainly some elements of medieval cuisine that have remained,[1] this claim is not without controversy. In my interview with the well-respected chef Ferran Adrià, for example, he was critical of the notion that the *sofregit* and *picada* which were to be found in these two medieval cookbooks were the same as that of today. On the contrary, he argued that they are completely different, and the connection placed upon them now was the result of 'socio-political movements' that put different interpretations onto food.

The *Libre de Coch* of 1520, by 'Mestre Robert', or Robert de Nola, the chef to King Ferdinand I of Naples, was the first Catalan cookbook to have been printed in Catalan, and to have a wide readership. Catalan writer Josep Pla began his *El que hem menjat* ('What we have eaten', 1972) with a chapter entitled 'Robert de Nola: A memory' to pay homage to this individual and work. Pla took pride in the book's widespread popularity yet bemoaned the lack of a Catalan edition at the time of his writing (under Franco). He considers this situation shocking, especially as it is one of the first cookbooks in the vernacular in Europe. From his tone, Pla seems to suggest that this lack is part of a more general decline in Catalan cuisine. When the founding texts of Catalan cuisine are unavailable to general readership, then the culinary identity itself suffers.

After the medieval golden age, with the end of the Catalan–Aragonese empire in the Mediterranean, and the centralisation of political power to Madrid, Catalonia entered a period of decline. Few books of any note were published in Catalan, though some cooking pamphlets of monastic origin did appear from the seventeenth century onwards. The first real Catalan cookbook of the modern period Catalan cookbook, *La Cuynera Catalana* (1835), is a bridge between medieval cuisine and that of the present day

(Martí Escayol, 2004), the sign of a rebirth in Catalan cuisine in the context of the renewed force of Catalan nationalism.

La Cuynera Catalana

La Cuynera Catalana was published anonymously in instalments from 1833 to 1835 by a Barcelonan publishing house, the Germans Torras. The title means the '*The Catalan Cook*', with the subtitle 'Useful, easy, safe and economic rules to cook well'. Note the use of the female form of the word ('*Cuynera*'), delineating that this book was aimed at women. These pamphlets were enormously successful and were finally compiled into a full edition in 1851 with 500 recipes. It was, and still is, very popular, going through many reprints and re-editions up to the present day. In her introduction to the most recent re-edition, the chef and food writer Carme Queralt calls it 'a great work, a patrimonial, lexical, historical and cultural reference' (Queralt, in Anonymous, 2009: 13), which sums up the reverence with which this book is held in Catalonia.

This cookbook is unusual in that it is written exclusively in Catalan. Most historians date the Catalan *Renaixença* to 1833, with the publication of *Oda a La Pàtria* ('Ode to the Fatherland') by Carles Aribau. This poem was the first visible manifestation of a vindication of the Catalan language. *La Cuynera Catalana* was published only 2 years later, when the *Renaixença* was still in its infancy. The first book of Catalan poetry of the era was published four years after, in 1839, when the first dictionary also appeared. The first Catalan language magazine (*Lo Verdader Català*) was founded in 1843.

Considering the context, to publish a serialised book entirely in colloquial Catalan was a bold undertaking, especially as the Catalan language had not yet been standardised. This decision was likely influenced by moves in Catalan literary culture. Indeed, in the original prologue, the writer admits that perhaps it is folly to start writing in Catalan, because those who cook may not have time to read such advice. Still, the writer claims this book can be useful to improve efficiency and knowledge of those who are badly trained, and that this must be done in a language that is used every day by those who cook ('written out in our own Catalan language, with the aim of general use, and suited to the capacity of all' – Anonymous, 1851: 6). This efficiency drive was to become a common theme in culinary literature of the time. The writer also states in the introduction that there must be good food but that it cannot go beyond the bounds of Christian propriety – another theme that was to appear in later cookbooks from the period.

The book's cuisine is still largely old fashioned, even medieval, with some modern touches. For example, it includes ingredients that were only recently incorporated from America, e.g. turkey and tomatoes, red pepper and chocolate. Extensive use of spices is still present, as in medieval cookbooks. The recipes probably came from a variety of sources, both verbal and written, but certainly from other books in other languages (Queralt, in Anonymous, 2009). There is an awareness of other cuisines and the internationalisation of recipes, e.g. *a la castellana* (Castilian), *l'espanyola* (Spanish – interestingly this is seen as different from Castilian), *l'italiana* (Italian) etc., whilst Catalan recipes are given a separate denomination as '*a la catalana*'. For example, *allioli* sauce is called '*salsa catalana*'. The writer of the introduction to the 1980 facsimile of the 1851 edition sees this as further evidence of the 'national affirmation' of the writer, because the writer is creating a culinary 'other' against which Catalan dishes can be contrasted.

One should remember that cookbooks provide fascinating social history. Like many of the cookbooks under discussion, *La Cuynera Catalana* was aimed primarily at the upwardly mobile Catalan bourgeoisie. As in other countries, they were also the earliest supporters of the nationalist movement. Vaczi (2016) has pointed out that many of the Catalan symbols of today were spearheaded by the Catalanist, bourgeois, intellectual elite in the nineteenth century. Applying this to food, it is possible that the recognition of certain national dishes in books like *Cuynera*, and in bourgeois cooking, has guaranteed their emblematic status in national cuisine to the present day.

Like many early cookbooks, the author of *Cuynera* is anonymous, and continues to be unknown. What is certain is that by choosing to publish in Catalan, the author is aligning themselves with the ideals of *Renaixença*, albeit not in the overtly literary sense generally associated with the poetic movement. Instead this cookbook should be compared to the work of folklorists and historians, who researched popular culture at this time as part of the incipient nationalist movement. This can be seen in the recipes, which, with the exception of some foreign ones, are clearly identifiable by their ingredients and procedures as belonging to Catalonia.

Later Nineteenth-Century Cookbooks

In 1857 the next cookbook to deal explicitly with Catalan cuisine and to use Catalan was published in Vic, '*Avisos o sien reglas senzilles a un principant cuiner o cuinera*' ('Advice or One Hundred Simple Rules for the Beginner Male or Female Cook') by Felip Cirera (also called Felip del Palau or Palacio, as he was the chef at the Bishops Palace in Vic). The four editions published over the rest of the nineteenth century suggest a popular acceptance of the book in Vic households, and demonstrate 'a public eager to instruct themselves in the art of economical cooking and baking in their own language' (Angelats and Vila, 2003: 35).

In the intervening forty years or so, the Catalan nationalist movement gained strength. The next text of interest appears in 1895, *Carmencita: o la buena cocinera* ('Carmencita: or the Good Cook') by Doña Eladia Maria, 'widow of Carpinell'. Although written in Spanish, it is interesting to note that the writer states she is familiar with 'Cuisine from Spain, Catalonia, Cuba, America, France and Italy', suggesting that Catalan cuisine was distinctive enough to be seen as separate from the rest of Spain. This cookbook includes the first recipe for *canelons*, which had come to Catalonia from Italian chefs and was to become a Catalan favourite (I discuss its role as a national food in the next chapter). The book's introduction glorifies the female Catalan cook, delineating its audience as housewives, rather than professional, male cooks, nor male gastronomes who give large, loud banquets. It was one of several cookbooks that my informants mentioned as an important book that they had seen used by older female relatives. This book was also known as one passed from generation to generation within families (Generalitat de Catalunya, 2005). It is now on its 39th edition, a testament to its enduring popularity (Anonymous, 2009).

The Twentieth Century

The most important work at the turn of the century was *La Cuyna Catalana*, ('Catalan Cooking') of 1907, by Josep Cunill de Bosch (the surname literally means woodland rabbit, a popular meat of the time, most likely a pseudonym). Again, this was expressly aimed at women cooks. The author's intention is to help others in 'the transcendental work of preparing, dressing and presenting dishes' (Cunill de Bosch, 1907: 5), a work they describe later as 'the greatest transcendence, both for the individual and the community' (ibid.: 7).

The author begins by referring to national dishes typical of Catalans, particularly the *escudella i carn d'olla* (a meat and vegetable stew). Cunill de Bosch claims that just as an Italian will never get tired of macaroni, so the Catalan will always have an affection for *escudella i carn d'olla*. Despite this Cunill de Bosch takes pride in saying that there are many different variations of the same dish, such as 15 of the aforementioned *escudella*.

Cunill de Bosch then sets out his basic argument, that is 'strong races are well fed races'. It is interesting that he refers to race, because racial arguments have been less prevalent in Catalan political discourse that those of other nationalist movements. Unlike the Romans, he says, one should not fall into gastronomic excess and eat only for pleasure. The ancient Greeks are idealised in this respect. People should eat to live, not live to eat. He sums up his logic for creating a healthy nation as follows:

Good cooks make good food;
Good food is eaten with pleasure;
Food eaten with pleasure is digested better;
Better-digested food leads to the conservation of the individual in good health;
The conservation of the individual in good health means their bodily functions are regular;
Regular functions make strong races;
Strong races go forth beyond others and in the end make themselves masters of the world (Cunill de Bosch 1907: 8)

With this final statement, the author is clearly linking this cookbook to the grander scheme of constructing a Catalan nation from its stomach. Good food is essential because it will make Catalans a great people. He concludes with a popular Catalan phrase, still used today, '*a la taula y al llit, al primer crit*' ('to the table and to bed at the first call'), leaving the reader in no doubt that this is a Catalan cookbook, situated in the popular, national culture of the time.

Next is the 1923 *Art de Ben Menjar* ('Art of Good Eating'), by Marta Salvia, subtitled as a 'Catalan Book of Cooking'. The name Marta Salvia was a pseudonym of Adriana and Sara Aldavert, the daughters of journalist and Catalanist politician Pere Aldavert (Armengol, 2015), further reinforcing this work's gastronationalist connections. The prologue begins with a brief introduction going back to the origins of the cuisine presented in the book, briefly referring to Homer and the cuisines of antiquity, as well as the principal historic texts in the Iberian Peninsula and Catalonia. This historical situating was a technique also used by Cunill de Bosch, placing the cookbooks within the context of an evolution from a historic past. As I have already described with medieval cookbooks, historical connections are central to the justifications of nationalist and gastronationalist movements, also recognised by MacClancey (2007), and Raviv (2013).

Salvia's intention is not to appeal to refined palates, but to contribute to the good preparation of dishes 'at the hearths of our native land', i.e. Catalonia. This use of 'our native land', ('*la nostra terra*' in Catalan), is a frequently used phrase to be found running throughout Catalanist discourse (DiGiacomo, 1987), and other Catalan cookbooks. The image of the hearth is also a potent emotional one, connecting the home and kitchen with the nation. The presence of these pro-Catalan phrases, the background of the authors, the subtitle of the book and the implied historical connectedness all suggest the influence of Catalanist ideas of the time.

For the *Art de Ben Menjar*, a review in the Catalanist magazine *L'esquella de la Torratxa* provides insight into contemporary reactions. Firstly, the reviewer states that it is enough that the book is written in Catalan to prove its patriotic credentials. The book is described as a 'demonstration that Catalonia has returned to being rich and full,[2] because only rich and full peoples are worried about good food ... Catalonia already has its own cuisine. Just as it has a history, a language, a dance, music, and painting, ... So too it has its own cuisine, over which we can now set the nationalist banner'. This is followed by a demand to the Mancommunitat (the Catalan government) to create a section for cooks in the School for Fine Arts, not for political banquets but for 'the cult of Catalan cuisine'. This review speaks for itself in demonstrating the connection between cookbook, cuisine and national identity in early twentieth century Catalan nationalist thought.

Ignasi Domènech, Chef and Cookbook Writer

No consideration of Catalan cookbooks is complete without mention of the works of Ignasi Domènech. Born in 1874 Domènech was apprenticed to the kitchen in his uncle's inn, and continued his training in Barcelona and Montserrat, where he learned Catalan cuisine. He continued to travel around Europe and Spain, and finally returned to Barcelona sometime in the 1920s (Lladonosa i Giró, 2000b), which coincides with the time he began publishing in Catalan. Domènech published over 30 cookbooks (the first in 1914 and the last in 1942) and edited two cooking magazines. Considering his extraordinary output, relatively few of his books were published in Catalan, however those that were have had huge popularity and influence up to the present day and are icons of twentieth century Catalan cuisine. His Catalan publications are *La Teca* (literally 'The Grub', 1924), *Llaminadures* ('Sweet Things', 1924), *La manduca: Un tresor de platets de gust* ('Nosh: A Treasury of Tasty Little Plates', 1926), *Àpats* ('Meals', 1930) and *El carnet de cuina de l'excursionista* ('The Excursionist's Cooking License', 1930).

Ignasi Domènech's decision to publish in Catalan at this time may well have been influenced by a heightened awareness of Catalan identity, an unexpected result of the repressive Primo de Rivera dictatorship (1923–1930). As Crameri (2000) has pointed out, the very decision to publish in Catalan can be a political statement. At the same time, language delineates the preferred audience to Catalan speakers. As the author of *La Cuynera Catalana* remarked back in 1853, a cookbook for everyday usage needs to be written in the language of everyday communication. We do not know Domènech's own views on the subject of Catalanism (he probably sought to avoid controversy, like many of today's chefs). The only mention of his attitude to Catalonia is in the introduction to *La Teca* (1924), where he remarks that '*La Teca* is a work resulting from the affection that I feel for our cuisine' and that 'Catalonia needs a simple book on cuisine, in which recipes will be well specified' (Domènech, 2005: 16). Domènech's decision to publish in Catalan was therefore probably a combination of the practical considerations of market demands influenced by popular nationalist sentiment.

La Teca has become a classic Catalan cookbook, and almost every household that I knew today had its own copy. It is probable that many of the most popular dishes today gained their privileged position thanks to inclusion in *La Teca*. Veteran chef Josep Lladonosa i Giró (2000b: 174) described the work as 'a treasure', while in the introduction to the most recent edition (Domènech, 2005: 13) chef Pep Nogué calls it 'an authentic treatment of the cuisine of the era. A cuisine based on traditional dishes'. Nogué continued by saying that it is now the book that every cook or student should have on their bookshelf, not only because of its legacy, but also because of its popularity.

La Teca contains a compendium of present-day Catalan classics, such as 'a good *carn d'olla a la catalana*' (ibid.: 41), along with a few international dishes from Domenech's visits to London and Paris. It also contains a list of the 'Festivals or Gastronomic parties in Catalonia', listing the principal saint's day of each month, and the best dish to eat for then (this feature is further developed in his later work, *Àpats*). This is significant, because many present-day informants saw the extensive association of foods with every feast day (the gastronomic calendar) as particular to Catalonia.

Alongside *La Teca*, Domènech's most remembered work in Catalonia is *Àpats* (1930). Much like *La Teca*, this is still a popular and widespread work. Twice whilst I was visiting households, one in Baix Empordà and one in Osona, a copy of this book was brought out to look over and discuss. It is an entertaining read. The book begins with a Gastronomic Calendar, more detailed than *La Teca*. It now includes several recipes for each month and more in-depth descriptions of the nature of each dish.

This is one of the first times that a contextualisation of recipes starts to appear within Catalan cookbooks. Food is associated with custom, and a Catalan culture and norms of behaviour, i.e. a gastronomic calendar. The importance of the gastronomic calendar to Catalan food identity will be discussed in Chapter Four, but the gastronomic calendar acts as a powerful unifying tool, because it means that, ideally, Catalans will be eating the same things on the same days. The information here would have been based on known habits of the time, using foods which differ from those of Spain. This gastronomic calendar can be seen as a claim to cultural difference by Catalans and a way of promoting national unity through shared performances and eating habits. For this reason, its inclusion here proves the Catalanist nature of the book.

Though there are some similarities between *La Teca* and *Àpats* (and some duplicated recipes), *La Teca* is undoubtedly a cooking manual written for everyday usage. *Àpats* on the other hand is more complex. It is a recipe book for the most part, but it has some sections that would be little use for preparing food, e.g. the information on the festive days and the gastronomic calendar, the history of popular Barcelonan restaurants, and the section on past menus for famous events. The latter includes dinners for Catalanist politicians and groups from the early twentieth century, such as the Lliga Regionalista political party (1906), the elections of two politicians to the Generalitat (1907) and the International Congress of the Catalan language (1906). A ten-course meal given by a Mr and Mrs de Claret on 30th January 1927 is also listed, described as being based entirely on Catalan cuisine, which suggests a self-conscious desire to promote the cuisine on the part of the bourgeoisie.

These sections are intended for leisure reading, outside a cooking environment. It should be read as a contribution to knowledge about the context of Catalan cooking and its cultural traditions, not just as a recipe book. Taking this idea further, it is important to remember that 'anthropological' material is also central to national movements. This includes books on 'traditions', 'village life', 'customs', agricultural procedures, popular festivals etc, as well as culinary traditions. This 'academicism' was and still is an important component of Catalanist literature, and we should consider cookbooks as part of this canon. This book could also be 'read' as a gastronomic text that moves cuisine from a base social fact to an intellectual and cultural field (Ferguson, 1988).

Àpats is a beautifully illustrated book, and it is worthwhile to consider its non-textual elements. It seems a shame to put it in the potentially messy environment of a kitchen, suggesting it was for reading outside a kitchen. This is unlike *La Teca*, which is a simple, unembellished manual. However, the most interesting of these non-textual elements is the picture used to separate each section of the book. It presents a typified, bucolic and idealised image of a family meal in a Catalan peasant kitchen. It is immediately recognizable as taking place in Catalonia, from the *barretina*-clad men, one of whom is drinking wine from a communal *purró*, to the large hearth with an *escudella* cooking pot (presumably containing an *escudella i carn d'olla*, or *sopa*), the flat *olla* pots around the fire for other stews, agricultural implements on the walls, *tomàquets de penjar* (hanging tomatoes, the best for making *pa amb tomàquet*) from the ceiling, and through the window the covered arches typical of town squares in Catalonia.

One cannot rule out the use of irony, as this book was destined for a Barcelonan readership, who may have found these images of rural life quaint. This may be a satire on rural versus urban life, of a Catalan publisher trying to gently poke fun at his readers and to encourage them to laugh at themselves and their ideals of the rural Catalan '*pagès*' who were so romanticised in the Catalanist movement. On a more prosaic level, this non-textual element again grounds the book in a Catalanist milieu, and perhaps even could be seen as a semi-'anthropological' attempt to demonstrate how Catalans lived and ate.

Furthermore, in a 1930s edition of *Àpats*, there is an open letter to readers at the start (the only description of the writer is 'Símon'), which performs a similar function to that of the introduction, and makes manifest its Catalanist nature. The book is described as 'a veritable treasure of home cooking. It will be highly useful for *Catalan* families for the variety of dishes that can be found there' (Domènech, c. 1930; emphasis added), in the creation 'of the most celebrated meals of our land'. Again, the wording 'our land' appears, connecting this cookbook with the territory that is the basis of the nation. The book is said to be especially useful for restaurateurs, inn keepers, and hoteliers, those who must know Catalan cuisine best, as well as home cooks. This is significant as these professionals would cater to Catalan *excursionistes*, internal tourists who travelled around Catalonia as part of the project of discovering the nation – and who expected to consume good Catalan food.

Llibre de la Cuina Catalana: A Nationalist's Cookbook

1928 saw the publication of the *Llibre de la Cuina Catalana* ('Book of Catalan Cuisine'), a work written purely with the intention of glorifying cuisine as a rallying point of Catalan nationalism. The author, Ferran Agulló, was not a chef; he was a well-respected member of the intelligentsia and political elite of the era and was associated with the right-wing Lliga Catalana. Journalist, poet and gastronome, he is reputed to have popularised the name 'Costa Brava' ('wild coast') to refer to Catalonia's northern coast. This is an example of a famous member of the Catalanist intelligentsia publishing a cookbook, demonstrating how a cookbook can be a tool for a nationalist writer. In the introduction to his book, he throws down the gauntlet for his defence of cuisine as a repository of Catalan identity. These are the first words of his book:

> Catalonia, just as it has a language, a right, customs, its own history and a political ideal, so it has a cuisine. There are regions, nations, peoples, who have a special, characteristic dish, but not a cuisine. Catalonia has that. (Agulló, 1999: 11)

And it has more, he adds. It has the power to assimilate dishes from other cuisines: '[Catalan cuisine] makes these dishes of other cuisines their own and modifies them according to their taste' (ibid.). Moreover, Catalan cuisine has a global reach through its adventurous inhabitants (the ideal Catalan of the time was one who travelled, made his wealth, then returned to enrich his homeland):

> The cuisine of Catalonia represented by a few of its dishes, has left its borders, conquering South America, Australia, Italy and a large part of the Iberian regions. It has been an instrument of expansion, and with the goodness of its dishes, Catalan cooks of sailboats, who upon their leaving the Catalan shorelines, installed themselves in the five corners of the world. (Ibid.: 11–12)

Agulló states that the purpose of the book is not to teach people to cook, but to promote Catalanism through its recipes. He is presenting a simple and economical cuisine, that applies to all the people in Catalonia, whom he has come to know from his travels throughout the country (as I stated a moment ago, both then as now, exploring Catalonia as an *excursionist* was an important activity for Catalanists). His introduction concludes by stating that he will 'demonstrate that Catalonia has its own cuisine, special, complete and for all tastes and dietary regimes' (ibid.: 12).

After the introduction, Agulló goes on to discuss food for daily meals and festive occasions in Catalonia, before going into the recipe collection. As in Domènech's *Àpats*, this chapter has an 'anthropological' feel to it, of a writer who has researched the facts, and set them down for readers. Once again, elements like these demonstrate how cookbooks can become guides to ideal behaviour for Catalans in a nationalist context. Like B. Anderson's (1983) printed newspapers, ideally Catalan readers would be reading the same information about how other Catalans behaved, and perhaps even identifying with it, situating themselves (and what they ate), within a Catalonia unified by these characteristics.

Next, Agulló talks of a set menu expected of all types of celebration, from baptisms to Festa Majors. Many of the dishes he describes for each major annual celebration are identical to those of today. For example, obligatory dishes for Christmas and New Year are turkey, chicken or capons, and *escudella i carn d'olla*. This section concludes with 'This is the tradition. If in the city it is not conserved, it still holds very much so, in villages, towns and settlements' (Agulló, 1999: 21). This is an idealisation of the rural, a common feature of nationalist movements, by claiming that 'true', autochthonous Catalan food culture has been preserved in a rural setting (like Sobral, 2014 and Yotova, 2014). As many of the readers would probably have been from Barcelona, aside from being informative the book may have also been a call to keep up those 'traditions', as a means of manifesting Catalanism (and glorifying a 'folk culture').

Throughout *Llibre de la Cuina Catalana*, Agulló repeatedly refers to the concept of the *Països Catalans*. At a cultural level, this means the inclusion or appropriation of some aspects of these areas, and this is especially true in discourses on cuisine. For example, dishes from Valencia or the Balearic islands are discussed in the book as if they are as Catalan as those from within the Principat. Agulló includes a great many recipes from the Balearics. In his section on sauces, he includes mayonnaise sauce as one of the principal sauces, which he underlines as being from Mahó – '*salsa mahonesa* called *maionesa*', which really should be called *mahonesa* because of its town of origin in Menorca.

The ideal of a wider reaching *Països Catalans* identity is subtly suggested by including references to it. Similarly, in the introduction, Agulló underlines the importance of variety and diversity that is seen to represent the different counties of Catalonia and the *Països Catalans*. In his own words:

> Just as the language has dialects, and the law has county modalities, and customs and dances are diverse in the different counties and ancient realms of Catalonia (Valencia, Mallorca, Provence, Roussillon), *Catalan cuisine is one*, but each one of these territories has special dishes, dishes that have taken the name of one of these counties. (Agulló, 1999: 12; emphasis added)

By referring to the Catalan-speaking areas, as 'ancient realms' he is bringing them into the fold of the overarching Catalan nation by including their cuisine as part of the larger 'one' of Catalan cuisine. The *Països Catalans* are an indivisible whole, and so too is Catalan cuisine, though regional variations are recognised. Like many of today's Catalan cookbooks, Agulló's recipe collection begins with an explanation of the sauces in Catalan cuisine. He recognises that there are many different variations, and then provides a basic recipe. Again, regional specificities and variations have to be accepted in the Catalan case, if a believable national identity is to be created, and one in which regional variation, not homogeneity (which was to become associated with Spain), came to be seen as another defining feature of Catalan culinary identity.

This work is intriguing from a contemporary perspective, as many of the features that Catalans today express as central to their cuisine are in this book. It is also interesting that the Draft Constitution of the Catalan Republic was written in the same year this cookbook was published, a document that was meant to act as the foundation for a Catalan state that never materialised. The *Llibre de la Cuina Catalana* should be seen as a culmination of this early twentieth century Catalanist sentiment when it comes to food.

The Republic and Cookbooks in the Franco Era

With the arrival of the Republican government in 1931, few other cookbooks of note were published, though existing cookbooks were republished.

Another source of gastronomic literature and education at this time was Barcelona's Women's Institute of Culture and Popular Library, set up by educationalist Francesca Bonnemaison in 1909. The Swiss-Italian chef Josep Rondissoni led cooking instruction from 1909 to 1937 (when the school was forced to close). There was a strong French emphasis in the recipes he provided in the cooking courses (weekly from October to June), however he included at least one Catalan recipe every month, in line with the demands of bourgeois Catalan households of the time (Rondissoni 1924, 1925, 1927, 1930).

A new alimentary reality hit Catalonia with the Spanish Civil War (1936–1939), which led to a new type of culinary literature. By popular demand, in 1937 the Generalitat published a recipe book with advice on wartime cooking, followed by several similar texts. In the Franco era, publications in Catalan were largely forbidden, though this was relaxed in the 1960s and 70s. Re-editions of popular and religious works, especially cookbooks, were permitted (needless to say, Agulló's *Llibre de la Cuina Catalana* was not one of them). Cookbook publications in Spain experienced a rise in popularity from the 1950s, and one of the most popular books of this time (published in Barcelona) was *Sabores* from 1945. In the 1960s, new Catalan cookbooks make an appearance, and were permitted because of their supposedly non-political nature as expressions of folk culture (Hall, 2001).

Ironically, this meant that one of the few ways that the Catalans could have access to new literature in their language was through cookbooks. These restrictions made Catalan books far more valued, and these came to be objects of covert Catalanist significance in the Franco era. Many families kept treasured Catalan libraries hidden in their homes (Llobera, 2004), and cookbooks formed part of these libraries. The role of these cookbooks in language preservation was brought home to me by Mon, a lecturer and professional cooking instructor in Barcelona. Not only did they become a symbol of Catalan identity through their language, they also helped to preserve Catalan names for particular foods. For example, the Catalan word for broth (*brou*) could have become the Castilian *caldo* if Catalan could not be spoken, leading to the loss of the vocabulary that contributes to distinctiveness.

Cookbooks are a seemingly uncontroversial form of literature, regardless of the language used. One could even argue that by allowing the publication in Catalan of certain seemingly non-threatening genres (e.g. folklore, dance, religious tracts, cookery etc.), the language could be trivialised as unsuited for serious topics such as politics or history. Inherent in this degradation is no doubt the association of cookbooks with female readers, thereby potentially placing Catalan in the private, inferior, feminine sphere (according to Falangist thought) through culinary literature.

However, some cookbooks published at this time may carry a hidden pro-Catalan subtext. In one of the Catalan language cookbooks published at this time (*200 Plats casolans de cuina catalana*, '200 home-made dishes from Catalan cuisine', 1969, by Antoni Dalmau), the author defends the notion that every region or village of Catalonia has its own dishes that distinguish the cuisine from the rest of Spain, much as Ferran Agulló had done 40 years earlier. Indeed, some of the points made by Dalmau mirror those of Agulló, for example, that Catalan cuisine is uncomplicated, and that it 'has left its frontiers, conquering those of the two Americas, Australia, Italy, and all the Spanish nation, being in its time a vehicle of expansion' (Dalmau, 1969: 5–6), thanks to the maritime exploits of its inhabitants. The parallels with Agulló are clear, though what is interesting here is the claim that Catalan cuisine has 'conquered' Spain. Considering the political situation of the era, the description here is a contradiction of the official image of a strong, centralised Spanish nation that had overcome regional identities. Reference is also made to the past glories, particularly to the *Libre de Coch* of Mestre Robert – another example of how this book is glorified as 'one of the first written cookbooks in the world' (ibid.: 5).

Dalmau also imitates Agulló's sentiment that Catalan cuisine is not a chauvinistic cuisine because, 'it has never suffered the sin of exclusivity and has adapted to universal modalities' (ibid.: 6). While listing the places associated with foods, like Agulló and Domènech, he remarks that days are also associated with foods. He concludes his introduction by saying that he hopes this series of culinary recipes will be shared throughout Catalan home kitchens, suggesting that like many other authors his aim was to promote Catalan recipes at a popular level. It is a hidden transcript (Scott, 1990) of both resistance and preservation. Another cookbook published at the same time, *Catalunya llaminera* ('Sweet Catalonia', Anonymous, 1968) also reinforces this stance by referring to the gastronomic calendar and regional specialities, just as Ignasi Domènech had done in *Àpats* (I should also add that sweet foods are also considered as something that differentiates Catalan cuisine from its neighbours).

It is important to remember that one way in which Catalans seek to differentiate themselves today from Spaniards is by this very diversity, held in contrast to a perceived homogenous Spanish identity. To glorify the specificities of Catalan food cultures was an implicit celebration of this Catalan identity. Writing similar sentiments outside of a cookbook would have been unthinkable in that time, showing how it was possible for culinary literature to became so associated with a defence of Catalan identity in the late Franco era.

An exhibition on cookbooks in Palau Robert from 2005 also noted another book called *Cuina Catalana* ('Catalan Cuisine') from 1971 by Maria del Carme Nicolau. Nicolau was a Catalanist, feminist journalist who pioneered Catalan women's literature in the 1920s, and which likely influenced her decision to publish her views in this cookbook. In Nicolau's introduction (entitled 'Every land ... does their cuisine'), the writer 'defends the taste of Catalan cuisine as its own cuisine and explains its evolution' (Generalitat de Catalonia, 2005: 25). In her introduction, Nicolau states that:

> It is an indisputable reality; you only have to put your nose into Catalonia, and you can tell that not only the *aesthetic of landscape*, the clothing, the customs and the *language* change, *so too does the style of eating*, the preparation and the condiments. (Nicolau, 1977: 11; emphasis added)

This extended quote brings up several interesting points. First of all, the author mentions the landscape, which is a potent point of national identity and difference, intimately connected to cuisine. She also states clearly that there is a different language; to state that Catalan was still a separate language that visibly differentiated Catalonia was bold indeed in the Franco era. As has been shown elsewhere, the Catalan language is the main justification of a separate Catalan identity. Here it is implicitly linked with the separate culinary identity.

Nicolau goes on to praise the *escudella i carn d'olla*, as 'the typical dish of our land ... with rice and *fideus* [pasta] ... What is the magic of this Catalan dish!' (Nicolau, 1977: 11). She is similarly effusive about '*seques amb botifarra*' (beans and sausage), seeing them as the best standard bearers of Catalan cuisine. Unlike other authors (both before and after) she is critical of the mixing of other cuisines with that of Catalonia, even going so far as to use the term 'our national cuisine', which is losing its good tastes to foreign influences. She then concludes in a similar manner to some other writers (like Agulló), by saying she is contributing to a furthering of the knowledge of the cuisine to prevent its disappearance. She is optimistic however, idealising Catalan cuisine as an unchanging cuisine that will always remain popular for Catalans. Although now these words may sound quaint, even chauvinistic, to claim in print that any aspect of Catalan national identity was going to continue to survive would have been almost unthinkable (anthropologists of the time, such as Hansen 1977, also predicted its disappearance). Even though these words relate to homely, familiar, dishes for Catalans, there is an unmistakable hint of national pride.

In this sort of environment, Catalan books, both cookbooks and other genres, came to hold a special significance as material objects. They became objects of resistance, and held a special reverence not just for what they said but also what they represented. When considering the relevance to the discussion of cookbooks as nationalist objects, the following story I heard from Jordi, a university lecturer in Barcelona, was especially moving. In his childhood under Franco, Jordi's mother kept Domènech's *La Teca* in pride of place in their kitchen, as a focus of Catalan identity in the domestic environment. These were Catalan recipes, written in the persecuted Catalan language, using Catalan words for foods. For his mother to cook the recipes for her family was a means of both transmitting Catalan identity, and quietly rebelling against the Francoist regime. He therefore came to see this cookbook as a rallying point in his early development as a Catalanist. One could even say that they are literary Proust's madeleines, intimately bound up with a past moment and memory that can be recalled on contact with them. Like food itself, books on food are powerful tools of memory.

Josep Pla and the Defence of Catalan Cuisine under Franco

Before moving onto culinary literature in the transition to democracy and post-Franco era, this is the ideal place to consider another writer, Josep Pla. Pla was one of the most readily-quoted Catalan authors amongst my informants, and undoubtedly one of the most important Catalan writers of the twentieth century. He was born in Palafrugell, Baix Empordà in 1897, and died in that same town in 1981, having seen some of the most tumultuous years in Spain's modern history.

He began his journalism career in 1919, travelling the world and reporting on politics from Madrid in the months leading up to the Civil War, when he fled the country. After returning in 1940, he based himself in his native Catalonia, and wrote extensively on his experiences, making his work an excellent source of information on Catalan life in this period. In his later works on his homeland, there is an element of salvage ethnography, because he was one of several authors of the time who felt that Catalan rural identity was gradually being eroded by Francoism,[3] modernity and tourism, and had to be recorded for posterity.

Unlike many of his contemporaries, he was politically neutral (though privately opposed to Francoism) and was able to continue writing during the dictatorship. This may be the reason why he managed to publish in Catalan after the 1950s, at a time when the language was largely banned. It is also for this reason that the post-Francoist Catalan literati snubbed him.

Food appears in many of Pla's works about his home country, and not all of them can be discussed in this book. In case of doubt when it comes to areas of Catalan life (including cuisine), Pla is the first port of call for Catalans. Like Chekhov in Caldwell's ethnography on Russian identity and the *dacha* (country home), Pla's works are seen as essential sources of information on many subjects in Catalonia, including culinary heritage. Caldwell (2011: 30) calls Chekhov a 'key informant – a person who, in anthropological terms, possesses extensive knowledge on a particular subject, can communicate that knowledge effectively, and enjoys widespread respect and acclaim for that knowledge', giving an account of everyday life. In this sense, Pla's work is similar to that of a primary informant, as a way of seeing inside the mind of a Catalan who had strong views about his identity, how it related to food and whose views are respected by other Catalans.

Perhaps his most famous work on food is his book *El que hem menjat* ('What We Have Eaten', 1972). This work follows his thoughts and experiences with food throughout his life, in 65 chapters dedicated to different aspects of Catalan culinary culture, particularly in Empordà, the area where he was born and lived for much of his life. The work is not really a gastronomic text, and Pla did not consider himself a gastronome (he did not enjoy eating), but it does contain his thoughts about cuisine, particularly traditional cuisine outside of restaurants and within the home. As I mentioned earlier, Pla's works are a source of information for Catalans on their own culture (a frequent saying to back up some cultural claim was 'Pla wrote about it'). This book is no exception and is now itself the basis of contemporary culinary literature.[4]

The tone of *El que hem menjat* is one of loss, and every chapter includes or concludes with a mournful diatribe about the impending disappearance of whatever is under discussion. His first sentence sets the tone, and also delineates that he will be talking mostly about Empordà, 'In this country where I normally live – in Empordà – there is a certain familiar cuisine that, undoubtedly, these days is gradually disappearing in a certain and inevitable way'. (Pla, 1972: 7). Idealisation of the past is key to his message, and he blatantly claims that 'before, everyone ate well, poor and rich' (ibid.).

Culinary Literature in the Post-Franco Era

With the coming of democracy, Catalan language and identity was now an acceptable medium and subject for publications, such as cookbooks, magazine and newspaper articles. There had already been some tentative attempts at promoting Catalan culinary identity, for example with the 1975 *Assortiment Gastronomic de Catalunya*, organised by now-retired chef Josep Lladonosa i Giró (a legend in his own lifetime in Catalonia for his contributions to Catalan cuisine). Culinary literature from this period is dominated by authors, rather than set books, such as the aforementioned Josep Lladonosa i Giró, Nèstor Luján, Manuel Vázquez Montalbán, Núria Baguena and Jaume Fàbrega, to name but a few. New editions could now be published of the first Catalan cookbooks that had a more obviously Catalanist tone, such as

Agulló's *Llibre de la Cuina Catalana* in 1978, and Rudolf Grewe's edition of the *Llibre de Sent Soví*, in 1979.

One work from this period that cannot be missed is *L'art del menjar a Catalunya* ('The Art of Eating in Catalonia'), by Manuel Vázquez Montalbán, first published in 1977. Firstly, the date of publication is significant, two years after Franco's death. Secondly, its subtitle, 'A Chronicle of the Resistance of Signs of Gastronomic Catalan Identity', positions it unambiguously as a book aimed at promoting Catalan cuisine as a sign of resistance against the old regime, and a symbol of identity to be preserved. This is a similar stance to Agulló's *Llibre de la Cuina Catalana* 50 years earlier, and Pla's *El que hem menjat*. This work may have contributed to the continued survival of Catalan cuisine and its regeneration in the post-Franco era by sensitising Catalans to cuisine as a national symbol. My informants frequently referred to it as an essential work on their cuisine. It was republished in 2004 with the subtitle 'the Red Book of Catalan Gastronomic Identity'. This change of title suggests a changed situation, where cuisine was no longer at threat of being lost as it had been at the end of the Franco period.[5]

Other essential figures include the modern chefs of this time. Indeed, it could be argued that no chef can really be taken seriously in Catalonia without publishing at least one cookbook. Some, like Ferran Adrià, the Roca brothers or Carme Ruscalleda, see these cookbooks as a key part of their output, and they are useful for the researcher seeking to understand their trajectories, inspirations and methods (and, for this work, supplement opinions expressed in field interviews). Ferran Adrià in particular often refers back to his first publication (*El Bulli: El sabor del Mediterráneo*, 'The Taste of the Mediterranean', 1993) to defend criticisms of excessive modernity that ignore the Catalan context, as this book explicitly demonstrated how Catalan cuisine inspired his earliest creations. On a more mercantile level, they are also useful cash cows and tools for self-promotion, and even act as personalised souvenirs of a visit to a celebrated restaurant. More recently, Michelin-starred chef Joan Roca has recognised the essential role of research and cookbooks in his personal cooking philosophy, which he calls '*academicism*' (Roca, 2013).

It is worthwhile to introduce other writers from the last thirty years who have played an important role in the development and dissemination of ideas about Catalan cuisine. One is Nèstor Luján, a journalist and gastronome. His works mostly catalogue the history of Catalan cuisine, and much like Pla his opinions are sacrosanct. He emphasised the historic continuity of Catalan cuisine, which Luján believed traced its origins back to the Romans, with titles such as *Mil anys de la cuina catalana* ('A Thousand Years of Catalan Cuisine', 1989) or *Vint segles de cuina a Barcelona* ('Twenty Centuries of Cuisine in Barcelona', 1993). Both Vázquez Montalbán and Luján had died over a decade before I arrived in the field, so their books provide an essential insight into their attitudes to cuisine.

Another author who is impossible to miss is Josep Lladonosa i Giró, organiser of the Catalan Gastronomic Assortment of 1975. This was an important moment for resurrecting Catalan cuisine towards the end of the Franco era. He himself is a very strong Catalanist and was very clear that he saw his protection of Catalan cuisine as a nationalist duty (to *'fer país'*, a popular phrase to describe such activities). He also published one of the first full length cookbooks on Catalan cuisine in the post-Franco era, appropriately entitled *La Cuina que Torna* ('The Cuisine that Returns', 1982), followed by other cookbooks (including one of today's classic cookbooks, *El Gran Llibre de la Cuina Catalana*, 'The Big Book of Catalan Cuisine', 1996 now in its third edition, 2005) and gastronomic literature (like Luján, these are mostly historic in focus). He also had a Barcelona restaurant called the 'Quatre Barres' (Four Bars), a reference to the *senyera*, which he opened on the day of the 1977 Diada protests, and was also manager of another famous Barcelona restaurant, 'Les Sept Portes' (The Seven Doors).

A final claimant to fame for contributing to the resurgence in Catalan cuisine is food writer Jaume Fàbrega. He alleges that he was one of the first to begin writing about Catalan cuisine in a public newspaper in the late 1970s, and he also gave the Celler de Can Roca its first review. As well as journalism, he has published over 200 books on Catalan cuisine. As a result, he is one of the most well-known Catalan food writers, and his work regularly appears in any bookshop or stall throughout Catalonia. As such, he is a recognised expert on these topics like Pla and Lladonosa i Giró.

In the last few years, with the rise of a new independence movement, expressing Catalan identity has begun to stretch to all parts of everyday life, and cookbook publishing is no exception. At gastronomic and national festivals, any Catalanist bookstall is incomplete without a sizeable cookery section peddling the popular titles of the last few years, and new editions of the older works. With names such as *100 Dishes of Catalan Cuisine That You Have to Try* (Guirado, 2012), *Catalan Cuisine for Festivals and Traditions* (Sano and Clotet, 2010, already in its third edition in 2012), *501 Catalan Recipes That You Have to Try Before You Die* (Garcia Massagué, 2012), they appeal to a Catalan consumer who is keen to promote and express their identity by investing in Catalan books and products. It is interesting that many books with titles such as those above appeared soon after the 2012 protest. Re-editions of old favourites, such as *La Cuynera Catalana* of 1853, Ignasi Domènech's *La Teca* and *Àpats*, and the *Llibre de Sent Soví* add to this popular literature on Catalonia's historic and culinary past.

The popularity of cookbooks as a genre (in particular those of celebrity chefs) in the early twenty-first century is not unique to Catalonia, but it has taken on a particular manifestations here due to the context of the Catalan independence movement. It is likely that cookbooks' contemporary popularity and visibility has contributed to the perception that cuisine makes an essential contribution to Catalan cultural nationalism today.

Notes

1. Not just in the *sofregit* and *picada*, but also in the Catalan habit of mixing sweet and sour flavours, *agredolç*, which was common to most of medieval European, court cuisine.
2. A reference to the second line of the Catalan national anthem.
3. Particularly historian Jaume Vicens Vives, who wrote one of the most influential histories of Catalonia in the twentieth century, *Notícia de Catalunya* (1954).
4. Celebrated chef Joan Roca, began the introduction to his first cookbook (on his mother's cuisine, it is important to note) with a reference to Josep Pla's *El que hem menjat*, quoting the claim that the cuisine he discusses is a 'familiar cuisine', and a good cuisine. Like Pla, Roca goes on to point out how much has changed since some idealised past time, how tourism has contributed to the abandonment of traditional cuisine and continues the litany of loss heard in Pla's work and others (Roca, 2004).
5. This realisation was also made separately by Garcia-Fuentes et al (2014), who note that this work provides 'an ironic and provocative if not heretical culinary parallel to the mission of protecting the language' (Garcia-Fuentes et al, 2014: 161)

Chapter 2
THE FOUNDATIONAL SAUCES AND NATIONAL DISHES

❧

Chapter One introduced several of the essential dishes and elements of Catalan cuisine, including the foundational sauces of *sofregit*, *picada* and *allioli*, and dishes such as the *escudella i carn d'olla* stew and *pa amb tomàquet*. The aim of this chapter is to unpack these elements further, to provide a rounded view of Catalan cuisine, its characteristics and the ideas and meanings that are attached to them. There will be a strong focus on cooked products in this chapter, rather than the ingredients themselves. While some ingredients and products may be unique to Catalonia, many are shared with surrounding countries and identities. To claim them as particular to Catalan cuisine would not be accurate. What is particular is their treatment when cooked, both in the eyes of my informants, and from an objective, factual standpoint. It is through the act of cooking that ingredients, often of non-Catalan origin, are acculturated with significance in a national context, and thereby become bearers of national identity. The style of cooking, the techniques, and the mixing of ingredients all contribute to the Catalanisation of a dish.

In the first section of this chapter, I will discuss several sauces essential to Catalan cuisine, which almost all my informants saw as central to the identity and specificity of Catalan cuisine, its basic foundations. In the second half of the chapter, I consider Catalan national 'signature' dishes. For my informants, these sauces and dishes were often related to other aspects of their culinary identity, such as their connection with a historical identity through cuisine, the openness of Catalan national and culinary identity, changes in contemporary cooking styles, and comparisons and contextualisation of Catalan cuisine with others in the Iberian Peninsula. Hence, this discussion will frequently branch into other topics that appeared in field interviews, following the associations and interpretations of informants.

The Foundational Sauces

A thing that differentiates Catalan cuisine from Portuguese and Spanish cuisine are the sauces. There is a great richness in sauces, primary bases of cuisine. Of the *sofregit*, that does not exist in Spanish cuisine, and in Portuguese very little and only in one place. The *picada*, which is the second base of a dish, and the *allioli negat* … Then, of the important sauces, the *romesco*, the best sauce in Europe. Because it is phenomenal, the sauce of the *xató*, or of *calçots* which are also variants.

—Jaume Fàbrega

This detailed quote from the beginning of an interview with Jaume Fàbrega, food historian and writer, introduces us to the foundations of Catalan cuisine, the sauces of the *sofregit*, the *picada*, the *allioli* and the *romesco*. As in my interview with Jaume, these sauces were often the first topic in any discussion on Catalan cuisine, firstly because of their claims to distinctiveness, and secondly because of their essential role in 'flavouring' a dish as Catalan, literally and figuratively.

Ferran Agulló, in his *Llibre de la Cuina Catalana* (1928), dedicates an early chapter to 'The basic sauces of our cuisine': the *sofregit*, the *samfaina*, the *picada* and the *allioli*. The *samfaina* admittedly is no longer included in this list today, perhaps because it is now considered a dish in its own right.[1] The *sofregit* is the starting point of any dish, made up in its most basic form of onion, garlic, parsley and tomato (according to Agulló, it can be done in different ways according to the dish being cooked). The *picada* is a paste of various herbs, spices and ground nuts with some liquid. *Allioli* and mayonnaise differ little from their British counterparts in terms of basic ingredients. The *romesco* is conspicuous by its absence, but this may be because the *romesco* was limited to the southern areas of Catalonia at the time. This is a spicy and versatile sauce, red-orange in colour and made up of *nyora*,[2] dry bread, almonds and other nuts, olive oil, *bitxo* peppers (very like chillies) and garlic (though, as many of my informants pointed out, there are almost as many variations as there are cooks, and this set of ingredients are only the basics).

The Michelin-starred chef Joan Roca (2004) also began his book *La cuina de la meva mare* (My Mother's Cooking) by talking about sauces. The first chapter, 'The Bases of Catalan Cuisine', is dedicated to the *sofregit*, *picada*, *allioli* and *romesco*. Like Agulló, Roca's first recipe is a *sofregit*, underlining its importance in Catalan cuisine. He recommends placing a finely diced onion in a pan of fat or oil, until it begins to brown, followed by the garlic (if desired) and tomato. Cook on a low heat until it has become like a sauce, to lessen the strength and bitterness of the tomato. During one of his presentations and in our interview, Joan Roca also recalled how his mother would prepare the *sofregit* on a very low heat overnight, leaving the onions to caramelise for hours before use the next morning in their small restaurant.

The Historicism of the *Sofregit*

That the *sofregit* is a starting point for many writers on Catalan cuisine is indicative of its importance. Throughout fieldwork, one of the most uniform responses to the question of what makes a dish Catalan, or what is the most important element, involved the *sofregit* or the *picada*. For Ramon Morató, a Vic chocolatier, he described Catalan cuisine as 'very much of the home, cuisine of the *sofregit*'. Barcelona chef Fermí likewise claimed that a Catalan dish is 'any that had a *sofregit*, the basic sauce from which to make our cuisine'.

The *sofregit* and *picada* are also often considered representative of Catalan cuisine's long history. For instance, when I asked Carles Gaig, a Michelin-starred Barcelona chef, what were the most important elements in Catalan cuisine, he selected the 'autochthonous' *picada* and the *sofregit*, saying that they 'define the essence of ancient Catalan cuisine'. I pointed out that this *sofregit* must have been without tomatoes, because they only entered Catalan cuisine in the nineteenth century. To support his argument for the *sofregit's* antiquity, he quoted from Catalan cookbooks:

> For example, the most ancient cookbook that we know is the *Libre de Coch* from 1400 ... there's a *sofregit*. The next oldest, maybe one of the oldest, was *La Cuynera Catalana*, from 1830–35, and there we find tomatoes, though very subtly, not being used much. But the *sofregit* is there, consisting of onions, garlic.

One can see in Carles' interpretation of the centrality of Catalan sauces the current of a historicism that frequently pervades discussions of Catalan cuisine. For many of my informants, their interpretation of contemporary cuisine is implicitly linked with that of the Catalan past, and how the preservation of characteristics of medieval cuisine acts as a window onto a golden age in Catalan history through its historic cookbooks, a concept already introduced in Chapter One.

Pepa Aymamí, the former head of the Fundació Institut Català de la Cuina i de la Cultura Gastronòmica (FICCG) and the main organiser of the bid for recognition under the UNESCO intangible cultural heritage scheme, is particularly keen that the history of Catalan cuisine be researched. Her reasoning was that, if not, there is a risk that Catalan cuisine might be misunderstood. A historical background sets it on a more stable footing and lends legitimacy to claims of a unique culinary identity for the campaign. The power of the past (whether actual or invented) in creating this legitimacy is a feature to be found in many nationalist movements, as well as claims to heritage protection. Barthes' claim that through national foods, peoples 'partake each day of the national past' (Barthes, 1961; 27), rings true for Catalonia. A common theme during fieldwork when my informants introduced and described dishes would be some background on its place of origin and history.

In this way, food can act as a touchstone with a historical past, in which Catalans can connect what they consume with this past, a past that is also the foundation and justification of their current national identity. Josep Sucarrats, the editor of the food magazine *Cuina*, after discussing the glob-ally-renowned chefs that Catalonia has produced in the contemporary era, returned to historical justifications for this situation: 'We share a country that has a very important culinary history, very rich and very identificatory from the Middle Ages until now. And which lives alongside some vanguard cooks who have been directly inspired by this very ancient cuisine that has evolved'. It is significant that vanguard chefs of the *nova cuina* are described as direct heirs to this rich history, implying a seamless transmission between past and present, which is not considered contradictory. This sentiment of living alongside an 'ancient cuisine' is a powerful image for culinary and national identity.

The importance of the *sofregit* as an identifying feature and its historical connectivity became salient during a cooking session with Jaume Fàbrega, where he showed me how the different sauces were used in the contexts of not just his cooking, but also with regards to his history and national identity. He compared the processes involved in making the dish we were cooking (*conill amb xocolata;* rabbit in chocolate sauce) with those of the medieval era. He introduced the *sofregit* preparation by saying 'in the medi-eval era, they used to do this'. Later in the cooking process, Jaume explained how the *picada* would give the dish a medieval character from its grainy texture. I pointed out that chocolate was something that would not have existed in the medieval era. This aspect was unimportant for him, just as chocolate was one of the more recent additions to the canon of ingredients one could add to the *picada*. In this way, an apparent contradiction to a tenet of gastronational identity could be swiftly refuted (a characteristic also found in Israel by Raviv, 2015). Chocolate was however important in Catalonia's more recent national history (I discuss this at the end of Chapter Five), so could still contribute to the historicism of the *picada*, albeit from another era. In this way, elements like the *picada* became a way of connecting with a timeline of Catalan history.

Sofregit as Culinary Differentiator

Returning to the distinctiveness of the *sofregit*, Jaume Fàbrega considered the way of making the *sofregit* as distinctly Catalan, differentiating Catalan from Spanish cooks, who use more tomato:

> When a Spaniard cooks [*sofregit*], you notice it. Because with a *sofregit*, it is forbidden to notice the tomato, but in the Spanish way, it is a tomato sauce. A Catalan never uses tinned tomatoes, it is unthinkable, but the Spanish way always uses them. So theoretically it is Catalan cuisine, but, like in Barcelona, they've never had an excess of that which is Catalan cuisine.[3] So the *macarrons*[4] [from Barcelona] taste wonderful, but I look at them and they're awful because with the Catalan ones you would not notice the tomatoes.

The components of the Catalan *sofregit* are therefore different from those made by the non-Catalan, Spanish 'other'. Indeed, in a somewhat essentialist way, Jaume suggested that a non-Catalan would find it harder to make a *sofregit*, because they have not grown up with the ancestral tastes – though it would not be impossible. Translation would also be an issue, as the usual translation in Castilian culinary literature for *sofregit* is *sofrito*. In reality, this describes another type of sauce, one with more tomatoes, which are fried, and which Jaume believed is rarely used in Catalan households (in practice, this is not entirely true). Their similarity might affect claims to culinary uniqueness, hence the need to draw attention to the presence of Catalanising features, such as the different use of tomatoes.

Two other chefs who did not wish to be named added that the celebrated Catalan chef Ferran Adrià did a terrible *sofregit*, in this 'Spanish' style with tinned tomatoes. One used this as the basis for his questioning of Adrià's true identity as a Catalan, because if he could not make the *sofregit* properly, then how could he be called a true representative of Catalonia's culinary tradition? This demonstrates well the centrality of the *sofregit*, because a chef's inability to cook it properly brought into question their very identity in the eyes of his or her peers.

The question of linguistic identity in translation is an interesting one in the Catalan–Spanish relationship, because the untranslatability of certain concepts (such as *seny* and *rauxa*) is often a mark of their distinctiveness. The difficulty of translating a dish into Spanish, or any other language, lends credence to a claim that the dish is exclusively Catalan. Similarly, several informants referred to the untranslatability of the Catalan use of the word *sobretaula* (literally 'around-the-table'). In its basic sense, it means discussing ideas around a table after a meal, continuing the sociable atmosphere and aiding digestion. The word in this sense can literally be translated as *sobremesa* in Spanish, and the concept is present in other Mediterranean contexts. Catalans however use the word in broader contexts, such as to describe public, roundtable events to discuss politics, independence or other civic issues, without a meal to precede it. The association with food and the sociability of a meal still remains, as a *sobretaula* implies a relaxed, homely atmosphere where anyone can speak up, compared to more formal debates, presentations or panels. Light snacks and drinks may also be served at *sobretaula* events, further playing on the associations of the word in the minds of informants.

Conversely, it should be noted that another of my informants, Mon, a cooking professor at Barcelona's tourism school, saw no difference between the *sofregit* and the *sofrito*. Both required frying onion and garlic in oil at the start of the cooking process, and included onions and tomatoes. How much of each would depend on individual taste. She also saw no problems using tinned tomatoes if the need arose. Similarly, Ferran Agulló in his 1933 description of the *sofregit* suggests using preserved tomato or tomato paste. The ideal *sofregit* can also be time-consuming to prepare (for instance, Joan Roca's mother preparing it overnight). This has led to strategies for speeding up the process. For instance, Irene, a woman in her twenties, would use pre-prepared, frozen *sofregit* that her mother prepared for her, as she rarely had time to prepare it in the 'proper' way. This way of speeding up the process was not always seen positively in the field, however it demonstrates how national identity performance changes over time, and how its performers adapt national objects (in this case, the *sofregit*) to new circumstances.

'We Are of the Onion': The Onion in Catalan Culinary Identity

The key element of the *sofregit* has always been the onion, and it is through the strong presence of onion that the *sofregit* can connect with medieval cuisine. The tomato was brought from the Americas, and only came into widespread use in the nineteenth century. Discussing the *sofregit* as the foundation of Catalan cuisine with Núria Baguena, a food historian, brought her on to the importance of onion to Catalan food identity: 'Everything we cook, we're accustomed to make them with onion. I have many Erasmus [Programme] students, and they define the Catalans as onion-eaters. Because we put onion everywhere … So, this *sofregit de ceba* is very Catalan, very done [here]. In other places they do it less'.

In this instance, identity is constructed in a general context of outsiders and their opinions. Núria later went on to discuss further the importance of the onion in Catalan cuisine. She compared Catalans with the Valencians and Valencian *paella*, claiming 'they do not put onion in the *paella*, it infuriates them! But here, a *paella* without onion, it cannot be'. These may be small differences, she added, but they are important distinctions for Catalan culinary identity. She also referred to the Catalans' use of onion in *truita* or *tortilla de patates*, best translated using the Spanish 'tortilla', an omelette stuffed with potatoes and other ingredients. Both the Catalan word '*truita*' and the Spanish '*tortilla*' are used interchangeably, without linguistic discrimination in everyday parlance. In Núria's words,

> The *tortilla espanyola*, we don't have it. We have *tortilla catalana*, the *truita de patates* with onion, that is something that people who come from outside like a lot … it is said the *tortilla espanyola* is done without onion, and has been adapted somewhat to Catalonia.

I cooked the *truita/tortilla de patates* with three women: Mon, Irene and her mother Concepció, and each said that the Catalan *truita/tortilla* has onions in it, which doesn't normally happen in the rest of Spain, where they only use potato. Like Núria they all felt the need to emphasise these minor differences from Spain through the *truita/tortilla* (even if some of those differences may be exaggerated, inconsistent, or out-of-date).[5] According to Mon, 'There are very simple things like the *truita de patates*, but with onion. The Spanish *tortilla* doesn't have onion in principle. When it has onion, for me, it is my *truita*, when only half of it is potato'.

During my interview with Núria, I asked her about the popular Catalan saying '*Som de la ceba*', literally 'We are of the onion', to describe someone who felt strongly Catalan. I was curious how this particular vegetable came to be connected to national identity, and whether it represented an intersection of national identity, territory, land and food. The general consensus was that this saying described an individual who took their Catalan identity seriously, and that it now means someone independentist, fanatical and stubborn.[6] The discussions around this phrase revealed the changes that have taken place in attitudes to independence, and its acceptance as a legitimate stance. When I discussed the phrase with a group of people from the Assemblea, they claimed that to be an 'onion' historically meant to be *catalanista*, and in the current climate meant *independentista*. Until about five years ago they would not admit to pro-independence sentiments, but now this is an accepted viewpoint. A group of younger *sardana* dancers I came to know felt that the phrase had always been associated with pro-independence senti-ments, even when these sentiments were less accepted, 'whereas now we're all of the onion'. The essence though is the same in all responses, that being 'of the onion' represents a strong connection to Catalan national identity.

As I had suspected, several informants linked the phrase's origins to the growing of onions, remarking on its connectedness with the land, to being '*de pagès*' (from a peasant/farming background). During a discussion with the group of Vic *geganters* (*gegant* carriers), one reasoned that 'because the onion comes from the land, it is a way of saying you're from the land. Very connected with the land. It is difficult to pull us out', suggesting resilience and rootedness. Another recalled that in his home village, a *casal independentista* (independentist meeting place) was called 'La Ceba' for this reason. All strongly independentist, the *geganters* linked this image with pro-independence leanings, and a history of needing to fight for their rights and defend their views as Catalans. For this reason, they need to be strong and resiliently attached to their territory, and by extension their nation, like the onion is attached to the ground. Marta, a Catalan activist who worked for Omnium, strongly identified with the phrase, using it to describe her position: '"I am of the onion", of profound and Catalanist convictions'.

Not many responses saw a connection with the onion's use in cuisine. Marta and a younger informant from Vic, Berta, admitted that they don't actually like onion, but admitted its important place in Catalan cuisine, for example, in the *sofregit*. Berta did not identify with the phrase herself, even though she was pro-independence. Similarly, Eloi, a student from Barcelona, claimed that he had heard it very little, and considered it old fashioned. He was the only informant to hypothesise that its origin may be thanks to the presence of onion in the *truita de ceba*. Still, the phrase expresses a connectedness with land, and the land as a source of food. These are difficult to disentangle from associations of nation, territory, earth and landscape; associations which I will continue to touch on throughout this work.

The *Picada*

The *picada* acts as the final addition to the flavours of a dish, a bookend to the *sofregit* in Catalan-style cooking. The cookbook writer Ignasi Domènech introduced the *picada* early on in his seminal work *La Teca*, claiming that 'The bettering of our stews is the Catalan *picada*', an addition which 'improves stews in an extraordinary way' (Domènech, 2005: 30). In a 1930s edition of one of his later works (*Àpats*), the writer of the prologue likewise described the base of Catalan cuisine as the '*picades*, truly original to our land', in contrast to other foreign (French) sauces. Possible ingredients include garlic, parsley, saffron, almonds, hazelnuts, pine nuts, biscuits, chocolate, chilli, chicken or fish liver, pieces of bread, biscuits – the list could go on. A liquid is added to the grainy mix, such as broth, white wine, vinegar, or even water. The *picada* thickens a sauce, making it more substantial. Based on this observation, several informants suggested an origin in subsistence cuisine (*cuina de subsistència*), thus linking it to the ideal of thrift, and historic cuisine in peasant households.

Figures 2.1 and 2.2 Preparing a *picada* with Jaume: ingredients in the mortar before grinding, and added to an almost-finished dish. Photographs by the author.

The *picada* creates a sensory experience particularly associated with Catalonia. Jaume Saborós, the chef of the Motel Empordà in Figueres, chose the *picada* as the fundamental element of his vision of Catalan cuisine. Food historian Núria described the *picada* with hazelnuts and almonds as the 'taste of the Catalans'. Magazine editor Josep Sucarrats saw the *picada* as the most important element in Catalan cuisine:

> It is a very big simplification, but it is graphic, [Catalan cuisine] is starting with a *sofregit* with onion, and ending with a *picada*, and in-between, things happen! It is an element, a detail, that seems like a supplement and that actually is very important because it gives a very Catalan personality to the cuisine.

Pep Palau, organiser of Fòrum Gastronomic, one of Spain's premier food congresses, saw the *sofregit* and the *picada* as 'traits that confer a clear identity on Catalan cuisine'. While the *sofregit* is a fundamental base because of its diversity as the foundation in many Catalan dishes, it was the *picada* that truly Catalanised the dish. In Pep's words:

> The *picada* includes those ingredients that allow us to finish the dish and add to it certain gustatory elements that differentiate these dishes from others done in different cuisines. We add the *picada* to a rice, and it makes it different. We add it to a stew (*estofat*), of veal for example, and it makes it different.

Rounding up the discussion, the *picada* identifies a dish as Catalan in contrast to any other cuisine, to give it that final point of particularity. The sensory experience is also a key part of the *picada's* capacity for Catalanising a dish. Finally, it also makes the dish look Catalan. As Pep explained,

> The *picada* makes it Catalan on sight. Thanks to this *picada* it will end up adopting browns, dark colours, particular to our dishes. Only the *picada* has almonds, roasted hazelnuts, *vi ranci*,[7] all these ingredients make sure that it has a different look, a different odour.

The *picada* is therefore not only about Catalanising the taste and texture of a dish, but also its appearance.

The *Allioli*

So far it should be clear that informants often talked about the pantheon of sauces together, like in cookbooks. Like the *picada*, the *allioli* makes extensive use of the mortar and pestle. Because these are the main implements used in making these essential sauces, they have become a symbol of Catalan cuisine. The most common type (indeed near universal in Catalonia) is made from glazed yellow pottery, with green splashes on the outside. Several of my informants remarked that this was one of the principal *estris* (tools) that they associated with Catalan cuisine from childhood, so much so that seeing one immediately made them think of *allioli*.

The name *allioli* (or aioli in English) describes what the sauce is, namely garlic (*all*) and (*i*) olive oil (*oli*), ground together at a steady pace until a creamy off-white paste forms. Making it is a delicate process, and several of my informants admitted they could not make it themselves and would instead buy the ready-prepared *allioli* in supermarkets (where it is cleverly sold in Catalonia in a plastic tub that imitates the shape and colour of the typical mortar). To help the mixture, there are various ingredients one can add (e.g. egg, lemon or cream), though these are the source of much controversy, because there are claims that this produces either an inferior version or something else entirely (Lujàn, 1990).

Despite its role as a major sauce, *allioli* was discussed less by my informants that the *sofregit* or *picada*, perhaps because it is not one of these principal bases of Catalan cuisine, and also because it has been globalised so extensively that it can no longer be called unique to Catalonia. Indeed, in one of the many popular food-related publications in recent years *El llibre de l'allioli* ('The Book of Allioli', Garcia-Arbós, 2005), *allioli* is described as an essential element of the cuisines of Catalonia, the Catalan-speaking countries in general, and of other Mediterranean cuisines, including Aragon, the rest of Spain, Provence and parts of Greece. The acknowledgement of its ubiquity in non-Catalan cuisines here, even while promoting it, suggests an admission of the problem of using it as a strong identificatory feature.

The *Romesco*

Finally, the last sauce in Jaume's list is the *romesco*. It originated in the south of the Principat, in New Catalonia, where the province of Tarragona is usually given as its original home. It is generally eaten with fish, added during cooking, though a variation (*salsa de calçots* or *salvitxada*) is eaten at the *calçotada* (spring onion eating), and another, *salsa de xató*, eaten with the winter *Xató* salad.[8] Like the *picada* and *allioli* the mortar and pestle are essential for making this sauce.

Contrary to a claim that Catalans rarely add sauces to their foods,[9] the *calçotada* is a prime example of this practice. When the topic of *calçots* came up, my informants generally praised both the convivial atmosphere of the event, and the sauce, rather than the spring onions themselves (which are unpleasant on their own). *Calçots* are spring onions, which have been dug up when sprouting in spring/summer, then buried again. For this second phase in autumn and winter, earth is continually heaped on the sprouting leaves, to blanche the stems.

By their *temporada* or eating season (January–March), they should ideally be about 8 inches long. They are wrapped in foil, then cooked over a brazier, carbonising the outside. Once cooked, the tender, white, edible inside is removed from the burnt outer layer (the diner grasps the sprouts to accomplish this). It is a messy process, and the blackened hands and faces were a central part of the experience, a source of amusement and complicity amongst diners. The *calçots* are dipped into the *salvitxada* sauce and lowered into the mouth from above (the characteristic gesture is a famous image associated with Catalan food culture). Food writer Pau Arenòs, waxing lyrical about the experience, describes the *calçotada* thus:

> The way of eating it, it seems hallucinatory for foreigners. To take up the blackened and dirty hands to eat it, the most informal thing in the world ... To eat it in the countryside, and always with friends, because no one does a *calçotada* alone ... but always is collective, always, always, always with people. Collective, territory, sun, the surprising way of eating it, this is Catalonia.

His remarks also suggest its usefulness for promoting Catalan cuisine to tourists. *Calçotades*, the occasions where these are eaten, can either be small groups of friends, or massive festive events attracting hundreds of attendants, such as the Calçotada of Valls, the town where they are said to have originated. The *calçot* was widely considered to be a product unique to Catalan cuisine. This was not only because the product itself and its manner of growing are unique to Catalonia (recognised as an EU Protected Designation of Origin), but also because of the way it is consumed. The *calçotada* is one of Catalonia's many '-ades', an addition to a word that describes communal eating occasions centred around the eating of a particular food. The communal nature of these events, related to the concept of the *sobretaula*, are highly significant in Catalan culinary culture, that I will discuss further later in this chapter.

A Catalan National Dish?

In November 2013, the food magazine *Cuina* created a campaign to find out which was the 'best Catalan dish', as part of the celebrations of the 150th issue. Calling on all readers, contributors put forward their answer via either Twitter or Facebook. While it was primarily a light-hearted social-media based promotion for the magazine, the results were interesting when considering what Catalans consider to be their 'signature dishes' (Mintz, 1996). The magazine itself has always been careful to side-step political Catalanism, but still places an emphasis on Catalan themes, locales and personages, and quietly promotes a pro-Catalan agenda. This campaign is therefore one of many ways of asserting a Catalan culinary identity by providing an outlet in which these ideas can be expressed, without being overtly political.

Three years later, in October 2016, the magazine ran a similar competition, this time called 'The Catalans' Favourite Dish', and tied it to Catalonia's role that year as European Region of Gastronomy. The source of the recipes was the *Corpus del Patrimoni Culinari Català* ('Corpus of Catalan Culinary Heritage'), a cookbook prepared by the Fundació Institut Català de la Cuina i de la Cultura Gastronòmica. Twenty dishes were selected by a board of four experts (important figures in Catalan gastronomy: the chef Carme Ruscalleda, the director of the Fundació Alícia Toni Massanés, the organiser of the Fòrum Gastronòmic Pep Palau and the editor of *Cuina* magazine Josep Sucarrats). Each of these dishes was then promoted by a well-known chef, and participants voted on which they preferred via a dedicated website. A series of further semi-finals reduced the dishes to eight, then four, then finally two, of which one was the winner. The competition was on a larger scale (120,000 took part) and with each vote participants could enter a raffle for gastronomic prizes. The entire campaign was an opportunity to promote Catalan gastronomy in all its forms, from traditional cooking, to contemporary chefs and restaurants, to food products.

In both competitions, the top four dishes were identical: *escudella i carn d'olla* (a meat and vegetable stew), *pa amb tomàquet* (bread rubbed with tomato), *canelons* (cannelloni) and *fricandó* (a veal and mushroom dish). Each one of these has different meanings and associations within Catalan culinary culture, and they were dishes that I regularly encountered in fieldwork. At the conclusion of the 2013 event, the virtues of each dish were defended by food writers, and in the 2016 event, the top two dishes, *escudella i carn d'olla* and *pa amb tomàquet* were similarly defended by two great figures of contemporary Catalan cuisine, Joan Roca and Ferran Adrià respectively. Adrià was a natural choice, as the *pa amb tomàquet* was the basis of an exhibition he created in 2016 ('Sapiens: Understanding to Create'), also connected to the European Region of Gastronomy. In both years, the winning dish was *escudella i carn d'olla*. The winner was announced at the Fòrum Gastronòmic in Barcelona by Carme Ruscalleda, who was supported by *Cuina's* editor, Josep Sucarrats, and the director of the Catalan Tourism Agency, Xavier Espasa (his presence underlined Catalonia as a gastronomic tourist destination, recognised by its European Region of Gastronomy status that year).

These two events engendered much debate in popular media (especially the 2016 campaign), with articles and televised discussions of the winning dishes, their merits and role in Catalan cuisine. According to Josep Sucarrats, the results in 2016 were a surprise, as they had not expected to see such clear results. The event was so successful, *Cuina* ran a similar competition in 2017, with a focus on preparing dishes using Protected Designation of Origin (PDO) and Protected Geographic Indication (PGI) foods, to raise awareness of these products and categorisation within Catalonia, of which there are twenty in the region. The winning two dishes were then provided as ready meals in supermarket chain Ametller Origen. In 2018 *Cuina* ran the competition a third time, on this occasion focusing on regional and local dishes in Catalan towns and villages. The intention of this iteration was to celebrate the diversity of Catalan cuisine (an important element of Catalan culinary identity that I discuss further in Chapter Four). The competition's aim apparently succeeded, as the runner up dishes represented most of Catalonia's different regions and cooking styles. The winning dish, the *Coradella de Molins de Rei* (lamb stew from Molins de Rei), came from the town of Molins de Rei outside Barcelona. The dish was connected with the history and identity of the town, a former trading hub, as it was the traditional dish of the muleteers that were once part of the town's economy.

The debates that these events engendered reflected popular subjects of discussion about Catalan cuisine's particular characteristics, what makes it distinctive and the meaning of the dishes in Catalan culinary culture. *Escudella i carn d'olla* is a hotpot of various ingredients, usually a selection of meats, a bone, sausage, meatballs (*pilota*), vegetables such as potatoes, cauliflower, beans and any other available ingredients. Finally, rice, *fideus* (tiny pasta sticks) and/or large pasta pieces (*galletes*) are added after several hours of cooking time and just before eating. This will often be served as a two-course meal, with the broth acting as first course (the *sopa*, or *escudella*, though there is not an exact consensus on whether the latter just refers to the whole meal), then the remaining, broth-soaked meat and vegetables served as the main meal (*carn d'olla*, literally 'meat of the pot').

Cookbook writers have referred to the Catalan love of *escudella*, sometimes considering it the national dish. In the 2013 competition, one of the presenters said 'We are in the land of *escudella*! That's all you need to know!', a comment that I had already heard in culinary literature and amongst informants. While the general consensus from my experiences speaking about *escudella* in Catalonia suggests common components (give or take some variations between households), the basic form of the *escudella* is not something unique to Catalonia. Interestingly, many of my informants voluntarily pointed this out, saying that there are many variations of this kind of a hotpot or stew around the world. Barcelona chef Carles Gaig openly admitted that:

> The most representative dish would be the *escudella*, our national dish. But if you look at it, *escudella* is no more than a *pot au feu*. Here there's one, in France, in Germany too. And everywhere, it is the dish that identifies, like with the Galicians, they have *pote gallego*, or in Madrid the *cocido madrileño* ... a subsistence dish ... So the *escudella* is the national dish of Catalonia, but it is a dish that you would say is born from necessity.

During the announcement of *escudella* as the winning dish in 2016, Carme Ruscalleda praised the dish's 'complexity', and added that 'it gives us an image of Catalans as people that can be bothered to put a dish on the hob' (ACN, 2016), implying that cooking had an important role in Catalan life. At the same event, Xavier Espasa also recognised that although the dish was 'difficult' to make and required long cooking times, it was the highest representation of Catalan cooking, and the ideal cuisine to represent Catalonia as European Region of Gastronomy (ibid.).

Escudella is the preferred starting point of another of the dishes, *canelons*. These are much like Italian cannelloni, tubular forms of pasta stuffed with minced meat or vegetables, and covered with a béchamel sauce, and sometimes grated tomato over the top. A version I have also experienced includes grated apple, or apple puréed into the béchamel, in line with the Catalan culinary practice of mixing fruit into savoury dishes. *Canelons* were originally brought to Barcelona by Italian restaurateurs in the nineteenth century, a fact readily admitted by most informants. This Italian origin does not affect the perception of *canelons* as a Catalan food. On the contrary, *canelons* were an example of the openness to new ideas idealised by informants.

Canelons are commonly associated with St. Stephen's day (26th December), where they ideally will use the leftover meat from Christmas Day *escudella i carn d'olla* or capon. Both these foods therefore well express the ideal of the gastronomic calendar that pervades Catalan culinary identity. At the same time, this association with a particular day also makes the role of *canelons* particular to Catalan culture, because Italians do not eat cannelloni on specific days. The same could also be said of the *escudella*, because although similar dishes are widespread across Europe, they do not have the same Christmas associations and practices as they do in Catalonia. This association is so entrenched, that when I showed this image of the *escudella* in photo-elicitation, the immediate reactions were all Christmas-related.

The *fricandó* had allegedly been in decline until a recent upsurge in popularity (symptomatic of a more general interest in 'traditional' Catalan dishes). This dish has already been introduced in the discussions of the *sofregit*, but to revisit, Vic chef Magda described it as 'veal, sliced very finely, first covered in flour and fried, then put in a saucepan with a good *sofregit*. Then add mushrooms, and this is simmered for a few hours'. Its use of the *sofregit* marks it out as a Catalan dish, despite some similarities with French dishes. The inclusion of mushrooms is also an intrinsic part of the *fricandó*, which is also seen as a marker of its Catalan-ness. The fondness (indeed, at times, obsession) for mushrooms in Catalan cuisine was also regularly referred to as a defining Catalan culinary feature, and as something that differentiated Catalan cuisine from the rest of Spain, where mushrooms are much less prevalent. Come autumn (and also spring), a popular pastime is mushroom gathering.

This standardisation of the *fricandó* recipe was something underlined by the speaker at *Cuina*'s 2013 event, in that its recipe was universal across Catalonia, whilst with the others, anything could be added depending on individual preference. The implication from this is that *fricandó* has a much greater potential as a unifier of Catalan food culture. He also claimed that the others have forgotten one important point, namely that 'it doesn't have a Castilian translation', because the *escudella* could be a Spanish '*olla podrida*' or '*cocido*', and '*canelons*' is the same in Catalan and Castilian. Once again, claims to linguistic uniqueness appear in Catalan gastronationalism, whereby concepts (including dishes) are identifiable to Catalonia alone because they are untranslatable, in particular into Castilian. The *fricandó* is also a historic dish. According to Joan Roca (2004), it can be found in recipe books from the seventeenth century and can thus also claim some historical continuity and connectedness.

The fourth dish in this pantheon of popular national dishes is *pa amb tomàquet*. However, I will leave discussions of this food until the end of this chapter, to first deal with some of the issues that have been raised by the three dishes that have been discussed so far. This includes ideas about subsistence cuisine and thriftiness as a national virtue, recovery of 'lost' dishes, the ideal of a cuisine of migrations, and regionality in cuisine.

The Ideal of Subsistence Cuisine

Often at the heart of the idealisation of *escudella i carn d'olla* were references to its former ubiquity as a poor, simple and subsistence dish, central to the history of Catalan cuisine, and of the Catalan nation as a whole (although as I have already pointed out, no one ever claimed it was unique to Catalonia). Even though it cannot be claimed as a unique culinary differentiator, *escudella*'s connection with a historical past makes it one of the top candidates for carrying Catalan identity. That said, I occasionally heard some claims to difference. For instance, at a pro-independence lunch, one of the organisers of the event explained that though other dishes may be similar cross-culturally, they were still uniquely interpreted in Catalonia. For example, the *escudella i carn d'olla* is similar, but not the same as the Spanish *cocido*, because the Catalan version was 'richer and tastier' than the Spanish version.

The *escudella* is filling and calorific, essential not only to agricultural labour in rural life, but also to work in the factories as Catalonia industrialised in the eighteenth and nineteenth centuries. The advantage of the *escudella* was that it could be left to cook over hours, so women were able to work without needing to tend the fire. Indeed, in childhood one of my informants recalled his mother telling him to go and remind his father to put the *fideus* pasta and rice into the *escudella* in the late afternoon, so their supper would be ready when she returned home from her factory shift. This connects the dish with Catalonia's social history, in this case the industrial past that has contributed much to the development of early Catalanism, contemporary identity and national pride. Like many Catalan dishes, it is also spread throughout all social classes, the only difference being that the ingredients differed depending on income.

In the photo-elicitation, many respondents also selected *escudella i carn d'olla* as a national dish (amongst others), if not their own personal favourite. One respondent hypothesised that it was because of its strong association with Christmas that *escudella* had such a prized position as a national food. As it is considered *the* food to eat on this day, according to the gastronomic calendar, Catalans have managed to develop a strong familiarity with it, making it a typical signature food (to follow Mintz, 1996). The dish also has strong familial associations, because it is over the *escudella i carn d'olla* that yearly Christmas meetings will take place (in the words of one informant 'you get to see mum, and taste her food').

The conversion of quotidian dishes into a festive, and later a luxury, cuisine has interesting ramifications in the minds of informants. The *escudella* has been converted from an example of subsistence cuisine, eaten every day as necessity, into a special dish associated with festive reunions. This situation is not unique to Catalonia and has been recognised in many other contexts (Wilk, 1999; Goody, 1982; Fajans, 2012; Ayora-Diaz, 2012). One should also not deny the importance of the role of such reunions as places where national identity is discussed and debated, nor the importance of the knowledge that other households in Catalonia are eating the same food at the same time, a culinary variation on Benedict Anderson's imagined communities (a situation also recognised by Fajans, 2012).

A Land and Cuisine of Migrations

I discussed *canelons* with Núria, a food historian, to learn more about their role in Catalan cuisine. She was keen to point out that though they may be Italian in origin, their usage in Catalonia differs as for Catalans it is a festive dish, 'the national dish for Sundays, since the nineteenth century'. She also claims that *canelons* are a national dish because it was a Catalan, a Mr Flor from the brand Pavó, who was the first to invent dried *caneló* pasta. This was a huge success in Barcelona and allowed *canelons* to be made in the home, hence its association with the city (following the tendency to associate place and food in Catalan culinary culture).

The adoption of the once-foreign *canelons* as a national dish is an example of how Catalan cuisine has adapted and adopted dishes from beyond its borders. This process was a common thread running through Catalan culinary discourse. Catalonia is described as a 'land of migrations' (*terra de pas*) through which many civilisations have passed and left their mark. In terms of cuisine, this means an acceptance, and even an emphasis, on the foreign origins of some ingredients or dishes, related to migratory movements. In the words of Ignasi, a chef in the mountains near Vic, 'there is this basis, there's not a [single] cuisine, they're all fruits of different invasions. For example, the Greeks brought vines, grain, a series of things. The Romans, a few others. Everyone brought things. And America brought us many things'.

In any everyday conversation about food, some mention of Catalan cuisine's diverse origins is unavoidable. Thus Catalans recognise their cuisine as a confluence of geo-cultural influences, from Arab, Iberian, Greek, Roman, Jewish, Italian cuisines, strongly affected by products from the Americas, and more recently by cuisines from other regions of Spain, and modern French cuisine. Josep Sucarrats, the editor of *Cuina*, placed contemporary culinary movements and influences as part of a longer trend in Catalan cuisine. In this way, the French-influenced *nova cuina* can be justified as conforming to historical influences and an accepted 'tradition of innovation'. This characteristic is also part of a cosmopolitan ideal, open to new ideas, especially from Europe.

The Barcelona chef Fermí likewise talked about the importance of external influences through history, pointing in particular to Roman influences. He contrasted this with the Basque country, which he also commended for its excellent culinary reputation, but claimed it had a limited *receptari* (recipe selection) due to its isolation in the Pyrenees. Fermí saw geography as a 'state of mind' which contributed to the openness of Catalan cuisine:

> We have had a particularly lucky geography. Others have a different geographical luck, but firstly we have had the sea. We've been a commercial people; we've been

envied many times. We've had many different cultures here and this has predestined us ... [Our geography] situated us in a place where people are passing.

Fermí refers to the 'commercial' nature of Catalans, another national ideal, which takes its origins from the maritime Catalan–Aragonese empire of the fourteenth and fifteenth centuries, lauded as Catalonia's golden age. From a gastronationalist perspective, because it was a time of trade, it fits into this discourse of a cosmopolitan, diverse culture. Once again, national ideals are related to constructions of history, so central to nationalist movements.

The notion of the '*terra de pas*' is also raised in the context of contemporary immigration to Catalonia. The comparison of the contemporary situation with an idealised characteristic of the historical past allows a justification of large-scale immigration and toleration in contemporary Catalonia. To accept migrants, and above all make them Catalan, is normalised as a natural part of the Catalan identity past and present. This view is particularly promoted by civil, cultural organisations Omnium Cultural and the Assemblea, and language normalisation programs.

It is also revealing that the first words to the Preamble of the much disputed 2006 Statute of Autonomy emphasise Catalonia's status as a land of migrations (Organic Law 6/2006 of the 19th July, on the Reform of the Statute of Autonomy of Catalonia: 1), 'Catalonia has been shaped over the course of time through the contribution of the energy of many generations, traditions and cultures, which found in Catalonia a land of welcome'. Isidre, a Vic chef, expressed a similar sentiment with regards to cuisine:

> One has to really respect and look after our customs and traditions, but remain open to everything. More than anything, Catalonia has always been a land of migrations (*terra de pas*), and a land of mixing. It has taken elements that were foreign, and that have arrived at being typical things of ours. Like beans (*mongetes*), *pa amb tomàquet*, because these have come from the new world.

There is a problem inherent in an ideology of openness when it comes to gastronationalism, namely the risk of losing a particular culinary identity because of a too rapid uptake of the characteristics of other culinary identities. However, very few of my informants believed that Catalan cuisine would ever be in danger of disappearing. For that to happen, Catalan identity would have to disappear entirely. There is a general acceptance however that its form may change. These concerns also relate to some of the complaints surrounding the cataloguing of Catalan cuisine, which I discuss in Chapter Three.

When eating with Catalans, the origins or background of dishes were often discussed or pointed out. The consumption of 'non-Catalan' food on a regular basis does not affect the self-perception of being Catalan. Several informants admitted that the food they normally ate in most contexts was 'Italian' in origin (i.e. pasta or pizza), and North African, Japanese and Peruvian cuisine has gained popularity, in line with food trends in the developed world. Indeed, one of my more unusual experiences was eating sushi alongside *pa amb tomàquet* and *truita de patates* with a group of young women in their twenties – the incongruity of the situation was not lost on them! The current popularity of Asiatic cuisine could be likened to that of Italian cuisine in the nineteenth century, which brought Catalonia many of its favourite dishes. Perhaps, one of my informants hypothesised, sushi will be seen as a characteristic of Catalan cuisine in a hundred years, as could couscous. At one masterclass in medieval Catalan cuisine given by the Fundació Alicia (a foundation dedicated to culinary research and education) at the Fòrum Gastronòmic in Girona, the presenter even suggested that sushi might be eaten at Christmas in a century. I also heard examples of how my informants integrated foreign ingredients into Catalan dishes, for instance the inclusion of curry with a *fideus* pasta dish. Another of my Vic informants expressed their fondness for the variety of north African cuisine now available thanks to the large immigrant population in the city. For him, this allowed him to 'understand our [Catalonia's] own diversity, as a positive value'.

Openness in cuisine was often paralleled to a general outlook that was positive to outside influence. Such openness was occasionally placed at odds with the perceived insularity of Spain. In this way, an open cuisine comes to express another perceived difference between Catalonia and Spain. Food writer Jaume expressed this in the strongest way of any of my informants, claiming that Catalan cuisine was 'the most mixed, combined cuisine in the world … a reflection of the country'. He scorned Spanish cuisine, by contrast, as a colonialist cuisine, which did not truly respect other cuisines.

While Jaume's remarks are those of a strongly pro-Catalan informant (even amongst his friends and admirers his research was criticised for his biased view), this favourable comparison with Spanish cuisine is not unique. At the Fundació Alicia, a conversation with a team of researchers on their own attitudes to the adoptive potential of Catalan cuisine revealed a more complex connection between this aspect of Catalan cuisine and national identity as a whole. While in favour of the notion of '*terra de pas*' ('land of migrations'), they pointed out that Catalonia is not unique in this respect (and in the literature, this ideal is celebrated in national foods in other contexts – Ayora-Diaz, 2012; Avieli, 2018; Fajans, 2012). What is different is that Italy and France have received migrant communities, but they have not had the openness to variation that Catalonia has had, because this would be an insult, not just to their cuisines, but also to their national identity.

Most interestingly, two of the Alicia team, Laia and Jaume, interpreted this openness in the context of the theories of a Catalan philosopher, Josep Ferrater i Mora, who wrote extensively on the Catalan national 'character'. He specified four characteristics, '*continuitat*' (continuity), '*seny*' (good sense), '*mesura*' (measure) and '*ironia*' (irony). *Rauxa*, the opposite of *seny*, was also a trait discussed in his work (Ferrater Mora, 2012). For Jaume and Laia, irony was a central part of the Catalan character, which meant that Catalans don't take themselves too seriously. While they have huge pride and respect in what they have, this also gives a certain perspective, and acceptance of new ideas.

According to Jaume, the point about *rauxa* is that 'it breaks all norms – but with *seny*. To break things with respect and in a good way' and create innovation. I also noted an unfavourable comparison with Madrid amongst the team. Some had worked with students in Madrid, to teach them dishes from El Bulli. However, these students lacked the concept of *seny*, or the desire to gain a deep understanding of the origins and inspiration behind the dishes. As a result, the finished product was rushed and sub-standard. Their attitude to difference was also more dismissive – difference was accepted, but only so far. '[Madrid] doesn't have a proper character, it is of too many places', i.e. its inhabitants didn't have a true identity, but instead a confused and unacknowledged mixture of Spain's multiple regional identities. In contrast, the group believed that awareness of the origins of their national foods was present amongst Catalans who took their identity seriously.

The reasoning that 'to be in Catalonia, it is all Catalan' was also a defence of *nova cuina* against its detractors, who claim that such cuisine cannot be called truly Catalan. The proponents of the *nova cuina* movement in Catalonia conveniently utilise this ideology of openness to market the cooking style as part of a general trend that has historical roots.

Time and again, this discussion has returned to notions of historicism. Before ending this section, it is worthwhile to consider the ideas of Pep Palau, the founder of the Fòrum Gastronòmic Girona. The ideal of a historical past enmeshed with the notion of openness and dynamism formed the basis of his worldview of Catalan cuisine. He began our interview with the following words:

> PP: Catalan cuisine has a characteristic, particular to a few great cuisines, of being very permeable to products that come from outside, or that Catalan travellers have discovered, and that they have incorporated into the cuisine.
> [VJ: Catalan cuisine is an open cuisine you mean, like Catalan identity?]
> PP: Yes, exactly. It is an identity open to the world and so it is a cuisine open to the world, This characteristic makes sure it is a very dynamic cuisine. And very rich at times, in the sense of diversity not luxury ... At the same time it produces a very great alimentary and culinary diversity.

His statements sum up many of the attitudes found in the ethnographic material presented in this chapter. What is most interesting about the discourse surrounding migration and the adoption of new foods in Catalan culinary culture is the way that it parallels more general ideals of Catalan nationhood and belonging. Just as foods can be adopted and integrated, so immigrants can likewise become Catalan through integration and the adoption of Catalan language and culture. The parallel is not absolute; food in itself does not have agency and is acted upon, whereas immigrants have the choice to learn Catalan and participate in Catalan activities, such as *castells* (Vaczi, 2016; Erickson, 2011). This take on Catalan culinary history manifests the ideal of *convivència* ('living together'), that food from different cultures and of different origins can exist side-by-side. The dining table is no longer only a place of social interaction, but a metaphor of society as a whole.

It is also possible to see the significance of acknowledging the origins of different elements of the cuisine. This not only demonstrates national knowledge (a crucial part of the Catalan identity), but also another aspect of the ideal of *convivència*, that of tolerance and awareness. Returning to the perceived problem of Madrid as a place of confused culinary identity for a Catalan chef and instructor, this identity was confused because its different elements (or ingredients, to use a culinary analogy) were not recognised. Jaume felt there was not enough awareness of which element belonged to which cuisine. In Catalonia however, there is a greater sense of self-awareness when it comes to elements of a cuisine, the origins of food, the techniques etc (this does not imply universally agreed facts, which are often the subject of lively and heated discussion). This may also reflect a society that, as with many minorities that have experienced persecution, is hyper-aware and hyper-vigilant in keeping cultural knowledge and specificities alive. More importantly, this awareness of the past means that change can be managed well, continually providing an inspiration or foundation. This is at the heart of many of the developments of the modern *nova cuina* chefs, who often have historical research as an important part of their philosophy.

Rediscovery of 'Lost' Dishes and the Preservation of Identity

Despite the apparent excellent health, clear presence and awareness of Catalan cuisine amongst the population of the Catalan Autonomous Community, I heard some Catalans bemoaning the loss of aspects of their cuisine. A regular complaint amongst older informants was that you could not find good *peus de porc* (pig's trotters) anymore, as they are not fashionable. Ditto the rich *cap i pota* (pig head and snout), perhaps because of the difficulty of finding the necessary ingredients, its complex cooking process, and the squeamishness of a younger generation of diners put off by its taste and content. This discourse of loss is a powerful one and is a convincing call to action to galvanise Catalans into participating in and protecting their own culture. It is also a useful top-down strategy by government bodies to try and promote their credentials as protectors of Catalan identity, as happened with the UNESCO campaign.

A large part of Catalonia's gastronomic literature centres on this premise, as did many of the events celebrating Catalan food in the years after the dictatorship. *El que hem menjat* ('What We Have Eaten') by Josep Pla (1972) was written as a swansong to traditional Catalan cuisine, specifically in the region of Empordà. In another work, *L'art del Menjar a Catalunya* ('The Art of Eating in Catalonia', 1977), in the context of the post-Francoist re-Catalanisation project, Manuel Vázquez Montalbán claims that 'amongst the symbols of destroyed Catalan identity are gastronomic symbols' (Vázquez Montalbán, 1977: 21). He adds that 'recovering Catalan cuisine today is almost an archaeological endeavour except in those areas that have conserved a great fidelity in their gastronomic identity ... everywhere else every exception confirms the rule and gastronomic memory has been reduced to one or two half-hidden dishes' (ibid.: 22).

However, all is not lost for dishes such as *cap i pota*. Magda, a cook in Vic, included *cap i pota* in her list of preferred Catalan dishes. Despite claiming the dish had been lost, she has tried to recover it in her restaurant. Indeed, the salvaging of *cap i pota* was often held up as an example of foods that have been saved, its recovery being a sign of increased interest on the part of Catalans in their culinary heritage and in preserving their historical cuisine.[10] For example, *peus de porc* was one of the *esmorzars de forquilla* (heavy breakfasts) prepared by Vic's hospitality guild in their gastronomic open days. Magda was keen to point out that there were several clients who came especially for this dish, because it was difficult to find elsewhere. She felt a sense of pride at having resurrected this dish, and that it was perhaps the most Catalan on her menu. The dish therefore serves a number of purposes on her menu: providing unique products to attract a devoted clientele, proving the Catalan credentials of her restaurant and allowing her to express and celebrate her Catalan identity as a chef.

There are several problems with the 'resurrection' of 'historic' or 'traditional' dishes. One is that they are high in calories, and not suited to today's lifestyles and official health recommendations, a complaint I often heard in reference to *escudella*. Frequently they also require long cooking times, or specific processes and techniques that are either too time consuming in the modern kitchen or too complicated for the average home cook. Another problem is that the ingredients required in some recipes, such as the *cap i pota*, are not easily accessible in supermarkets and shops, and need a special trip to a particular supplier, again adding to the time needed to make them.

Many of these older dishes therefore cannot be eaten or made in their 'original' form by most members of the population on an everyday basis. It is for this reason that chefs have taken on the task of researching these dishes and preparing them in line with modern tastes. According to a member of Vic's hospitality guild, this is the greatest contribution contemporary Catalan chefs are bringing to the cuisine. He explained that 'what chefs today have done is take this product, and made a format, some new textures, but the taste has the memory of what it was'. Preservation is therefore not always about exact replication, but equally an attempt to preserve a memory and taste, which is enough to provide a direct link with the past. This connection has been suitably updated to contemporary tastes, and therefore allows consumers and promoters to participate (in some way) in the senses of their national past (Barthes, 1961).

The editor of *Cuina*, Josep Sucarrats, set this preservation even more firmly on his agenda, seeing it as a key task of his magazine and its promotion of Catalonia:

> It is that we want to reflect the Catalan cuisine of today. And an important part of this is the preservation and revaluation, the divulgation of the cuisine from the past. And another part with contemporary cuisines that evolve, is that they do this cuisine with new things … There's no contradiction in this. We don't like to speak about the past as if it was a piece in a museum. Nor that the past doesn't interest us or that we don't like innovation.

National Dishes and Unusual Combinations

During an interview with the Vic chef Magda, she explained that she always tried to add a 'very Catalan dish' to her restaurant's weekend *menu* (three course set meal), such as *canelons*, *cap i pota*, *botifarra i mongetes* (sausage and beans) or *escalivada* (roasted vegetables). The weekend of our interview, this was calamari stuffed with meat, an example of *mar i muntanya* cuisine. This type of cuisine, literally 'sea and mountain' came up time and again in my conversations with informants as being truly characteristic of Catalan cuisine. In the context of the resurrection of dishes, another local chef, Manel, in the neighbouring town of Manlleu, described how one of the most important elements of Catalan cuisine was the combination of meat ('chickens, geese, pork, veal') with vegetables and fruits, claiming that 'we work a lot with fruits'. He was referring in particular to a dish local to Manlleu, sausage with pears, which he was also proud to have rediscovered, and an example of *agredolç* (savoury-sweet) cuisine.

During conversations about what makes Catalan cuisine distinctive, after describing the foundational sauces, my informants would then often mention the habit of mixing fish and meat, meat and fruit, and sweet and savoury flavours. Straight after her remarks on the *sofregit* and other sauces, the former head of the FICCG Pepa Aymamí claimed, 'we mix foodstuffs [that seem strange], it is very important, it gives a special touch to things. We put fruit into a dish, and we do many of these mixes'. The Michelin-starred chef Carme Ruscalleda made the same point, linking it with the notion of the open cuisine and the ideal of an open national identity:

> I think the Catalans have a very open way of thinking. Because we've always had a very eclectic and varied cuisine. We have always made cold and hot, sweet and savoury, meat and fish ... It is for the many cuisines that there were. For the mixing of cultures. The contrasts. If we look at the cuisine of Castile, it is a more limited cuisine, they have a much shorter recipe list, and ours is very long and varied. We've been mixing things for a long time.

Carme was not the only informant to make this parallel, and it was often in this context that the aforesaid migratory influences on Catalonia as a *terra de pas* were discussed, with lists of the different groups who had left their influence on the cuisine. Concerning the actual origin of *mar i muntanya/agredolç* cuisine, there are a number of theories, and it is possible there is no one explanation. These different ideas are useful to consider however, as they have the potential to tell us much about regional identity construction and how this relates to Catalan social history, landscape and the interplay of regional and national identities.

Food writer Jaume Fàbrega suggested a fairly recent (nineteenth century) origin amongst the cuisine of Empordan fishermen (this style of cooking is particularly associated with this region). It was a cuisine based on necessity, of combining whatever was available such as a piece of chicken, potatoes, beans or any other vegetables. Cooking professor Mon also suggested an origin in subsistence cuisine, perhaps related to Catholic food prohibitions whereby fish was required on certain days, but meat was also available, and was 'disguised' as fish, or needed to be eaten before it rotted. This justification suits the cuisine in the interior, where fish was scarce, or where preserved cod was the only fish available. Another informant who was based in Empordà related its origins to the social and cultural history of the region, as younger sons of fishermen or farmers entered the cork industry that developed in the nineteenth century, and each brought foods from home to communal meals.

One of my older Vic informants, Montserrat, a woman in her 90s, claimed that this popularity in *mar i muntanya* is only a recent trend throughout all Catalonia, of the last two or three decades. Her daughter, Sat, disagreed, claiming that some dishes were 'of all one's life', such as 'chicken with lobster' or 'meatballs with calamari', and used their mention in Josep Pla as a justification that it certainly went back to the nineteenth century.

It is interesting that Empordà is often considered one of the most Catalan areas, because it is geographically furthest from Spain, is the place of origin of the national dance and was also celebrated by many Catalan writers and painters (Josep Pla especially). I was often told that Empordà was a microcosm of Catalonia itself, particularly in the huge variety of landscapes to be found within this small area. As the recognised place of origin of a universally recognised trait of Catalan cuisine, I suggest that this may also have contributed to Empordà's standing as a nationalist centre, much as *llonganissa* and the sausage industry has done with Vic.

Sat and her mother's remarks also show a common feature of the discourse of my informants, which is the awareness of the place from which certain dishes or ingredients originated within Catalonia. Empordà is also associated with *agredolç* cuisine. Montserrat remarked that this was something she particularly associated with Empordà, and less with Vic. Her daughter added though that in Vic, *coca* (sweet, sugared flatbread) 'has always been' consumed with *llonganissa* sausage, a characteristic other local informants also remarked upon (one former Barcelonan even admitted he had to 'acclimatise' to this taste). Other examples of *agredolç* cuisine Sat and her mother gave included combining sugar with beans, hare with chocolate, liquor and forest herbs, cod with sugar or sweet pigs' trotters.

For the hare, both gave an extensive account of the recipe and how it would be made, another commonly occurring feature in informant discourse, showing how clearly processes of culinary preparation are ingrained in conceptions of food. The sweet pig's trotters were regarded as something lost. Sat explained that her recipe was from 'Can Monset', the home of her French paternal grandmother's home, and that this dish was shared with French Catalonia. This demonstrates a connection made in everyday discourse with the cuisine of other Catalan-speaking countries, with the aforementioned awareness of locality and origins, suggesting a strong awareness of regional variations within Catalonia.

Another product that the older Montserrat strongly associated with the area of Girona (lower Empordà) was the *botifarra dolça*, literally 'sweet sausage', where sugar is combined with meat in the sausage casing. This dish has remained localised to the region, and the two occasions on which I was able to try it were both in Empordà. On both occasions, it was prepared as a dessert, gently fried in a saucepan with cooked apples, bread and milk, and a little sugar, to caramelise the apples (to this day, it remains one of my most unusual and delicious experiences from fieldwork).

Unlike *mar i muntanya*, the *agredolç* cuisine has a longer history, and my informants almost universally recognised its roots in medieval cuisine. *Agredolç* cuisine is probably one of the most obvious examples of the presence of historically-documented cuisine being consumed today in Catalonia. It is therefore a potent symbol of the consumption of national past (Barthes, 1961). The description of this kind of food as 'characteristic' or 'determining' was usually followed in informant discourse by a discussion of its place in history, and if the informant was knowledgeable enough, some discussion of Catalan medieval history, and how influential Catalan cuisine was in Europe of the era.

Regionality and Richness in Diversity

Geographically, Catalonia is characterised by huge variations in terms of both produce and cooking styles. Both my informants and the culinary literature described Catalonia as 'rich', 'varied' and 'diverse'. What is interesting is that this variety is often contrasted with Spain, which is presented as monolingual, intolerant and conformist, refusing to accept the variety of identities within its borders. In other words, Catalonia is identified as more tolerant of its constituent regions' differences than Spain. In this section, I will introduce a concept that I will elaborate upon in Chapter Four, namely the importance placed upon an *awareness* of these varieties, and their particular locales. In doing so, Catalans display their knowledge of their national landscapes and patrimony, which are not just sources of pride, but also signify knowledge of the nation, its characteristics and its symbols. For a cultural nationalism, such knowledge is key to self-identifying as a Catalan.

This 'richness' in variety came through in discussions of national dishes. While the discussion so far suggests some consensus on a national dish, others were sceptical of the claim that there was one single national dish. Even if it could be narrowed down to a small selection, there would be many different variations throughout Catalonia. Throughout my interview with Pep Palau, founder of the Fòrum Gastronòmic, he placed continued emphasis upon diversity and richness, and before our interview he stated clearly that he found a question such as 'what is Catalonia's national dish?' to be out of place. To ask such a question was an affront to the complexity of Catalan cuisine. Food historian Núria explained why she felt the same way:

> It makes it [the cuisine] poor. Because a cuisine is not a dish, it is a way of doing. A way of eating, of understanding. Catalan cuisine can never be defined by one

dish alone, nor can any global cuisine. Nor by a single product, because we're very rich in products. And in seasonality, which are what makes the products.

Aside from bringing up Núria's earlier point that it is the act of cooking ('way of doing') which makes a dish Catalan, this 'rich in produce' (*ric en producte*) was to become a common theme throughout food-related discourse in Catalonia. Oriol, a graphic designer of food-themed T-shirts, considered diversity to be the most important element in Catalan culinary identity. Localism is also important, and in fact it was probably the most commonly recurring theme in my interviews.

The best description of Catalonia's regional variety came from an interview with Barcelona chef Carles Gaig, who explained that 'one must understand that Catalan cuisine is not a single cuisine. There are various cultures within Catalonia'. He divided Catalonia into five main areas: Barcelona, the northern coast, the southern coast, the centre and the Pyrenees. As a chef of the *nova cuina*, he linked this diversity with the rise of vanguard cuisine, and the way Catalonia has remained at the forefront of new culinary developments.

There were times when this attitude seemed to contradict the idealisation of subsistence cuisine. I explained as much to food writer Jaume Fàbrega, who argued that whilst richness in produce was indeed true in that there was a great deal of variety, this represented a little of everything rather than bountiful quantity. It was this 'diversity' that should be idealised, in the form of different varieties in vegetables, fruits and grain, breeds of livestock, fish, mushrooms etc. Moreover, there is an almost competitive conversational game in Catalonia, of naming as many varieties as possible of a particular fruit or vegetable when in company. For instance, when I showed a picture of the Vic market to a group of *sardana* dancers (mostly in their teens and twenties), they began taking it in turns to name all the varieties of tomatoes available in Catalonia, both from what they saw in the photo and from their own knowledge. They tried to out-do each other with how many they could name, both of local varieties (such as the Montserrat tomato, significant because it associated with the shrine of one of Catalonia's patron saints), and other more generic ones, such as the cherry tomato, or the *tomàquets de penjar* (hanging tomatoes) for use in *pa amb tomàquet*. Other times it would be oil, and the different types of olive and their localities within Catalonia. On a few occasions the theme would be how many dishes one could name using a particular ingredient. Tallies were not kept of who had said what, but they were a means of showing knowledge of Catalan products, and by extension, national knowledge.

This attitude to variety/poverty may have been inspired by Josep Pla, who dedicates a chapter to this phenomenon in *El que hem menjat* ('What we have eaten', 1972). He admits that the popular dish for decades (if not centuries) was *escudella i carn d'olla*, though he bemoans the elevated cost of the dish and its decline in popularity (still a pertinent complaint). Despite the appearance of monotony however, there is actually 'enormous diversity' (ibid.: 228) in local and county cuisine. He even claims, 'this diversity is so fabulous, that I don't think one could ever do a cookbook of Catalan cuisine. This type of book wants a particular generality, and this can never happen. It is a country that has a palate that is often by county, if not only locale' (ibid.). This might not be unusual in any country, but it is extraordinarily so in Catalonia, he argues.

The gastronomic calendar, which is the focus of Chapter Four, provides another element of variety. Pla claims that the seasonal cuisine of the year is 'so diversified', that there is a clear cuisine for spring, summer, autumn and winter (to which he dedicates several chapters for each one), and that this progression of seasonal products is clearly visible within markets. This parallels a comment made by several of my older informants who remembered eating *escudella* regularly in their youth, that at least the dish varied with seasonal ingredients, so the monotony was bearable. Pla concludes his argument thus (ibid.: 228–229):

> One can say that our traditional cuisine is mediocre, often precarious, often very thrifty … the country has never been rich enough to do a cuisine separate from that of the popular current, rich, substantial and thought out like in France … Its monotony has been modified by the elements of diversity already discussed. In a culinary sense, each county is a world. Afterwards, there are the seasons of the year.

Apparent monotony is therefore counteracted by huge regional variation, of which most Catalans have at least a basic awareness, so much so to at least be able to associate a particular area, town or county with certain products or dishes. Jaume was quick to point out that this diversity was in strong contrast to Spain, which had little variety in either produce or dishes, part of his negative attitude to the Spanish state. His view though was far from unique, and informants would regularly compare the huge and varied list of Catalan recipes (*receptari*) with that of Spain, or more commonly with individual regions of the Spanish state.

The contemporary Catalan chef Carme Ruscalleda defines the Catalan as 'someone who doesn't want to be bored at the table … There is an aptitude particular to the culture that knows how to put in this charm, this creativity. For that reason we have a *receptari* that is so rich, varied and plural'. She also drew attention to the diversity of Catalonia's land- and foodscapes in contrast to that of the rest of Spain, particularly in Castile, describing that region as 'a more limited cuisine. They have a much shorter *receptari*, ours is very long and varied'. Later in our interview, when I asked her what she believed to be the distinctive features of Catalan cuisine, she reiterated 'this richness. Richness in produce, and in the combination of foods. From our own initiative, in what is sometimes so simple and poor, we excel'. These remarks show how diversity and Catalan cuisine's extensive recipe list act as markers of difference.

It was interesting that when discussing Spanish cuisine, my informants tended to divide Spain into its distinct communities and discuss them individually. It seemed an indirect way of questioning the Spanish state's legitimacy, and its cultural unity. One chef in Barcelona even claimed 'there is no Spanish cuisine, just a cuisine of the autonomous communities'. In this comparison, Castilian cuisine is frequently mocked for its perceived dullness and monotony, compared with the variety of landscape and microclimates within Catalonia.

Returning to the question of whether there is a national dish, one could argue that in Catalonia, such a dish would depend on the area, due to the inherent regional variety and diversity. The manager of Vic's Omnium Cultural, Pep Vila, even suggested that I should consider what would be the best dish for all the *Països Catalans*, in line with Omnium's stance of promoting a greater Catalan identity to include all the Catalan speaking areas. Interestingly, he suggested the *paella*, despite its associations with Spain, because it was a dish that varied so extensively from region to region, and season to season. Even the rice selected could represent Catalonia's regional diversity, because, in his words 'the rice [dishes] from Pals [Empordà's rice producing region] has nothing to do with that in the mountains, from Berguedà, or the typical *paella* from the zones of the coast, with seafood, or the *paella mixta*'.

Pep's response shows a habit of visualising other parts of Catalonia and its landscapes through their products and associated foodstuffs, in this instance the town of Pals or the county of Berguedà. Returning to the regional variation in choosing national dishes, I saw this attitude borne out depending on the origin of my informants. In Osona, it was often pork-based cuisine, such as *botifarra amb mongetes* , and also truffle products. Pepa Aymamí, the former head of the FICCG, saw the *romesco* sauce local to her place of origin in the Ebro Delta as a fundamental feature of Catalan cuisine. Informants who lived in Empordà, in the northeast, or had connections there, would emphasise the *mar i muntanya* or *agredolç*.

The ambiguity posed by regional variation in the creation of unified national cuisines is a common theme, and evidently Catalonia is no exception (Ferguson, 1988; Appadurai, 1988; Mintz, 1996; Fajans, 2012 to name a few). Yet, for Catalans, it is this diversity that is an essential claim to their culinary particularity, and its recognition is in fact a unifying feature.

Awareness of this variety is a form of national knowledge, showing knowledge of landscapes, territories and nation, a contrast to the perceived attitude of Spaniards. Spain might have regional diversity but will only accept this provided it does not affect the overarching Spanish identity, which should command the most important feelings of national loyalty. Even when individual autonomous communities are referred to by name, for example the Basque country or Castile, they are seen as poorer in diversity than Catalonia.

The Ideal of Thrift, and Pork-Based Cuisine

Throughout the discussion so far, the ideal of subsistence cuisine (*cuina d'aprofitament* or *cuina de subsistència*) has continually been flagged up. A popular Catalan phrase is '*ens aprofita de tot*' – literally, 'we make use of everything'. This concept was a common theme in discussions about Catalan food, as it ties in well to other concepts. For example, subsistence cuisine and the re-using of resources was central to two of the national/signature dishes discussed at the start of this section, the *canelons* and the *escudella i carn d'olla*. One of the ways that Catalan *canelons* were differentiated from Italian *cannelloni* is that the meat for the latter should be specially prepared for the filling, whereas in Catalonia it should use leftovers. *Pa amb tomàquet*, another highly identificatory food, is also based on the ideal of subsistence. It involves rubbing tomatoes onto hard bread, to make it palatable. As I have already discussed, dishes that have been 'revived' or 'rediscovered' are often praised for their origins as thrifty dishes that upheld this ideal of *aprofitament*.

This attitude appeared in everyday remarks and meals. In the unusual meal consisting of *pa amb tomàquet*, *truita de patates* and sushi that I shared with a group of young women in their twenties, one of the party started to eat the squashed tomato that she had used to make *pa amb tomàquet*. These tomatoes were normally thrown away, and the other diners protested in revulsion. She brushed off the criticism by saying 'We're Catalans, *ens aprofitem de tot*'. This casual usage of both national and culinary identity to defend quotidian behaviour shows well how ingrained these attitudes are, and moreover how closely national ideals and cuisine are interconnected in everyday life.

This ideal of thriftiness is related to several of the ideals of Catalan national character. As I explained in the introduction, it is often claimed that Catalans are miserly, avaricious or penny-pinching in the anti-Catalan stereotypes from the rest of Spain. Since its foundations in the nineteenth century, it was generally agreed by most of its early ideologues that common sense, industriousness and a good business mind were essential parts of the Catalan character (Llobera, 2004). The attitude of *ens aprofita de tot* is a culinary manifestation of this ideal.

I have already hypothesised that the reputation Vic has as a stronghold of Catalan identity may be due to its association with the pork industry and a product (sausages) regularly seen as characteristic of Catalan cuisine. The signature dish *botifarra amb mongetes*, a simple combination of sausage and broad beans, encapsulates this ideal of *aprofitament*. Several of my informants said that if they invited a non-Catalan to dinner, this would be the dish they would serve, because it represented one of the typical rural meals, from the environment of the countryside so idealised by early Catalan nationalists (DiGiacomo, 1987, Pi-Sunyer, 1987). In line with the *cuina d'aprofitament* ideal, the beans should ideally be cooked after the sausages, in the same pan, to make use of the leftover oil. It is a fairly easy meal to cook today and in modern kitchens, unlike the *escudella i carn d'olla*. The differences between Catalan and Spanish sausages are also frequently underlined. For instance, in Spain sausage meat is preserved using paprika, like the chorizo, which was entirely different from Catalonia, where salt and pepper were the only additions. Climate and locality also played its role, as my informants recognised that Catalonia was cooler than other parts of Spain, thus creating some uniqueness in the drying of sausages given by landscape and territory.

The key point to realise however about pig-related products is that they are excellent examples of *cuina de subsistència*. Pigs were a popular animal to raise in small spaces,[11] thus making them ideal for home consumption because they could be fed on leftovers. Once they reached maturity, all parts of the pig could be used, and nothing wasted. Sat recalled that even now, she took pride in taking the offal and other edible waste products from a particular pork factory in Vic where she knew the management. In this way, she continued the tradition of *aprofitament* of all parts of the pig. These include the blood, trotters, loin, bacon, lardons, lard, offal and intestines for sausage casings, liver, belly, ears and snout. Some of these are the sources of recently revived signature dishes, such as *cap i pota* (pig's ear, snout and trotters), or sweet pig's trotters, as well as a variety of *botifarres*. Of these, the selection varies from region to region (and, as Pla himself noted earlier, from town to town). The main varieties include: raw sausages (*per a coure*), which must be cooked, cured sausages (*curats*, of which the Vic *llonganissa* is one), and finally cooked sausages (*cuits*), that can be divided into those with and without blood (Torrado, 1985).

This variety also ties in to the ideal of regional, local and even familial variety in Catalan cuisine. Pork products such as these also have historical connectedness. The keeping of a pig was associated with a more rural lifestyle, that of the *pagès* farmer. For obvious reasons, subsistence cuisine is closely related to the past, a perfect example of an attempt to consume a national past through food. One chef I spoke with related this cuisine to Catalonia's place as a *terra de pas* (land of migrations): Catalonia had experienced many wars and plunders by passing armies, which had contributed to the need for a *cuina de subsistència*. Historic connectedness was also key to other explanations of *botifarra* and pork products as carriers of national identity. Francesc, the coordinator of the hospitality guild in Vic, argued that if he had to pick a Catalan national food, it would have to be the *llonganissa*, for three reasons. Firstly, because it was from pork, which had huge culinary importance, 'the most important in Catalonia'. Secondly, it had a history stretching back to Roman times, so 'has a tradition', and finally because it is an industry that brings wealth to the area.[12]

For Concepció, another informant from Vic, the *cuina d'aprofitament* was central to her understanding of Catalan cuisine. Like Sat, she took pride in using more marginal food products in her cooking, such as offal, bones, and hooves. The latter two generally ended up in her *escudella i carn d'olla*, her favourite dish, and for her the national dish and symbol of the Catalan nation. She herself related it to a bourgeois sensibility in Catalonia, placing it in line with the tradition of common sense and the power of the middle classes (this may also have been connected with her personal background, as the daughter of a self-made industrialist from a modest background, who had married into an old Vic family). She also emphasised its rural origin in some of our discussions, a dish that her ancestors had eaten. Her reason for this choice of the *escudella* as a signature dish was therefore because the dish represented the two intertwined ideas that have already been discussed at length here, that is its manifestation of the Catalan ideal of thrift and *aprofitament*, and also the connection with a historical past where such dishes were common.

The *matança de porc*, or pig killing, is a mythologised event, spoken of with awe. Until the last few decades, the *matança* was held in the autumn or winter months, and were opportunities for celebratory get-togethers amongst friends, relatives and neighbours, as large numbers of people were needed to properly prepare the sausages, bacon, cuts of meat, offal, scratchings and fat for each pig. A celebratory meal would then be held, to consume more perishable products, such as liver and blood. Nowadays, these events are difficult to arrange, due to official requirements ensuring the health and welfare of the pig (especially that it is not infected with trichinosis), permission from the local authority and other bureaucratic hurdles. Still, most Catalans try to attend at least one per year, held by friends or acquaintances, or even a 'symbolic' *matança* at a pork festival, such as at Manlleu's autumn Pork and Beer Festival, where a pre-killed pig is brought to the central arena, and carved up as in a traditional *matança*.

It is impossible to overemphasise the importance of this event in renewing and strengthening social and kinship ties. Not only does the event itself require physical labour from participants (though more in a symbolic sense today than in the past, as professional butchers are brought in), it is also an opportunity to catch up with friends and family. Simultaneously, one is participating in an activity that has a strong rootedness in the past, and thus recreating in some way a national past and historic forms of sociability. The activity also involves the creation of national, signature foods and symbols in the form of sausages. At the end of the day, with the carrying away of the resulting products, social ties are upheld through the exchange of food. As the food is consumed throughout the year these kin or social ties will be remembered and commented upon, coming to represent the event and people themselves.

The act of gathering together in a festive, ludic setting around food is also key to the national ideologies which surround the signature dishes of *escudella i carn d'olla* and other communal meals and food-centred occasions. Christmas and the *matança de porc* are both occasions at which social and familial ties are regenerated, occurring through interactions mediated by food. Food provides the sensory background to these emotional bonds. It is also in these contexts that ideas about national identity and national events come to be discussed, formulated, and articulated. In Catalonia, food-related events act as the means by which inhabitants of a nation can come into contact with one another, and make the imagined community into a reality.

Related to both communal consumption and *aprofitament* is the ideal of following the seasons (and related to the gastronomic calendar, which I discuss in Chapter Four, whereby certain foods are eaten on certain days). Pep Salsetes, a retired chef and cooking show host, emphasised this point, which was especially relevant at the time of fieldwork due to the economic crisis. He believed that Catalan cuisine must use 'produce from the season, everything in its proper place. This process of *aprofitament*, today in the crisis, I think it is a return to the past, a return to using more things that were thrown away'. Once again, his words show a desire to evoke a past approach to cuisine, adapting it to contemporary realities.

Subsistence cuisine may seem a far cry from vanguard restaurant cuisine and the *nova cuina*, but even there this ideal is still very present. One of the most important modern chefs in Catalonia, Joan Roca, talks about this topic in his first book. At the outset, he lays down his views that Catalan cuisine is fundamentally based on its products and good primary materials. Home cuisine has never been sophisticated, but is 'made with things from home, which are there at that precise moment in time' (Roca, 2004: 9). He relates the notion of a subsistence cuisine to the Empordan fishermen's cuisine, who made use of whatever fish could not be sold for their daily meals in soups, broths or *suquets*, and which he ties to the proximity to the Mediterranean. Place is therefore also central to *cuina de subsistència. Mar i muntanya* cuisine, for him, was a result of this need to use all available materials, something unnecessary today, but which he claims to still bear in mind in his contemporary creations. This could be self-promotion, a marketing ploy to appeal to Catalan values, but even then, his choice of introductory words is still revealing in showing the importance of a subsistence, thrift cuisine mentality to Catalan culinary identity.

During an interview with another Michelin-starred chef, Nandu Jubany, Osona's proponent of the *nova cuina*, I was able to witness the ideal of subsistence cuisine and the re-using of leftover ingredients first hand. Our interview took place in the evening, straight after supper with his family. He insisted on rustling up a quick supper for me of the remaining peas, pork and vegetables, presented beautifully in a wide rimmed bowl. He then used this as a starting point for our interview, to demonstrate the presence of subsistence cuisine in contemporary Catalan cuisine. In the background, his sous-chefs prepared the restaurant's particular *llonganissa*, which would be cured on site, and given to customers as a farewell gift. He also prepared *pa amb tomàquet* to eat throughout our interview, another manifestation of subsistence cuisine.

Pa amb tomàquet: A Catalan 'We Food'

At this point, it is essential to describe a food that has repeatedly occurred in the ethnography thus far: *pa amb tomàquet*. It consists of rubbing a ripe tomato into a slice of bread (an action called '*sucar*', juicing or moistening), ideally using bread that is a few days old so is slightly hard, allowing the juices to soften the bread. Salt and oil are usually added to conclude, but other ingredients can be added depending on individual preferences, such as garlic. It is commonly the base for sandwiches, and combined with cold meats and sausages. From talking to informants, most claimed to eat it every day, or at least every other day, either as a snack or a light meal. Of all the signature dishes identified by Catalans, *pa amb tomàquet* is probably the most regularly eaten. It is a common side dish or starter at festive events. To fully underline its symbolic importance, it is served in Catalan homes when there is a Barça football match (alongside Estrella Damm beer and *llonganissa*), thus ensuring the gustatory association between this food and other essential symbols of national identity (à la Sutton, 2001).

More than a signature dish in Mintz's (1996) sense, I prefer to use the term 'we food', to show how *pa amb tomàquet* is a gastronationalist symbol of Catalans. This term was used in Schacht's (2013) chapter on Makushi

Figure 2.3 *Pa amb tomàquet*, served at a food festival. Photograph by the author.

food identity as an indigenous term to describe the cassava plant and its 'complicated history of conflict, colonisation, and upheaval that has at times destabilized a people' (Schacht, 2013: 16). The cassava thus encapsulates both the historic events and the contemporary identity which that history has created. While all signature dishes so far discussed in the Catalan case could be described as 'we foods', my interpretation of 'we food' in this instance is something that comes to personify the Catalan people. Like the cassava amongst the Makushi, *pa amb tomàquet* is consumed (or at least encountered) on a quotidian basis by Catalans, so has a familiar and integrated place in Catalan contemporary identity.

Pa amb tomàquet sums up many of the features and ideas surrounding Catalan culinary identity that have appeared in this chapter. First and foremost, it is a prime example of the *ens aprofita de tot* attitude. In the words of one respondent in photo-elicitation, when she saw an image of the *pa amb tomàquet*, she immediately said 'the Catalan doesn't throw anything away!'. According to my informants, the dish first appeared in the nineteenth century, probably to soften hard, inedible bread to make it more palatable (though no cookbook or gastronomic text mentions it until Vázquez Montalbán in 1977, although Luján (1990) found reference to it in a poem from 1884). I was also told it used up old, over-ripe tomatoes, so contributing further to its reputation as a way of using up whatever ingredients were available.

It is also claimed as unique to Catalonia, though its spread to other regions of Spain has altered this conception somewhat, and now the emphasis is placed upon the process used to make it, that of rubbing the tomato in, rather than pouring on squashed or sliced tomato. However, the key point is that *pa amb tomàquet* is recognised as distinctly Catalan *by non-Catalans* within Spain. It is therefore a point of self-identification that is reinforced by interactions with outsiders.

For example, the retired chef Pep Salsetes recalled that the moment in his life that he felt most different, as a Catalan, from Spaniards was while making *pa amb tomàquet* in an all-male bar in Andalucía. After hearing he was Catalan, one of the other patrons recalled trying 'something called *pan con tomaca*' in Catalonia. This association shows how strongly connected the food is with Catalans by other inhabitants of Spain. Pep offered to show them how, and all the other patrons fell silent and gathered round to stare. The concept was completely alien to the spectators, and several remarked 'the Catalans are a strange people, they're people from the frontier', highlighting their sense of otherness in the eyes of non-Catalans within Spain. *Pa amb tomàquet* is equated with Catalans, both by insiders and outsiders, continually reinforcing this connection.

Its component ingredients contribute to this position. The tomato, as both a central component of Catalan cuisine and a product from the Americas, manifests the ideal of an integratory cuisine open to new influences. Bread is a basic staple in Catalonia, and has received some attention with the recognition of *Pa de pagès* ('Peasant bread') as a food with Protected Geographical Indication within the EU. Its description even explicitly states that it is ideal for *pa amb tomàquet*, officially enshrined as part of a 'traditional' foodway. Oil also represents a point of pride as one of Catalonia's main exports, and varies hugely from region to region, thereby acting as an example of the ideal of regional diversity and variety.

One should also consider *pa amb tomàquet* as Catalonia's 'we-food' because it can be found in all areas of Catalonia, a cultural unifier cross-nationally. This role is particularly important in Catalan food culture, due to the inherent diversity in cuisines that has already been discussed, which could contradict a claim of culinary unity in Catalonia. While visiting the Ebro Delta, in the extreme south of Catalonia, which is an area sometimes seen as more influenced by Spain due to its location and history of immigration from other parts of Spain, my host Gustavo claimed the fact that they ate *pa amb tomàquet* regularly proved that the Delta was part of Catalonia.

This symbolic association of *pa amb tomàquet* with Catalans has become such a commonly held assumption that it is even held as a cliché by some of my informants. When talking with Sat and her mother Montserrat, Sat suggested that along with *botifarra amb mongetes*, to 'outsiders' (i.e. Spaniards), *pa amb tomàquet* would be the food that was seen as most characteristic of Catalans. For them, its supposed uniqueness to Catalonia was a reason for its status as a we food. Sat noted with amusement that in a Madrid restaurant she had seen the words '*Pam tomaca*', and its recent appearances outside Catalonia in the rest of Spain were limited to restaurants, not homes. Still, another of my informants, Barcelona-based university lecturer Jordi, remarked that *pa amb tomàquet* is not as unique as Catalans would like to believe, like Sat pointing to its presence in Madrid under a different name.[13]

Others, however, noted that saying *pa amb tomàquet* is 'the' most representative dish is almost a cliché. Even though it can could be said to differentiate Catalans from their neighbours in Spain, it does not contribute to the Catalan economy, unlike pork-based cuisine. Several of my informants saw *pa amb tomàquet* as an extension of poverty cuisine into everyday life in the modern era, despite its relative recentness in the historical timeline. This was a fact that did not go unnoticed, but rarely dented its esteem. *Pa amb tomàquet* is perhaps the best example of how the emphasis on historical continuity going back centuries can be overlooked in preference for other national virtues if the food is convenient and ubiquitous enough.

Pa amb tomàquet is also a dish that is hard to produce beyond the borders of Catalonia. While any hard bread can be used, the preferred variety of tomatoes for making *pa amb tomàquet*, the *tomàquets de penjar*, are harder to find outside Catalonia, especially in other European countries. Other tomatoes can be used, but the end product will not conform to the 'proper' *pa amb tomàquet*. While Irene, a student in her twenties, was living in the UK for example, she said that she even brought these tomatoes from Catalonia, because the varieties found in British supermarkets either had too little juice or an unsuitable flavour (an experience I myself have also had). She eventually gave up trying. Likewise, Ricard, the son of Catalan expatriates who lived in the UK for twenty years during the Franco dictatorship, never made *pa amb tomàquet* in their home, as they could not recreate the flavour. Even in Catalonia, using supermarket-bought tomatoes is frowned upon, because they will not produce enough juice. Markets are considered the ideal location for buying the 'correct' type of tomatoes. At popular food festivals throughout Catalonia *pa amb tomàquet* is almost always handed out as the festive food on these occasions. The presence of *pa amb tomàquet* in these contexts reinforces the importance of these arenas for consuming national foods.

With its recognised ubiquity and symbolic power, it is not surprising that *pa amb tomàquet* is used as a metaphor for Catalans within the independence movement. For example, when I asked Joan, a restaurateur in Vic, whether he thought there was a connection between cuisine and independence, he was sceptical of a connection, but noted that there were some people who were 'very *pa amb tomàquet*', to describe that they were strongly in favour of independence. On this note, it is interesting that in a photo album handed out by the Vanguardia newspaper to commemorate September 2014's pro-independence Via Catalana demonstration, there was a page dedicated to T-shirts from the march, one of which was a cartoon image of *pa amb tomàquet*, alongside others representing patriotic slogans such as 'I'm Catalan, so I'm not Spanish', 'Independence' and 'One people, One language'. As a national symbol, *pa amb tomàquet* is just as powerful as any more obvious symbols, such as language, history or territory. Catalunyam, a company that created T-shirts inspired by Catalan food, designed a T-shirt with a cartoon strip of pictorial instructions on how to make it. Company owner and designer Oriol described his motivations for making the design:

> It is the most common, what everyone does. If I invite you to breakfast, we'll do a *pa amb tomàquet*. If I invite you to supper at home, we'll do *pa amb tomàquet*. Or if we go to a fancy restaurant, we'll do a *pa amb tomàquet*. It is transversal, all hours of the day, for everyone who wants it. I don't know anyone who dislikes it. A dish that is so democratic, universal, is a dish that identifies us in this sense.

Oriol explained that part of his inspiration was manuals for children, teaching them how to make *pa amb tomàquet*, as part of a general responsibility to pass on Catalan culture to the next generation (the packaging describes how these T-shirts make sure that 'our traditions will not disappear'). The other part was to teach outsiders (especially tourists) about Catalan culinary culture, and how to make *pa amb tomàquet*, a tongue-in-cheek way of spreading awareness of Catalan symbols to a non-Catalan audience.

During fieldwork, another indication of the importance of *pa amb tomàquet* was the reaction of Catalans to *my* making of this food. Their responses to first seeing me making it were very like the reaction to my speaking Catalan, pleasantly surprised that a non-Catalan was participating in such in-group activity. Was this a way of becoming a Catalan, I asked Oriol, through the making of *pa amb tomàquet*?:

> I think that with this, it is a bit like language. I think that, thanks to our history, we're accustomed to being Catalans in private. Like, in a collective. With another Catalan, it is normal to speak in Catalan, to do a *pa amb tomàquet*. But when someone non-Catalan speaks to you in Catalan, it pleases you. You note that this person has done a voluntary act of identifying themselves. *Pa amb tomàquet* is a bit of the same. It is as if this person has incorporated themselves in this cause.

Pa amb tomàquet can also be related to Catalonia's political movement in the form of satire. On 9 May 2013, in the midst of the controversy surrounding the Spanish Constitutional Court's ruling in March that Catalonia's proposed independence vote was unconstitutional, newspaper *la Vanguardia* published a cartoon that used *pa amb tomàquet* to poke fun at the situation. A Catalan (obvious by his bright red *barretina*) considers all the outrageous acts against Catalonia that the 'Tribunal Curtitucional' (a play on *'Tribunal constitucional'*, suggesting their short-sighted policies) could do. These include renaming Catalonia the 'Community for Spaniards of the North-East', or reassigning all the election votes amongst anti-Catalanist parties. He finally concludes by suggesting, 'prohibit *pa amb tomàquet?'*, to which a voice off-side calls out 'don't give them any ideas'. The message is that as a basic signifier of Catalan identity, much like language or territory, the prohibition of *pa amb tomàquet* would be an insult to the Catalan people, tantamount to removing their right to vote or refusing to acknowledge Catalonia as a geographical entity.

There have also been claims in Spanish media that deny the Catalan origin of *pa amb tomàquet*, or that emphasise its cross-Mediterranean nature. For instance, a 2014 article in pro-unionist newspaper ABC claimed that the dish originated from Murcian migrants who built the Barcelona Metro, and also drew attention to the *escudella*'s similarity to Spanish dishes (m.j.c., 2014). To paraphrase DeSoucey (2010: 433), this attack against a nation's food practices represents 'assaults on heritage and culture, not just on the food item itself'. As an aside, this behaviour occurs in food-related discourse amongst pro-unionist Catalans that I knew on fieldwork. For instance, one strongly pro-Spanish family from Barcelona who had a holiday home outside Vic would often point out to me how similar Catalan foods were to those of Spain. When discussing wines with one member of the family, Luís, he implied that the current success of the Catalan wine industry was thanks to the influence of knowledge from other Spanish wine-producing regions, which he felt were superior. They would also buy from shops in Vic that were known for *not* promoting themselves as 'Catalan'.

In the arena of *nova cuina*, *pa amb tomàquet* has even had recognition. Michelin-starred chef Joan Roca includes a recipe for a sophisticated 'lamb and *pa amb tomàquet*' in the 'memory' section in his work *El Celler de Can Roca* (2013). The dish was inspired by a recipe his grandmother used to make him as a childhood treat, *pa amb tomàquet* with small chunks of lamb sandwiched between the bread. Despite the new interpretation of the dish, it demonstrates the important role of *pa amb tomàquet* in Catalan food memories. *Pa amb tomàquet* was also the starting point of a 2016–2017 exhibition ('Sapiens: Understanding to Create') developed by Ferran Adrià and the elBulliLab. In the publicity, the dish was described as 'iconic', and one of the Adrià's favourite dishes.

'Bad' *pa amb tomàquet*

While the discussion this far has centred on foods with which Catalans identify because they represent some aspect of being Catalan, it is also worth discussing foods that Catalans reject. *Pa amb tomàquet* should be made by rubbing a tomato into the bread, and some of my informants contrasted this with making it in the 'non-Catalan', 'Madrileño' or Andalusian way, by pouring sliced or mashed tomatoes onto bread. However, at a few festive events I attended in Vic, this was precisely the way in which the dish was prepared for large groups of people, because it is more time-efficient than rubbing in tomatoes.

During a *gegants* festival in Vic, I was able to witness this first hand, as I helped to prepare *pa amb tomàquet* in this way. Our ingredients were several large piles of sliced *pa de pagès*, and two or three containers of a thick tomato juice-like substance made from crushed tomato, olive oil and salt. This mixture was poured onto the bread with a spoon, and the finished product stacked onto large trays and distributed with a *botifarra* at the end of the event to 200 participants.

The end result was far inferior to the *pa amb tomàquet* made in the 'proper' way. The bread was too moist, and easily fell apart. I was surprised that such a 'non-Catalan' means of making this was employed at festive events, such as the *gegants* festival, considering that these events are a focus of national identity expression. In this instance, convenience won out over culinary self-identification. I was curious about what Catalans felt about seeing this way of making *pa amb tomàquet*, and I included some of the images I gathered from the event in photo-elicitation (Figure 2.4).

The reactions provided a fascinating insight into what Catalan culinary identity was *not*. While recognising the food itself, most saw the images in an extremely negative light, with comments such as 'how disgusting', 'this is nothing', 'it is not *pa amb tomàquet*', 'you've got to choke on it', 'it looks like it comes from a can', 'they do this in cheap restaurants' and 'McDonalds of *pa amb tomàquet*'. Some of my respondents even criticised me for includ-ing the photos in my images of Catalonia. The younger group of *sardanistes* called it 'industrial *pa amb tomàquet*', but they admitted that even they had sometimes done it to make enough for a large gathering. Ironically, the very *geganters* with whom I prepared the *pa amb tomàquet* also hated this image, and even asked where I took it. That it was from their event elicited an awk-ward silence and embarrassed laughter. They then admitted that, despite the negative associations, it is done in Catalonia.

It can be seen from these responses that *pa amb tomàquet* made in this way is associated with public events as a quick, cheap and easy food to make for large groups, whilst cutting on quality. This is in contrast to the more

Figure 2.4 'Bad' *pa amb tomàquet*, as prepared and served at the *gegant* festival. Photograph by the author.

intimate *pa amb tomàquet*, done at home or with close friends, where the tomato is rubbed into the bread. This 'proper' way is also in contrast to the negative 'industrial', 'McDonalds', 'fast-food' and mass-produced associations elicited by the 'bad' way of making *pa amb tomàquet*. This reaction has some similarities to Pratt's (2007) description of the false dichotomy between 'the mainstream and the alternatives' (ibid.: 285), where the industrial food industry acts as a negative counterpart to the more 'local' or 'authentic' foods with a 'history' (ibid.) that are supposedly produced outside this industry, when they are in fact simply branded in a way to appeal to these values. While the parallel is not total with *pa amb tomàquet* (even in the case of the 'mass produced' variety, no attempt has been made to produce *pa amb tomàquet* on an industrial scale), the situation shows well how this false dichotomy works in Catalonia, and that despite these negative attitudes, these practices still continue, even in the context of 'traditional' events.

Pa amb tomàquet as *tapas*

In terms of manifestations of Spanish culinary identity outside its borders, *tapas* is perhaps the most enduring and commonly recognised. *Tapas* are small appetisers that are served together to form a meal, generally consumed sitting at a bar, and are especially associated with the southern and central areas of Spain. *Tapas* is not native to Catalonia, but there are numerous *tapas* bars in Barcelona (mostly catering to tourists) and most towns and cities in Catalonia have at least one. Catalonia's relationship with *tapas* is a complex one, because it is strongly associated with Spain. In the first cookbook in English on Catalan cuisine, *Catalan Cuisine: Europe's Last Great Culinary Secret* (1997), Colman Andrews describes Catalans' indifference to *tapas*. It is consumed by tourists and other Spaniards, not Catalans themselves. This is certainly the impression in Barcelona, and one of my informants from there, Oriol, admitted to becoming angry when outsiders think Catalans eat *tapas*. However, in practice, many Catalans do eat *tapas*. Some Catalans may prefer to use the term *pintxos*,[14] which describe the Basque-style *tapas* that has become very popular in Barcelona thanks to several chains offering Basque cuisine. It is interesting that the Basque variety of this food is preferred over the Spanish one, because Basques are seen in a more favourable light by Catalans due to their similarly difficult relationship with Spain.

An experience I had early on in fieldwork is enlightening when trying to understand the contexts in which Catalans consume *tapas*. On an evening out with a group of *sardana* dancers, they took me to a popular *tapas* bar in Vic for our meal. I was surprised at the choice, having thought that *tapas* was distinctly un-Catalan. They explained to me that this choice was not unusual for them, as it was convenient. There were several other places they liked to meet in Vic: a sandwich bar, a Sicilian pizzeria, or a French crêperie. As they talked about these other restaurant options, it became clear that the *tapas* restaurant was placed into the category of 'other' foods, i.e. foreign and non-Catalan. So, while *tapas* comes from the same state, it is still classed in just as foreign a category as cuisine from Sicily or France. When I asked the group whether they would choose a Catalan restaurant, they said that Catalan food was reserved for family occasions, or large formal dinners organised by the *sardana group*, when the group met as *sardanistes* and performers of a Catalan cultural heritage. The contexts for consuming Catalan food are more valued and formalised, while 'foreign' foods (like *tapas*) are better suited to informal outings.

However, it is not just what is eaten in *tapas*, but also the way of eating, that is alien, and has had to be changed at the popular level to be 'palatable' (in more ways than one) to Catalans. When we ordered in the Vic *tapas* bar, I realised the extent to which *tapas* has been Catalanised, as each of the dishes were of Catalan origin. There was the ubiquitous *pa amb tomàquet*, sliced Vic sausages, *empedrat* (bean and cod salad) and *llonganissa* sausage croquettes. The foods at the meal were also important during another *tapas* meal I had with a group of older Catalans. They admitted that it may seem odd they were eating in a *tapas* restaurant, particularly with the arrival of *patates bravas* (potatoes with a spicy sauce), which they jokingly called 'very Catalan', because they were so ubiquitous. However, when the *pa amb tomà-quet* arrived a moment later to oohs and aahs of contentment, one remarked 'ah, even more Catalan now'. With the presence of the *pa amb tomàquet*, the Catalan-ness of the meal was re-established.

During our *tapas* meal, the *sardanistes* also pointed out that we were eating at a table, not at a bar, the usual way to eat *tapas* in Spain. This preference for eating at a table, be it for *tapas* or anything else, was a common refrain throughout Catalonia. Andrews (1997) relates how Catalans don't feel they have eaten until they sit down at a table. Returning to my conversation with Oriol, I mentioned that earlier that day I had eaten a dish of *patates braves* with a friend, contradicting his claim that Catalans don't eat *tapas* dishes. His first reaction was to ask whether we were sitting at a table, which we had. This proved his point, that though we called it '*tapas*', it was being eaten in the Catalan way, at a table.

Several other informants raised the importance of the '*sobretaula*'. The phrase 'we always get together around a table' was one I often heard when referring to Catalan social and eating habits, that is that Catalans will eat to socialise, rather than go to a bar for a drink or small *tapas*, unlike Spaniards. The Catalan medieval writer Francesc Eiximenis, who wrote of the Catalans' table habits in 1384, claimed that Catalans eat better than other nations because they sit at a table, amongst other reasons (Contreras, 2006). Considering that Catalans often refer back to writings on themselves for identity construction, it is possible that my informants' statements were influenced by their knowledge of Eiximenis.

The Character of a National Cuisine

This chapter has provided an overview of some of the key themes in Catalan culinary culture, identity and signature dishes. These themes and dishes are essential to understanding the rest of the work, because they will reappear frequently throughout. These include the relationship between food and the independence movement, the gastronomic calendar, landscape and locality, and other aspects of national, festive and pork-based dishes. Each of these elements of culinary nationalism feed into each other (literally as well as figuratively), creating a rich tapestry of symbols and associations that allow Catalans to interact with the nation through food, in many different contexts.

Notes

1. *Samfaina* is almost identical to the French *ratatouille*, so is perhaps not such a good candidate for the bearing of unique culinary identity. In situations where connections with prestigious French cuisine are to be emphasised however, the *samfaina/ratatouille* connection does come up.
2. A variety of small red bell peppers particular to Catalonia, dried for use in cooking.
3. Note this dismissive attitude to Barcelona, which has experienced much greater levels of immigration from elsewhere in Spain, and where Catalan identity has been 'diluted'.
4. Catalan pasta dish using macaroni, but where the pasta is normally baked instead of boiled.
5. While Catalans may have designated a *tortilla de patates* with onion as a marker of culinary identity, in practice it is not exclusive to Catalonia. Including onion in the *tortilla* is a controversial decision in the whole of Spain, much debated in gastronomic circles and online forums. It is perhaps because of the uncertain status of onion in *tortilla* in the rest of the Peninsula that Catalans have chosen to make their position plain. It would be interesting to see a geographic spread of attitudes to onion in *tortilla* throughout Spain, suggesting possible differences by autonomous community. Similarly, the presence of onion in *paella* is a source of heated debate in Spain, as are most ingredients of the 'true' Valencian *paella*, which is the one described by my informants, and is different to other types of *paella*, e.g. seafood *paella*, *paella mixta* (mixed seafood and meat *paella*) etc.
6. It could parallel in this sense the saying that 'He's a donkey', which refers to a stubborn individual, and has now come to be a metaphor for the Catalan people in their relationship with Spain. The donkey is now one of the symbols of Catalonia, much in the way the Osborne bull is for Spain (Strubell, 2008).
7. Literally 'stale wine', a kind of dessert wine with a strong flavour, that has been submitted to oxidised ageing.
8. The *Xató* is a salad associated with the seaside counties of Garraf and Baix Penedès, south of Barcelona. Its ingredients include endive, anchovies, cod, tuna and olives, with the essential addition of the *Xató* sauce (to which the word *Xató* sometimes refers alone). It is a winter dish, consumed between January and April, which is when *Xató*-eating events and festivals (*xatonades*) take place. Unlike *calçotades*, which now take place all over Catalonia, *xatonades* are largely limited to the *xató's* area of origin.

9. I was often told that Catalans don't normally add sauces to already cooked foods, except for the *allioli* as a side sauce, as the sauce should already be present during the cooking. For my benefit in particular, this was contrasted with the perception of northern Europeans (specifically English tourists, apparently) who are seen to smother cooked food in sauces like ketchup or mayonnaise.

10. This trend has been noticed elsewhere, for example in the increased consumption in Barcelona markets of butcher's off-cuts and offal (Contreras, 2007).

11. Today this is a thing of the past, thanks to the concern for trichinosis, foot and mouth and other diseases, which makes raising them prohibitively expensive, and the accompanying limits on housing.

12. While Francesc was unable to give exact figures on this, there was a general consensus in Vic that the importance of the pig and alimentary industries had meant that Vic was less affected than some other cities by the recent economic crisis.

13. David Sutton in his *Remembrance of Repasts* (2001), also describes a similar kind of food, which his informants (ironically) also considered unique to the islands:

> Bread is also used as a mid-morning snack, dribbled with olive oil, rubbed with a juicy tomato and sprinkled with salt. This snack is considered by many to be a particularly Kalymnian food, and people recalled bringing it with them to school, along with a few dried figs. Workers still use this as a coffee-break snack. (Sutton, 2001: 33)

14. These *pintxos* (literally 'punctured') are slices of crusty bread with the toppings pressed in by a toothpick, hence their name.

Chapter 3
CATALAN CUISINE IN CONTEXT

ے౨ۍ۞ﻪ౨ے

Now that the principle characteristics of Catalan cuisine have been established, it is relevant to consider the broader context of this culinary identity. This includes connections with neighbouring regions in Spain and the Mediterranean, and international institutions such as UNESCO (United Nations Educational Scientific and Cultural Organisation), and how food mediates these connections. Considering the importance of heritage cuisine to gastronationalism, one cannot ignore the campaign to recognise Catalan cuisine as a UNESCO intangible cultural heritage of humanity. In 2010, UNESCO granted this accreditation to several food-related cultural manifestations, including the 'Gastronomic meal of the French', North Croatian gingerbread making, and traditional Mexican cuisine. This was the first time that gastronomy had been recognised as a distinctive measure of heritage status in its own right, instead of part of some other intangible heritage expression. This has led to other food-related designations since 2010.[1]

An accreditation by UNESCO brings many potential benefits to stakeholders involved in tangible or intangible cultural heritage. Intangible Cultural Heritage is defined by UNESCO as 'practices, representations, expressions, knowledge, skills … that communities … recognize as part of their cultural heritage' (UNESCO, 2003), which are recreated in every generation, and construct group identity. The main aim of accreditation is to safeguard these practices, thus preserving (according to UNESCO) cultural diversity in light of increasing homogenisation through globalisation. An obvious benefit too is the educational impact of raising awareness, both within and without the community. In doing so, communities can be empowered and galvanised by the campaign and resulting accreditation, especially in cases where this heritage has been historically marginalised (Cruces Roldán, 2014). The controversies inherent in such campaigns can make an intangible heritage newly relevant, occasionally in opposition to organisational bodies involved in the UNESCO campaign – an unintended consequence, but a feasible benefit, nonetheless. Potential economic benefits to communities who safeguard intangible heritage are also undeniable, such as funding from the state and international agencies, development of tourist industries, local investment and employment creation (Lourenço and Rebelo, 2006; Talaya et al, 2008; Nett, 2013). Despite the many positive elements of UNESCO, accreditation has its flipsides. Organisations leading accreditation campaigns and related stakeholders may have ulterior motives to that of 'protecting' threatened heritage. Nation states and NGOs have frequently co-opted such campaigns for their own ends (Cruces Roldán, 2014; Ichijo and Ranta, 2016).

The recognition of food culture as a UNESCO intangible cultural heritage spawned a campaign to gain this status for Catalan cuisine, initiated in 2012 by the Fundació Institut Català de la Cuina i de la Cultura Gastronòmica ('Foundation-Institute of Catalan Cuisine and Gastronomic Culture' – FICCG). The FICCG is a private non-profit organisation that has been in existence since 1994, one of the results of the 2nd Congress of Catalan Cuisine (1994–1995). The Foundation added the name 'Institute' to its title in 2012 to coincide with the UNESCO bid, to emphasise its role as a research organisation. The crisis of autumn 2017 placed a break on the application process to UNESCO (which had already been delayed several times since 2012), and made it clear that such an application could not be made via Madrid in the current political climate. In line with the findings of Ichijo and Ranta (2016), the Spanish state appears to be using its influence to prevent the recognition of Catalan cuisine by UNESCO. However, the Catalan campaign also shows how non-state actors (i.e. nations within a state) can attempt to use designations such as UNESCO to assert their existence on a global scale. The FICCG underwent a change in management in January 2018, which has chosen to focus more on initiatives within Catalonia, such as the Third Congress of Catalan Cuisine in 2018–2019.

To begin I give an overview of the activities of the FICCG, and their approach. My main interest here is the reaction of my informants to these efforts and to the FICCG. Such reactions reveal some of the controversies that arise when an official body claims to become a legitimate authority on a particular symbol of identity. The connection between Catalan cuisine and expressions of pro-independence sentiment is also considered. This moves onto an update of how Catalan cuisine has been mobilised following the contested independence referendum of October 2017, using data gathered in January 2018. Finally, I consider some statements regarding the connections (or lack thereof) between Catalan cuisine and other cuisines in the surrounding geographic areas, e.g. Spain, Europe and the Mediterranean.

These provide an insight into the self-perceptions of Catalans in relation to surrounding food identities.

Catalan Cuisine: UNESCO Intangible Cultural Heritage

The FICCG has been involved in several projects related to the UNESCO campaign. These included continual research for the recipe book created by the foundation, the *Corpus del Patrimoni Culinari Català* ('Corpus of Catalan Culinary Patrimony', 2011), as well as other publications such as *La cuina del 1714* (a collection of recipes to remember the tercentenary of the Siege of Barcelona) and in 2014 a small English-language book aimed at tourists (*Catalan Cuisine*) to raise international awareness (Pomés Leiz, 2014). The organisation's activities included research for the *Corpus*, now in affiliation with the Food Observatory (ODELA) at the University of Barcelona, and public promulgation of Catalan cuisines, in particular in schools and museums. The organisation also gave support to initiatives related to gastronomy, hospitality or tourism promoted by member groups (the Gastronomic Coordination and Promotion Service). Another project, related to the *Corpus*, was (and continues to be) the *Marca Cuina Catalana* designation for establishments who provide Catalan cuisine.

During my interview with the founder and former President, Pepa Aymamí, she explained that the aim of the institute was to 'promote and consolidate Catalan gastronomic culture'. The aim is not just to internationalise Catalan cuisine with the UNESCO bid, but also 'make sure there's a permanence'. This emphasis on preservation is unsurprising considering that the main argument for the bid is that cultural heritage is at risk. It is this emphasis on creating permanence which has motivated the categorisation of Catalan cuisine in the form of the *Corpus del Patrimoni Culinari Català*. This is a compendium of 1,136 recipes officially recognised by the FICCG, alphabetically ordered, which the FICCG advertised as 'the most complete inventory of Catalan recipes in existence' (FICCG, 2015a). Originally published in 2006 (as the *Corpus de la Cuina Catalana*), the most recent edition came out in 2016.

The fear of loss lies at the heart of UNESCO's preservation initiative, that some aspect of human civilisation is essential to preserve in the face of the homogenising influence of modernity and globalisation (Man Kong Lum and de Ferrière le Vayer, 2016). As in many nationalist movements, there is also a discourse of loss at the heart of Catalanism – one which was not far from reality in the post-Franco years. If it is lost, Catalan national identity will disappear forever. To preserve Catalan identity, cultural manifestations must be continually performed, re-enacted, and preserved by either popular or official channels. Such is the motivation that pervades many of the encouragements for the continued performance of cultural acts on a government level (Crameri, 2008), and also a personal and individual one. Cuisine is also pervaded by this sense that certain culinary 'traditions' are at risk of being lost, or have already been lost, despite a concurrent recognition of 'revivals'. While highly unlikely to happen today, these cultural losses (sometimes called 'cultural genocide') were a real concern by the end of the Franco dictatorship. All the same, this sense of impending doom lends an added urgency to the performance of Catalan cultural acts, or attempts to protect them.

Pepa admits that now Catalan cuisine is not at risk, claiming that many restaurants were doing 'traditional cuisine'. However, continual work was needed to reduce any risk of loss, aided by the guarantee of preservation that UNESCO recognition could offer. In particular this has meant correcting some of the misconceptions about 'traditional' Catalan cuisine, for example that it is fattening and unhealthy for contemporary lifestyles. This is why many of their promotional activities have emphasised the connection with the Mediterranean diet (already recognised by UNESCO), and products such as oils and heritage vegetables. Pepa made a clear delineation between the modern cuisine of the *cuina nova* developed by Ferran Adrià, and 'traditional' Catalan cuisine, which is what she was protecting.

These measures generally receive a favourable reaction in Catalonia, not just because of the touristic economic potential they give to an area, but also because this international recognition furthers and even celebrates awareness of Catalan identity outside its borders. The ruling party (CiU) could demonstrate to their electorate that they were involved in promoting and protecting Catalan heritage. Recognitions of heritage by external bodies are also part of the game of one-upmanship the Generalitat plays with Spain, which can be held up as examples of a unique Catalan identity as sanctioned by an impartial, outside group with global prestige. This explains why the Generalitat put its support behind the campaign for Catalan cuisine almost since its inception in 2012. It also explains why the campaign later met difficulties going through Madrid.

The UNESCO campaign, was originally intended for 2013 recognition, but was continually put off over the next five years. A UNESCO delegation visited the University of Barcelona in June 2012 to see a fourteenth-century copy of the *Llibre de Sent Soví* (the underlying importance of this book to the bid was discussed in Chapter One). According to the University of Barcelona's reporting of the event, the act showed that University was putting its support behind the UNESCO bid.

On the UNESCO front, there were originally nine members of the scientific committee in charge of researching and organising the bid, but this has since increased to fourteen. Common to many campaigns for UNESCO's Intangible Cultural Heritage (ICH) status in cuisine (Di Giovine and Brulotte, 2014), academic specialists from a number of Catalonia's most prestigious universities (especially the University of Barcelona) make up this committee, lending credibility to the campaign. They included the president of the Institute of Catalan Studies, several historians and medievalists, two anthropologists, two nutritionists and a sociologist. Some of these academics had also been involved in the campaign to recognise the Mediterranean Diet as UNESCO ICH in 2013.

The effort to recognise Catalan cuisine as an intangible heritage is not the first in Catalonia, and there have been several successful campaigns, including the Patum of Berga (2005), the *Castells* or humans towers (2010) and the Methodology for inventorying intangible cultural heritage in biosphere reserves: the experience of Montseny (2013), there providing a precedent for recognising Catalonia's cultural heritage. However, the FICCG's application was politically awkward, as it can only be presented at a state, not a regional, level. This presentation had to officially be done from Madrid (via Spain's Permanent Delegation to UNESCO, and relevant NGOs), which is complicated by the negative attitudes to Catalonia's independence movement, the current government and Catalan identity in general.

Complications also arose within Catalonia because the campaign will be presented as a *regional* food identity (i.e. as part of Spain), not a national one. It is possible that this may be why there has been little support from Catalan cultural groups such as the Omnium Cultural or Assemblea, though I did not hear this view expressed outright. The FICCG might have avoided any association of this kind in case it damaged the campaign's application process from the central government.

The UNESCO project was separate from Vic's (now failed) application to UNESCO's Cities of Gastronomy (part of its Creative Cities designation), though Pepa regarded it as helpful to the FICCG's campaign. Osona's Hospitality Guild is one of the bodies grouped under the FICCG, and they promoted each other's respective agendas.

The project '*Marca Cuina Catalana*' (Catalan Cuisine Brand) was created in 2001. Its first phase consisted of putting together the recipes that became the *Corpus*, first published in 2006. After this, the FICCG then began recognising establishments that cooked Catalan cuisine according to the recipes within the *Corpus*, who could then be given a plaque to place outside their restaurant. Most establishments are restaurants, though some are shops and hotels. The establishment has to show that at least 40 per cent of the dishes served are from the *Corpus*, using the exact same recipe and name as in the book. Restaurants can also apply to be members of the FICCG without being part of the Marca, though some are both. Although Pepa was unclear on the difference, it seems that 'La Marca' restaurants serve 'traditional cuisine' that are 'typical of the country', and others in the FICCG can be more experimental and work on 'investigating Catalan cuisine'. As of 2018, there were 230 restaurants registered throughout Catalonia. Restaurants under the *Marca Cuina Catalana* have to place the FICCG's logo next to each dish from the *Corpus* on the menu.

On the FICCG website, the objectives of the *Marca* are listed as 'guaranteeing the continuity of Catalan cuisine', creating a marker of quality for both Catalan restaurants and associated products, developing a network of establishments which will defend and offer 'gastronomic cultural patrimony', and finally provide opportunities for the 'conservation of alimentary biodiversity, the promotion and defence of the rural area' (FICCG, 2015a). In line with these aims, establishments are advised to use seasonal products, their 'own products' (i.e. Catalan-made) and Catalan products recognised by the EU's PDO/PGI scheme, which are made following 'methods respectable to tradition'. The goal is to 'encourage awareness and preservation of autochthonous products' (FICCG, 2015b).

The FICCG used to be very strict about the names, ingredients and preparation of dishes in project's early years, and establishments had to use the precise recipe. However, it soon became clear that there was a huge variation in names, and that there had to be some poetic license. For example, one restaurant had served a dish called '*pollastre de la iaia*' (grandma's chicken) for many years, which was identical to a recipe in the book under a different name. When the establishment first joined, they were required to remove it or change the name. When the restaurant refused to serve it using the name in the *Corpus*, the FICCG came to a compromise and allowed them to call it '*pollastre de la nostra iaia*' (*our* grandma's chicken; emphasis added). Still, an application for such a change has to be made to the FICCG. According to Pepa, they have informants continually passing through restaurants to monitor compliance.

Since 2016, the UNESCO bid has stalled, due to the unwillingness of the necessary Madrid-based organisations to take up the project. Since that time, the FICCG focused on raising local awareness of the campaign within Catalonia, as well as on promoting Catalan food-based initiatives, with a special emphasis on raising awareness of local products and producers, and food education in schools. The possibility of a third Congress of Catalan Cuisine was suggested in 2017, however this project was delayed, due to lack of funding and the political situation. Pepa Aymamí retired as head of the FICCG in 2017, and the role was filled in August 2017 by chef Sergi de Meià (he began his responsibilities in January 2018).

During an interview with Sergi de Meià in January 2018, he revealed some of his plans for the future of the FICCG. As a chef, his vision for the FICCG focused more on promoting Catalan cuisine amongst younger chefs and seeing it in restaurants. Unlike Pepa, he bemoaned that very few restaurants actually described themselves as doing 'Catalan cuisine', even if they used local products that contributed to the local economy (this is a key tenet of his definition of the cuisine), a situation that is especially acute in Barcelona.

De Meià also restarted preparations for the third Congress of Catalan Cuisine, which took place from September 2018 to the end of 2019. The Congress had six main themes: Culinary Heritage, Gastronomy, the role of chefs, culinary knowledge in Catalonia, cuisine industry and work, and finally cuisine and society. Early in his tenure, de Meià set up five teams spread throughout Catalonia (based in Metropolitan Barcelona, Outer Barcelona and the central counties, Tarragona, Lleida and Girona) to create a space to share cross-regional experiences about the variations in cuisine, its promotion and touristic potential. These teams have now become territorial commissions to manage the Congress cross-regionally. The aims of the Congress have been three-fold. Firstly, consolidate the world leadership of Catalan cuisine and ensure its continued place at the forefront of global culinary innovation. Secondly, define the key actors in Catalan cuisine and gastronomy, encouraging communication and collaboration across sectors. And finally, perhaps the most important is to define and promote a strategy for Catalan cuisine with a focus on the years up to 2025, called the 'Gastronomic Horizon' (Tercer Congrés Català de la Cuina, 2019).

As for the UNESCO candidature, four years of political instability had 'paralysed' the initiative. According to de Meià, all the relevant documents were in order for the application, but they were still awaiting a response from the Madrid-based Permanent Delegation to UNESCO. The lack of clarity on funding from the central government (via the Generalitat) had also created a challenging environment for many Catalan-based organisations, not just the FICCG (this was a common complaint during my January 2018 visit). He characterised the current situation as surreal, as there is a sense of being held hostage to the whims of Madrid. The application has therefore not entirely stopped, but remains in limbo. The situation also reveals how politicised food-related expressions of national identity can become, in a case of a contested nation-against-the-state situation.

Reactions to the UNESCO Campaign

Attitudes towards the FICCG and the UNESCO campaign reveal fault lines and a fundamental questioning both of the situation of Catalan cuisine, and of who has the right to 'manage' it. The reactions to UNESCO amongst my informants were mixed. In principle, there was a positive attitude to the preservation and promotion of any aspect of Catalan culture, cuisine included. However, they found it hard to fully accept the notion that Catalan cuisine could be controlled and managed by an organisation, even if it was backed by the Generalitat.

In practice the codification inherent in the 'UNESCO-isation' of cuisine also raises concerns about cuisine's ability to change and adapt to contemporary and future realities, or whether it will remain relevant to practitioners. Noyes (2011b) sums up these concerns in her article 'Traditional Culture: How Does it Work?', including issues of stability, stakeholders and the responsibility to perform and learn traditional arts. If this responsibility is assigned to some 'supervising authority', incentives to learn them could potentially disappear within their original practitioner group. While this is unlikely to happen in the case of Catalan cuisine, and the FICCG is not well known as an authority in Catalonia, such concerns are worth considering in this context. I discussed this with Barcelona chef Carles, whose family have been innkeepers since 1868, and whose restaurant is a reference point of Catalan cuisine. He felt positive about the UNESCO recognition, but hoped that it would not cause Catalan cuisine to become 'a work of art from grandma, which is hung up and does nothing. UNESCO provides awareness, but if you do not keep using and adapting it, then the cuisine will die'.

A journalist who has worked extensively with the *nova cuina* movement was particularly sceptical of the UNESCO bid, and also the Marca Catalana system for restaurants (he did not wish to be named when expressing this view). He could see the importance of globalising Catalan cuisine but felt that the UNESCO candidature risked turning it into 'the offerings of a museum. Because it doesn't move, it is immutable, codified'. Moreover, another criticism stemmed from the application of the Marca Catalana. As I have explained, to give a restaurant the Marca Catalana, 40 per cent of the recipes have to be Catalan, and from the *Corpus*. Yet how, he asked, can a restaurant be registered as Catalan if the other 60 per cent includes foreign dishes that have no connection with Catalan cuisine (a problem that resonates with de Meià's comments on the dearth of restaurants doing purely 'Catalan' cuisine)? All in all, while he believed that the *Corpus* could be updated, improved and adapted, successful UNESCO recognition would stunt this process. As he explained:

> If you say that it is Patrimony of Humanity, this recipe cannot evolve, because it is final … I understand the idea of giving support, visibility, but the way of saying, this is the dish and you cannot change it, that I do not like.

Another area of controversy surrounding the Corpus has been the refusal to include dishes that were of Spanish origin, but which have become popular since mass-immigration in the Franco-era in the 1950s and 1960s. A prime example is the tomato and vegetable soup *gazpacho* (or *gaspatxo* in Catalan), popular throughout Spain but associated primarily with Andalusia. It is widely consumed throughout Catalonia, especially in the summer months, despite widespread recognition that it is not Catalan cuisine. This raises a vital question: at what point is a food Catalan or not Catalan, especially if it includes ingredients grown within Catalonia?

The situation is not unlike Pilcher's (1998) descriptions of government officials dictating the content of Mexican cuisine, by refusing to accept indigenous, pre-Columbian dishes as Mexican, a trait that has also been recognised in other contexts by Ichijo and Ranta (2016). One could wonder whether the FICCG, which has been promoted and sponsored by the Generalitat, has been carrying out a subtle enforcing of national culinary ideals. However, I found no evidence to state that the Generalitat attempted to have any influence on the FICCG's policies in this way.

I put the same question to Pepa Aymamí during out interview. She clarified that only when a food clearly has over 50 years of recognition and popularity in Catalonia can it be included, 'when it has enough tradition in Catalonia'. Allegedly the FICCG did a study into whether *gaspatxo* was done in Catalan homes, where it was done much less frequently than in res-taurants. This she compared with its use in Andalucía, where it is consumed regularly within homes. This does back up a remark from an older informant in Vic, Sat, who remembered only making her first *gaspatxo* at home in the early 2000s. Her mother, in her 90s at the time, had only a vague awareness of *gaspataxo* as a soup with tomato.

Still, there were others who did cook *gaspatxo* at home, and felt that it was well incorporated into Catalan cuisine. Isidre, a middle-aged chef and cooking instructor in Vic, recalled that at first *gaspatxo* was looked upon with suspicion, a dish of 'foreign people, even though they were of the same peninsula', indicating the way in which other Spaniards (aka *gaspatxo*-eaters) were viewed. Still, he added 'we're a land that has received much influence, including from the lands of our own peninsula', and that, in his view, it had totally integrated. Once again, the inclusion of *gaspatxo* fits into the culi-nary ideal of an open Catalan cuisine. Likewise, the editor of *Cuina*, Josep, recalled how his grandmother had learned how to make *gaspatxo* from an immigrant from Seville. He strongly emphasised that his grandmother never recognised the dish as Catalan, and always regarded it as an Andalusian dish. This returns once more to the theme of the recognition of otherness of for-eign foods in Catalonia, and respect for their origins. However, he admitted that now it had become ubiquitous in Catalonia:

I do not know if the Andalusians do it in a different way, they do it in many ways, and Catalans do it in a thousand ways. In summer, we have all the right products to do *gaspatxo* here. They might be used differently, but we can do it with products from here.

The dish could be made Catalan by using products from Catalonia, and Josep also implied that the 'process' and recipe might be different, an aspect that delineates culinary identity. For example, a restaurateur in one of the counties closer to Barcelona described how he'd made his own *gaspatxo*, by adding cherries and red fruits. Through the use of fruit, a Catalan culinary trait, he had Catalanised a 'foreign' dish and adapted it to his own culinary identity. Still, this example was in a restaurant not a home, returning once again to Pepa's requirement that a dish be prepared regularly within the home.

During a cooking session with Mon, a professional cooking instructor, she expressed scepticism of the FICCG and its attempts. Their Catalan credentials and intentions were undeniably sincere, but for her they seemed more interested in publicity and photo opportunities with the Catalan President and other dignitaries, than really helping Catalan cuisine in any practical way. I raised the issue of codification through the *Corpus*, and the story of *canelons de la iaia*. Mon replied that this was just one example of (she felt) the FICCG's focus on technicalities. Earlier in our conversation, she had clarified the differences between the *salvitxada*, *xató* and *romesco* sauces. This kind of subject was discussed with academic rigour at the first two Congresses of Catalan Cuisine in 1981–1982 and 1994–1995, which led to the creation of the FICCG. While an interesting discussion, she felt that it drew attention away from the actual cooking, the skill that the FICCG claims to protect. All in all, Mon concluded, if she had to choose who was doing the most for Catalan cuisine at present, between the FICCG and Ferran Adrià, then Ferran Adrià would win.[2]

More important though for Mon was the quality of recipes. According to her, she had tried two or three from the *Corpus*, which were disastrous. If there is to be codification, it is acceptable (though not ideal) to have a book with antiquated recipes, but at least they should be of a high standard and workable. This question of quality was similar to a concern raised by the retired chef and writer Josep Lladonosa i Giró. While in favour of the global promotion of Catalan cuisine via UNESCO or similar campaigns, he admitted that there were many restaurants that served poor quality Catalan cuisine. If one is to promote Catalan cuisine globally, standards of excellence must be maintained within the country itself. He was unimpressed with the system of plaques erected outside restaurants that prepared dishes based on *Corpus* recipes, not just because it did not guarantee a high standard, but also because it reduced the diversity of recipes (the wide *receptari*) inherent in Catalan cuisine.

Barcelona chef Fermí held an opposite opinion. He even defined Catalan cuisine as the recipes collected in the *Corpus* (i.e. the sort of cuisine he cooked himself). He later explained that his support for UNESCO recognition came from a desire to see a separate Catalan identity recognised by an official, world-recognised entity that was outside Spain:

> In the sense that UNESCO protects the differentiating facts (*fets diferencials*). Like with French or Italian, if a cuisine has all these historic elements that can be protected, in order to be considered as a cultural fact (*fet cultural*), then it is Catalan cuisine. The thing with us, is that we've had a hostile state, and we haven't been able to raise our voices, to communicate [to the world] things that have a certain merit. For this reason, Catalan cuisine is not so well known, because many people associate it with Spanish cuisine. Notice up to what point it is political. That in Spain right now, the two important places that have the maximum culinary quality, both in restaurants and Michelin stars, as well as products and related businesses, are Catalonia and the Basque country. *That's because we are nations without a state in a political conflict with Spain.* (Emphasis added)

Fermí therefore saw the bid for UNESCO intangible cultural heritage recognition as a means of asserting Catalan existence and political rights within the context of a hostile Spanish state, as a kind of cultural one-upmanship. UNESCO becomes a means of gaining international recognition for Catalan cuisine.

I made use of photo-elicitation to probe opinons about the UNESCO bid amongst closer informants. I added two promotional images of the 2013 bid within Catalonia, both of which prominently displayed the logo and title of the campaign. The first had a wooden plate and cutlery, and the tagline '*tothom a taula*' ('everyone to the table'), a popular saying. The second showed a *crema catalana* from overhead, a spoon dipping into it invitingly, with the tagline '*Som el pais de la crema catalana*' ('we are the country of *crema catalana*').

With several groups, the first reaction with the first picture was to talk about similar food-related sayings in Catalan, and the UNESCO campaign did not even occur to the interviewees. When I pointed out the UNESCO campaign, many were unaware of it, and uninterested. Some even expressed surprise at the existence of such a campaign. For instance, when I did this group interview with members of the Assemblea cultural group, they claimed that while cuisine was important for Catalan patrimony, they could not understand why it would be so for global patrimony. Still, they were not averse to a campaign that raised awareness of Catalan culture (via cuisine) in the world generally.

In line with this promotional aspect, the most enthusiastic response to the campaign amongst my friends and informants was from Marta, who worked for Omnium Cultural, one of the principal Catalan organisations. The main aim of the organisation had been to promote global awareness of the Catalan independence movement. Coming from this angle, Marta saw the UNESCO campaign as one other way of promoting Catalan identity. As she said:

> I think that Catalan cuisine deserves to be a patrimony of humanity. I think it is very important, it is a deserved recognition, because it has its own very important personality, since the medieval era, and it has been adapting to the times. After all, it is still evolving, it is one of the most innovative. A historic recognition.

Several of my informants found the use of wooden cutlery and dishes from the first image strange, because they are not in regular usage. One woman, Cristina (in her early sixties) even said that it made her feel embarassed, as they seemed too folkloric to be a proper advert for Catalan practices, implying they were a backward people. When I showed this image to Pep, the manager of Vic's branch of Omnium Cultural, he responded positively to the first image, but not the second. He agreed with others that the wooden plates idealised a heavy and old-fashioned view of Catalan cuisine, but felt the image to be 'traditional ... very connected with Catalan cuisine'. Moreover, the phrase '*tothom a taula*' implied a space for discussion, be it of identity, or of cuisine, in the tradition of the *sobretaula* (i.e. to be continually discussing what Catalan identity means). Pep still considered the UNESCO recognition to be 'a commercial strategy', a view shared across many of my informants when I raised the issue. It may be useful for economic or political promotion, but it is superfluous to the individual experience of Catalan culinary identity.

With the second image also from the campaign, 'We are the country of the *crema catalana*', this prompted even less reaction to the UNESCO labelling, and led to more discussion of the *crema catalana*. However, one woman in her late-fifties was outraged, saying that 'we eat *crema catalana*, but that's not who we are. We're so much more', suggesting once more that the approach of the UNESCO campaign and the FICCG in this instance was too reductionist to truly represent Catalan cuisine. From the two images I showed, she and her cousin Cristina, and daughter Irene (in her 20s), were unimpressed and disappointed by what they saw of the UNESCO campaign.

One can see that there is a general disinterest in the UNESCO campaign, though many informants highlighted its usefulness in promoting Catalan identity to a global audience. It can therefore be used as a weapon to assert Catalonia's existence as a political and cultural unity beyond the borders of the Catalan Autonomous Community. After I left the field, the FICCG began campaigns to boost support around Catalonia, so it is possible my informants later became more aware of the campaign. Still, the concerns surrounding the homogenisation of the diversity of Catalan cuisine, one of the ways in which its proponents self-identity and differentiate it from other cuisines, will still remain. This also applies to issues of quality, and the matter of who the agent tasked with preserving a cuisine should be: a public organisation, an international body, or the people who prepare it?

Cuisine and Independence

The discussion on UNESCO raised the issue of the politicisation of cuisine in Catalonia. That is, how cuisine is a salient aspect by which Catalans can differentiate themselves from Spain, and the importance of official recognition of this at a global level via UNESCO. One question that intrigued me during fieldwork was whether the current rise in pro-independence sentiment in Catalonia was in some way connected to attitudes or behaviours around food. I have already described that those who were very pro-independence can be called 'very *pa amb tomàquet*'. Such a connection is hardly new in Catalan cuisine, as Ferran Agulló's introduction to his 1928 book *El Llibre de la Cuina Catalana* demonstrated.

In many interviews and everyday discussions, I directly asked my informants whether there was a connection between Catalan cuisine and the independence movement. I received a wide variety of opinions, but many suggested a deep sense of disillusionment with the current political situation, and also a perceived separation between everyday life (the world of food), and the world of politics. More importantly, the answers to this question revealed much about the connection between the cultural and political aspects of Catalan nationalism. For instance, one can be pro-independence and pro-Catalan but dislike the political parties that support this view (a finding also supported by Crameri, 2014).

The general view was that cultural aspects such as cuisine feed into pro-independence sentiment by acting as a wellspring of Catalan identity which can be mobilised in developing and enforcing pro-independence sentiments. I found this expressed in various ways, from academicised expressions of the general role of food in identity, to comfortable recognition of how food is an accessible way of feeling Catalan. An example of the former can be found in the polished perspective of Pep Palau, the organiser and founder of large-scale trade fair Fòrum Gastronomic ('Cuisine, which is one of the fundamental cultural factors of this collective, as a people, as a nation, logically it is and will be one of the best expressions of this claim to independence ... It is one of the ways of best expressing, most agreeably, how we are as a people, through how we eat'.), or the 'food as language' sensibility of food journalist Pau Arenós, 'food is culture, and food forms a part of language. You speak, you think, and that facilitates the identity of a people. Language is a vehicle, and food is also a language'.

In the latter mode, there was not always an explicit recognition of the relationship between food and independence, but as one chef based outside Vic explained, 'with independence, it makes you feel a bit more Catalan, you have it inside, no? And this includes everything with food. That instead of choosing something foreign, you'll choose something from here'. This view reflected an attitude of increased awareness of Catalan products and foods, engendered by the political situation. A member of the town council of La Garriga (a town between Vic and Barcelona) who organised the town's food festivals held a similar view, that it has a role to play as a cultural symbol and differentiator:

> I think it is all cultural no? Culture manifests itself in many ways, and gastronomy is another. The identifying Catalan traits (*el tret identitari català*) we're restoring it a lot, because we have in our background a cultural fact (*un fet cultural*) … We have differentiating traits that are different from the rest of Spain, that in this movement, it makes us get together more, because [the Spanish government] makes us forget them.

Catalan cuisine is therefore 'an identifying trait' that differentiates Catalans from Spaniards, and can be mobilised to lend support to the independence movement. Magda, a chef in Vic, also did not draw an explicit connection, but believed that cuisine and food 'all forms a part of this sentiment that we have as Catalans'. Independence sentiments can therefore be harnessed and connected to any other aspect of Catalanism, to use it to emphasise those differences that make Catalan identity separate. A feeling of belonging to a cultural collective is central to the independence movement. Through attending pro-independence events where food almost always played a central role, it became clear that, as my informants explained, this cultural collective is formed in parts by food.

The pro-independence movement is not without controversy, a situation that has worsened since my original fieldwork in 2012–2013. Some cooks even refused to enter into discussions of national politics altogether. Joan Roca, perhaps the most important chef in Catalonia today, responded to a question on the labelling of his cuisine as 'Spanish' by placing himself outside the debate, but making clear his identity as a Catalan nonetheless:

> I am a Catalan, and I want to be Catalan with dignity and without confrontations. I don't want to enter into political debates, I want to be able to understand

cuisine and continue doing my own cuisine as it has always been done, which has Catalan roots because it is the cuisine that we know, with the people with whom we've learned, and with which we've evolved. And evidently it is an open cuisine, open to the world, to new influences from our voyages.

Joan Roca's comments bring up once more the ideal of openness in cuisine. Still, there were others who connected Catalan cuisine and the independence movement more explicitly. Barcelona-based food historian Núria claimed that, at the time of our interview in April 2013, there was little connection, but during the tercentenary celebrations of the Siege of Barcelona in 2014, there would be. The year was dedicated to seventeenth-century-themed events, including in cuisine. She was designing menus for restaurants to serve 'food before the Castilians came!'. This particular aspect of historical memory is perhaps the most explicit way in which food has been connected with the independence movement, as will be discussed in detail in Chapter Five.

Many informants made a clear differentiation between cultural and political aspects of Catalan nationalism. There are some areas of alignment, however. For instance, well-known chefs have been the recipients the St. George's Cross, an award the Generalitat gives to those who have defended Catalan identity in civil and cultural settings. Like most of my other informants, Barcelona chef Carles Gaig saw Catalan cuisine as 'a cultural patrimony', that was not a political patrimony. Despite this, culinary culture could be taken on and used by politicians when it served their interests. He recalled that several chefs, himself included, had banded together in the 1980s to petition the President of the Generalitat at that time, Jordi Pujol, to help with their efforts to promote Catalan cuisine. Carles recalled bitterly how they arranged conferences and events (he may have had the 1981–1982 *Congrés de la Cuina Catalana* in mind) but their efforts came to nothing, as cuisine as culture did not seem useful in a political dimension. Nowadays on the other hand, 'they do see a cultural potential, and when there is any event or any political question, they try and put cuisine to the fore'.

This comment parallels many of the views on the UNESCO campaign, which is that food is beneficial to explaining and introducing Catalonia to an outside audience. Cuisine is more appealing than the fraught topics of secessionist politics and nationalism today. Yet, as my informants noted, perhaps through the attractions of culinary idylls, non-Catalans will start to have an awareness of the cultural reasons behind the independence movement, and come to sympathise with the movement. This approach can be seen in touristic promotion of the region, such as the 2010 campaign 'Catalonia is gastronomy' (Massanés, 2010), Catalonia as European Region of Gastronomy in 2016, and events such as the 'Taste of Catalonia' event in London, organised by tourist agency Catalunya Experience in July 2017. These events are promoted by the Generalitat, and though subtle, can contain hidden transcripts (Scott, 1990) that by celebrating the region, implicitly promote Catalan difference and separate identity.

Food and the Independence Movement since 2017

The events of autumn 2017 were undoubtedly a traumatic period for Catalonia. The reaction of the Spanish state with the police crackdown, arrest of most of Catalonia's leading politicians, and imposition of direct rule engendered a sense of shock and uncertainty. This has been compounded by the European Union's indifferent reaction, and concerns about the financial and economic repercussions of the independence vote. When I visited in January 2018, many friends and acquaintances described walking around in a sense of shock from late October to December – 'we have passed some very strange days' one remarked to me. They noted a general sense of disappointment, disillusionment, and an uneasy calm after the storm. According to some of my informants, in September and the early days of October, there were noticeably more food products sporting Catalan flags, and Catalan companies emphasised their connection to promote products. After November, there was a conspicuous decline in this kind of promotion, as shops and producers seemed to hide the *senyeres* in fear of a potential backlash. For instance, in the popular bakeries of pastry chef Carles Escribà in Barcelona, a seasonal '*senyera* croissant' (a croissant decorated with four coloured strips) was offered during the two weeks either side of the Diada. In 2017, they were kept in shops for longer, until mid-October, a response to demand engendered by pro-independence awareness. Yet by November, demand had dropped so low that they were discontinued.

One of the most visible results of the events of October 2017 has been the presence of yellow ribbons in public places, as clothing pins, or on graffiti.[3] This has become a new symbol of pro-independentism, as a symbol of the Llibertat Presos Politics ('Free Political Prisoners') campaign led by Omnium Cultural, to support Catalan politicians and activists who were imprisoned in October and November 2017, and later in March 2018, on charges of rebellion, sedition and misuse of public funds.[4] So prevalent did this symbol become, that the Spanish Electoral Council even demanded that Barcelona city council remove the colour from fountain and Christmas lights in the city (Badcock, 2017).

This campaign has spawned a number of awareness and fundraising initiatives, some of which have focused on food. For Christmas, one was the *Nadal Groc* (Yellow Christmas), where supporters were encouraged to place a yellow scarf or ribbon at an empty chair during the Christmas meal, to represent one of the prisoners. The intention was to bring home the emotional significance of these individuals' empty chairs, as they remained imprisoned over Christmas. Participants posted images of their Christmas tables and food on Twitter with the hashtag #nadalgroc, with messages of support.

The symbolic potential of this act should not be underestimated. An aspect of the Catalan independence movement was explicitly linked with an important festive moment in the Catalan gastronomic calendar, where food is central to its celebration – and not just any food, but the recognised national dishes such as *escudella*, *canelons* and other popular seasonal dishes. The performance of the *Nadal Groc* is related to the table, a popular symbol of Catalan sociality (the *sobretaula*), and the site where national cuisine is consumed. In creating a symbolic chair for significant members of the nation, seen by many as unjustly persecuted martyrs for the Catalan cause, one can sense the creation of a fictive kinship with these individuals through the Catalan nation, by providing them with a place at the Christmas table, a place for the strengthening and celebration of commensality and family ties. This could also perhaps be an interesting development of the 'imagined community' (B. Anderson, 1983), as specific members of the nation are imagined to be present through food.

Later in December, after the 21 December elections that ended with a technical victory for the pro-independence coalition, a popular image appeared on social media, called '*Menú de Nadal*' (Christmas Menu). It represented a play on the traditional Christmas menu, with courses related to the independence movement and recent events. This included entries such as *Musclos amb Patates* (mussels with chips), that were 'made in Brussels', a reference to Carles Puigdemont's exile in the city; *Amanida Victòria* (Victory Salad) because 'we won the 21 December'; *Caldo de memòria* (Memory soup) – 'we will not forget the 1st October'; and a *Ració de llibertat* (portion of liberty) 'for the political prisoners'. In this instance, food once again became a way of making a political movement more familiar (MacClancy 2007) and associating it with a popular festival.

A related food-focused event was the *Sopar Groc* ('Yellow Supper'), created by well-known (and pro-independence) chef Ada Parellada, at her Barcelona restaurant Semproniana, on 9 January 2018. Each of the five courses was inspired by the colour yellow, and used yellow foods, such as scrambled eggs with chanterelle and yellow food mushrooms, yellow pepper stuffed with polenta, sweetcorn and saffron sauce, battered cod with mustard sauce, chicken curry and lemon cake with caramelised *crema catalana* topping and pineapple, decorated with a small chocolate yellow ribbon. Two types of beer were on offer, one Catalan and one Belgian, to remember the Catalan politicians in Brussels, and the wines were of Catalan origin.

Following the announcement of the event in December, Ada Parellada experienced a wave of harassment and calls to boycott the restaurant from pro-unionists. A series of critical, one-star reviews appeared on TripAdvisor (who later took them down), Google Business and Facebook as part of this campaign. Over the busy New Year period, half the reservations made to the restaurant were fake, no-show reservations. She also received threatening emails from fake accounts, asking for reservations in the names of the arrested officials. Once this activity became known to the Catalan media in early January (via word-of-mouth on a WhatsApp group amongst Parellada's friends), she became a dramatic cause célèbre, an 'affair of state' as Parellada described. Supporters of her restaurant flocked to post positive reviews, and the debacle raised the visibility of Parellada and her restaurant to new customers – January 2018 was the busiest month in the restaurant's 25 years. In the end, an anti-Catalan smear campaign became a free advertising campaign for the restaurant.

The supper itself, according to Ada Parellada, was intended to be a festive, celebratory event, to share food and ideas, and a meeting place for likeminded individuals in solidarity with the prisoners, not a political protest. For the menu, she was inspired by the concept of market cuisine (i.e. what was available in season), instead of Catalan cuisine and as a result the menu contained many 'non-Catalan' ingredients and dishes (e.g. polenta and chicken curry). She was also inspired by the Catalan concept of '*mesura*', that is measured, calm, good sense. On the night of the event, fellow diners felt that the menu was not 'typically' Catalan, although it contained Catalan elements such as mushrooms, cod and *crema catalana*. As is common in dining contexts, discussion of the menu moved onto other food-related topics, such as the variety of yellow foods in Catalonia (not many, except for *allioli*, which lead to a debate of its 'real' colour), and Catalan cuisine as a Mediterranean cuisine, the influence of history and geography, culinary differences with surrounding regions like Valencia, and the upcoming *calçot* (spring onion) season. During the speeches by representatives of Omnium Cultural and the Assemblea, the speakers drew attention to how this dinner represented the national virtues, such as creativity, *associacionisme* (to mobilise in a group), strength and generosity and the ability to do a job well despite obstacles. The event demonstrated that Catalonia is a 'country of solidarity', with 'great professionals' in cuisine and elsewhere, and 'people of great initiative'.

Ironically, the harassment campaign raised awareness of the *Sopar Groc* across Catalonia, and the event was transformed into a focus of the *Llibertat* campaign. The event has inspired similar events, including 'yellow dinners' in private homes, and an Omnium- and Assemblea-affiliated series of suppers in Reus, at the restaurant Olor de Color de Poma. Another restaurant owned by a pro-independence comedian, Toni Albà, in seaside town Vilanova i la Geltrú, also experienced a similar boycott and harassment campaign in January 2018 because he insulted the leader of the Ciutadans party (Alcàzar, 2018). However, these have been exceptions, as few in the restaurant industry have come out in favour of independence (even if they privately support it). Mon, my cooking professor friend, pointed to a Catalan saying 'at the table, never speak of politics', which is the attitude of most chefs in the region. However, there are exceptions, for instance Ada Parellada has claimed (Minder, 2017) that her clientele is attracted to Semproniana and her two other restaurants because they know her politics and agree with them.

The political crisis has had deleterious economic effects on the region (and on Spain), in a number of different sectors. The most obvious effect has been in the tourism and dining sectors. Even before the unrest in October, a terrorist attack in Barcelona on 17 August 2017 had already led to a reduction in tourist numbers, a major worry in a region where tourism is a major industry. The number of Catalan holiday visitors fell by 4.7 per cent in October, the only region in Spain to experience a decline in the same period (Stothard, 2017). In January 2018, the World Trade Organisation (WTO) announced that tourism in Catalonia had decreased 15–20 per cent in the final quarter of 2017, as a result of the 'political problems', the August terrorist attack and negative attitudes to tourism amongst Barcelona residents (ACN, 2018b).[5]

Restaurant reservations saw a noticeable decline from November, and over the normally busy Christmas season in December compared with previous years. In most establishments 21 December, normally one of the most popular dates in a restaurant's calendar, was disappointingly underbooked (Castàn, 2017), perhaps because it was the same day as the elections. Discussing the issue with local informants inside and outside the food world, the consensus was that Catalans have preferred to stay home and go out less due to the uncertain and depressive mood in the region. Uncertainty about economic ramifications of the political crisis has ensured that Catalans are tighter with their disposable income. One of my informants also remarked that fewer people wanted to meet for Christmas gatherings, a common practice during the season, as the conversation would likely revolve around the depressing topics of the elections and referendum, thus causing arguments among friends with different views.

When I spoke with Oriol, the owner of Catalunyam, the food-focused T-shirt business, he admitted that Christmas 2017 was the worst the company had experienced in their seven years of business, despite starting at the height of the economic crisis in 2010. Oriol noted that since 1 October, there had been a 'certain depression' which has affected the once buoyant market for Catalanist T-shirts and other products. Fewer people wanted to talk about independence, reducing demand for independence-related products for Christmas. Catalunyam had not been founded with political connotations and was simply part of a general trend of pro-Catalan, individual initiatives and businesses that began in 2010. Now, as polarisation has occurred between anti- and pro-independence Catalans, such companies are associated with a political angle, despite efforts to the contrary. Oriol added that he was fed up with being labelled as 'pro-independence', the automatic label if anyone states that they are Catalan.

One way that the Catalan food industry has been affected is through boycotts of Catalan products in Spanish markets. Spain represents about 40 per cent of Catalonia's export market, a market that has been steadily declining since another round of boycotts in 2004–2006. These boycotts originally focused on cava, as a reaction on the part of Spanish consumers to Catalan opposition to Madrid's Olympic city bid, and calls from the Catalan government for greater fiscal control (the origins of the current political crisis). In the long run, the boycotts had positive ramifications for Catalonia, as Catalan businesses realised that they could no longer rely on the Spanish market, and expanded their markets to the European and global markets.

The most recent round of boycotts began soon after the political crisis broke, led by social media. Mobile apps were developed to help Spanish consumers avoid Catalan-made products (Andrews, 2017). The main focus was on Catalan food and drink, one of Catalonia's most important exports (in 2016, the food industry provided 12.3 per cent of exports, the third largest sector – Generalitat de Catalunya, 2017), aiming at products like cava, and brands such as Estrella Damm beer, water producers Vichy Catalan and Font Vella, and foreign multinationals headquartered in the region such as Nestlé and Unilever. A recent study by the Reputation Institute estimated that 23 per cent of Spaniards outside Catalonia have boycotted Catalan products following the referendum, and that 21 per cent considered doing so in the near future. In the case of effective independence 49 per cent would stop buying Catalan products (Johnson and Carretero, 2017). However, the reality of Spain's industrial food system has meant that these boycotts had negative repercussions for businesses in the rest of Spain, including the regions of Extremadura, Andalucía, Aragón, Murcia and Valencia, which provided ingredients and packaging for boycotted companies (Andrews, 2017).

Another disheartening result of the political crisis is that by the end of November 2017 2,500 companies moved their legal headquarters out of Catalonia due to political risk (Stothard, 2017). Foreign investment in the region has also stalled, despite a record increase in exports for January 2018 (ACN, 2018a). This apparent abandonment by Catalan companies was frequently mentioned in conversations with Catalan informants in 2018. Many are iconic Catalan brands, such as cava producers Freixenet and Codornriu, or banks Caixabanc and Banc Sabadell, national symbols in their own right.

My informants expressed disappointment that companies who once trumpeted their Catalan credentials and were symbols of their own personal and national identities have now abandoned the region.

The effect of the political crisis on small to medium-sized enterprises (SMEs) in the food and drink sector was brought home to me in a discussion with Marta Amorós, the head of the Catalonia Gourmet Cluster in Barcelona, a collective of SME high-end food producers that forms part of the Generalitat's Agency for Business Competitivity. For the companies affiliated with the Cluster, they could be divided into three groups, depending on how they have been affected by market conditions.

Firstly, the companies that have suffered the most are those that were obviously Catalan, and whose main markets are in Spain. Their name may be obviously Catalan, or their products were tied to the Catalan image and locality (e.g. a particular location, such as olive oil). Brands easily substituted for other products or brands have been most affected. This is especially so of cava (which can be replaced with champagne or sparkling wine) and brands with Catalan orthography. The timing of the crisis during the Christmas season was damaging for these businesses, when their products are in demand for Christmas hampers that Spanish businesses send to customers. Secondly, there are those who have their sole or main market in Catalonia. By contrast, they have been affected little, and even felt positive effects. According to Marta Amorós, 'now more than ever, Catalans want to buy and protect local products'. This effect has been muted in some cases, due to economic uncertainty reducing Christmas spending. Finally, companies within the Cluster that sell principally outside Spain have been hardly affected by the crisis.

Food is not only used in the service of the pro-independence movement. It has also been used in pro-unionist events and protests. During pro-union protests the weekend after the 1 October referendum, a banner that read in mixed Catalan and Castilian *'me niego a comer 'pa amb tomàquet' sin jamón'* ('I refuse to eat *'pa amb tomàquet'* without [Iberian] ham') became a popular image on social media and in news sites (Rodés, 2017; Redacccció, 2017). For pro-union Catalans, the notion of Catalan *pa amb tomàquet* and Spanish *jamón* served together represented a culinary symbol of their own identity on a plate, to be both Spanish and Catalan. This combination is a source of debate within Catalan circles, some claiming that it is not 'properly' Catalan (in everyday consumption, Iberian ham is one of many possible additions to *pa amb tomàquet*).

On 14 November 2017, a public dinner called '*Quedamos a dinar. Quedem per comer*' ('We meet to eat' in both Castilian and Catalan) was organised in Madrid by a group of anti-independence Catalans in collaboration with the Madrid city council, several Madrid associations and the Barcelona restaurant association. The meal, which included a number of well-known public figures from both Catalan and Madrid communities, was intended to showcase Catalan and Madrid foods together, and encourage dialogue. Food served included Madrid *cocido* (stew) with Catalan *escalivada, empedrado de garbanzos* (chickpea salad) and *botifarra amb mongetes*, and two milk-based desserts, Madrid's *leche meregada* and *crema catalana* (El Periódico/Efe, 2017).

Connections with Neighbouring Cuisines

So far, there has been some mention of the many contexts of Catalan cuisine: Spain, the *Països Catalans*, the Mediterranean and the rest of Europe. Catalans see themselves as aligned more with Europe than with the rest of Spain. A common theme when discussing Spanish cuisine with Catalans is that they would divide Spain up into regional entities, rather than referring to Spain as a whole entity. Some even denied that 'Spanish cuisine' existed as a legitimate entity. Barcelona chef Fermí had much to say on this topic. I include the entirety of his remarks on the subject here, as they reveal many of the interlocking factors involved in this subject:

> There is something really clear: the concept of Spanish cuisine, it does not exist, it is a political concept. The concept of 'Catalan cuisine', yes, it exists, it is a cultural concept. It is not political. Why? It is very simple, because you have to know the history. Cuisine is culture. Catalonia has been generating its own cuisine, from a geographic area, which takes in the area of the south of France ... which has been a passing of routes. And all the cultures that have arrived in Catalonia have left a part of their origins. The Phoenicians, the Greeks, the Romans, the Arabs, the Visigoths, everyone. So this cuisine has a lot in common with the cuisine of Toulouse and Languedoc, and Marseille.
>
> The Mediterranean, it has a lot more in common [with Catalonia], including language, that Catalonia hasn't with Castilian![6] For that, the cuisines have a unity, a cultural proximity. The cuisine of Valencia, of the [Balearic] Islands, clearly, they're cousin-siblings with Catalan cuisine. We had a political unity at one time, it is no coincidence that there is cultural unity.

Fermí's extended quote raises several interesting points. Firstly, the claim that Spanish cuisine does not exist is implicitly connected with the claim that a united Spain does not exist. This in itself is one of the major arguments of the Catalan independence movement, that is that Spain is too centralist and homogenising. The acceptance of regional identities within Catalonia is a direct contrast to this attitude. Fermí also referred to the ideal of the 'land of migrations', which in this instance is used to show connectivity with other (non-Spanish areas), particularly France.

The French connection is an interesting one, because this close proximity undoubtedly aided the rise of the *nova cuina* movement in Catalonia that was inspired by *nouvelle cuisine*. The Basque country also played a part in this development, which is significant considering this area's similarly fraught history as part of the Spanish state. France is also a state, so to compare Catalonia and France in this way is to suggest Catalonia is on a level footing as a distinct entity. It is also interesting that in Fermí's comment, the past 'political unity' between the *Països Catalans* is seen as more legitimate than the 'political concept' of the Spanish state today.

Two older informants, Sat and her mother Montserrat replicated this view. Sat was keen to point out dishes that French (specifically Roussillon/French Catalonia) and Catalan cuisine shared, and they particularly emphasised how they had once been united, and together for many centuries, as *Països Catalans*. Whilst showing me her family's cookbook library, she drew my attention to several French cookbooks, and took pride in the fact that her grandmother had come from Roussillon, north of the border. She discussed recipes that were similar, if not identical, such as *ratatouille/samfaina* and the popular technique of stuffing vegetables to be found in both areas. Towards the end of our tour of the library, she added:

> I think Catalonia is one of the parts of Spain that has changed most in terms of food ... My impression is that we got more from the French than from the rest of Spain ... We have had lots more contact with Europe. Here we have a good bit of frontier. And of course, the rest of Spain seems so far away.

She therefore hints that Catalonia is perhaps more innovative, and more closely related to France and the rest of Europe than to Spain. Her mother, who was sitting with us, added 'There are lots of people in Spain who know nothing about Catalonia'. This was an attitude I heard elsewhere which heightens the sense of distance from a Spain apparently uninterested in Catalonia.

While I often heard denials of the legitimacy of Spanish cuisine as a whole, I rarely heard derogatory comments about other cuisines within Spain (though occasionally I heard negative comments about 'boring' Castilian cuisine in central Spain). There is a habit in Catalonia of referring to Spain by its individual autonomous community, including by its cooking styles. This suggests a worldview whereby Spain is divided into different areas, not unified. It is pertinent that Vázquez Montalbán (1977), in his polemical work on the defence of Catalan cuisine, continually referred to 'Cuisines of the Spanish state', not 'Spanish cuisine'.

It is as if by suggesting that there is no such thing as gastronational unity, there is a denial of the unity of Spain as a political and culturally justified entity. Considering that such claims to a unified cuisine have been used by the Spanish state in the past to cement Spanish identity at the expense of Catalonia's, both in the nineteenth century (L. Anderson, 2013) and during the Franco period, this denial of such unity is unsurprising. Toni Massanés, the founder of the Fundació Alicia, explained to me that that in the Franco era, food was used to express unity, not diversity within Spain. Tourism within Spain was encouraged to 'get to know the Francoist soil', and that sameness and unity were emphasised in this experience. There would be lists of recipes with no recognition of their point of origin within Spain. If there was some recognition, it was as a folkloric curiosity, and then each part of Spain would be limited to a few set dishes, essentialising them (this may explain another reason why some informants disliked claiming one dish or a few dishes as particularly Catalan). However, as Toni added, 'The *suquet* was still the *suquet*, a Catalan dish, and always would be'.

Furthermore, the connection with the Mediterranean was evident in informant discourse, which also relates to the *Països Catalans* ideal, and to Catalonia's golden age when the Catalan–Aragonese empire ruled this area. Once more, my informants expressed an eagerness to connect themselves to any country aside from Spain. Fermí's quote earlier suggested connections with Greeks, Romans and Phoenicians, and I heard Catalan cuisine paralleled with Greece, Turkey, Italy (notably all state entities), and even Algeria and Morocco.

Food historian Núria said of Mediterranean identity that it was all related to the historic connections between the *Països Catalans*, as well as places like Sicily. She remarked that 'the Mediterranean seems like my home. I see [other Mediterranean countries] as siblings and very close'. This notion of a kinship with the Mediterranean is an interesting one. Returning to Fermí's comment, he referred to Valencia and Balearic cuisine as *cosines-germanes*. Literally 'cousin-sibling', this is a kin relationship in the region that describes a family connection between first or second cousins, who are like siblings because they have grown up together, and share an intimate, emotional connection. This implication of blood ties is different from the kinship metaphors used to describe the relationship of Catalonia and Spain: often seen as a marital relationship in informant discourse and popular media – and one in which the woman (Catalonia) is asking for a divorce.

Other features that Catalonia shares with the Mediterranean area include olive oil, in contrast to butter-based cuisines (in this case, a difference from France is suggested). This difference was a fairly recent one, I hasten to add, because olive oil was not always widely available, and pig fat was often the preferred cooking oil due to its ubiquity. Awareness of the 2013 recognition of the Mediterranean diet as UNESCO intangible cultural heritage may have contributed to this affiliation with the Mediterranean diet. Both official promotional discourse (generally from Generalitat sponsored initiatives) and my informants, often made comparisons between Catalan and Mediterranean cuisine in the context of the latter's healthful properties.

A consideration of the question of the *Països Catalans* in Catalan food discourse would be incomplete without some discussion of the *paella*. *Paella* is of Valencian origin, and therefore from a Catalan-speaking area,[7] and is a rice dish with added ingredients, cooked in a large pan (ideally) over an open flame. Duhart and Medina (2006) have discussed the origins of *paella* in nineteenth-century Valencia and its strong local identification with that area, even while it has also spread to other parts of Spain (to become part of the Spanish tourist experience), and become a global dish. *Paella* is regularly cooked in Catalonia, though informants normally differentiated between *paella* and *arròs*, the latter being a non-specific rice dish.

There are a number of differences between *paella* and *arròs*. Firstly, different receptacles are normally used. In Catalonia a wide ceramic or cast-iron pan is preferred. However, thin metal pans are more ubiquitous further south in Catalonia, closer to Valencia. The preference for the ceramic pan creates another difference, which is that Catalan rice dishes allow for slower cooking, and all the juices do not have time to evaporate. As Mon remarked, 'in the case of pots, in Catalonia we use the *cassola* [wide ceramic pot] because we like rice with more liquid, and with the *paella* you cannot'. Older informants explained that the arrival of *paella* in central and northern regions of Catalonia was fairly new, starting about forty years ago.

A final point of (alleged) differentiation between the Catalan and Valencian *paella* is the actual ingredients used. There are widespread debates about this subject (i.e. outside Catalonia), which is a point of pride for many Valencians (Duhart and Medina, 2006). In both regions there are many different varieties of *paella*, thus the difference is more about different rules for combinations. For instance, *mar i muntanya* cuisine is a characteristic of Catalan cuisine, and a Catalan *paella* typically uses this combination. However, Catalans claim that Valencians dislike this mixing, who will only cook either meat or seafood, never together, in any variety of *paella*. In reality, the factualness of this claim is debatable, and may even be a stereotype, as *paella mixta*, a popular variety, is known to combine meat and seafood. It may originate due to a conflation of *paella valenciana*, the 'typical', Valencian paella of chicken, rabbit, saffron and vegetables, with other types of *paella* to be found in the Valencia.

Conclusions: Cuisines, Contexts, Controversies

The discussion about *paella* and other foods reveals how Catalans circumvent the presence of foods that are shared with other cuisines in Spain, and underlines how similarities can be emphasised or differences magnified depending on the identity politics situation (a trait recognised by Harrison, 2003). For instance, in contexts where the *Països Catalans* relationships needs to be emphasised, then the connectedness and shared elements of the cuisine will be stressed. This happens in politicised events to provide an alternative narrative and organisational structure to that of Spain, such as at Omnium Cultural's Diada lunch in 2011, where *paella* was the main course, cooked in a massive pan several metres across and stirred with large wooden paddles. This style of cooking the dish for large numbers is popular in Valencia, where it originated. Images of a united *Països Catalans* as floating maps (Urla, 1993) were popular at the event on clothing, posters and memorabilia, again stressing this alternative political unit. Yet highlighting parallels with Valencia is not always appropriate, in particular due to the (until 2015) majority of the pro-Spanish Partido Popular, and complex identities politics that have sought to differentiate Valencian and Catalan identities (Castelló and Castelló, 2009). In this case, real or imagined differences become a focus.

The discourses surrounding *paella* are just one example of the flexibility of food that I have demonstrated in this chapter, and the multiplicity of divergent meanings attached to food, depending on the political, geographic or emotional contexts. The controversies surrounding the inherent categorisation necessary in the initiatives of the FICCG and UNESCO campaign bring out fundamental questions of agency and ownership of cultural acts like cooking. One sees this flexibility too in the ways different actors have put food to use in the Catalan independence movement, both for and against the cause. The denial of a unified, real Spanish cuisine as a metaphor for a denial of the Spanish state's legitimacy is an interesting one. It is the existence of ideas and discourses such as these that reveal how food can reflect the politics of the nation-within-the-state, and help to elucidate the bigger pictures within identity politics.

Notes

1. These include: In 2013, 'Washoku, traditional dietary cultures of the Japanese', Turkish coffee culture, traditional Georgian Qvevri winemaking and the Mediterranean Diet. In 2014, 'Lavash, the preparation, meaning and appearance of traditional bread as an expression of culture in Armenia'. In 2015, Arabic coffee, and Kimchi (preserved and seasoned vegetables) in Korea. In 2016, 'Flatbread making and sharing culture: Lavash, Katyrma, Jupka, Yufka', Oshi palav (pilaf) in Tajikistan, Palov in Uzbekistan and beer culture in Belgium. In 2017, Neapolitan

'Pizzaiuolo' (pizza-making), and the Dolma making and sharing tradition in Azerbaijan.

2. It is also worth pointing out that many leading actors in the world of Catalan cuisine were not involved with the FICCG under the pre-2018 management. This surprised me at the start of fieldwork, but I later heard from a number of sources that they had felt alienated by the approach taken by the FICCG. This may have changed with the new management's focus on chefs and restaurants.

3. I heard several reasons for why this colour was chosen. The most likely is that it was the only one not already affiliated with a Catalan political party. Many of the ANC and Omnium campaigns have also used the colour yellow. It is also the base colour of the *senyera*, and (allegedly) was the colour of the Austrian side in 1714, so a symbol of past Catalanism.

4. This includes 'the two Jordis', Jordi Cuixart (President of Omnium Cultural) and Jordi Sanchez (ex-president of Assemblea Nacional Catalana) imprisoned on 16 October 2017; Oriol Junqueras (leader of Esquerra, former vice-president of the Generalitat), Joaquim Forn (ex-minister of the Interior) on 2 November 2017; and the Generalitat ministers Raul Romeva, Josep Rull, Dolors Bassa and Jordi Turull, and Carme Forcadell (President of the Catalan Parliament 2–15-2017) on 23 March 2018.

5. I do not have space to tackle this issue here. For more on this in Catalonia see Johannes (2018a), and Pi-Sunyer (1978).

6. He is referring to parallels between Catalan and neighboring romance languages, such as French and Italian, and claiming that they are linguistically and culturally closer to Catalan than Spanish is to Catalan.

7. Despite recent controversy on whether the language spoken there should really be called Valencian.

Chapter 4
THE GASTRONOMIC CALENDAR
SEASONALITY, FESTIVITY AND TERRITORY

Now that the broader context of Catalan cuisine has been considered in detail, it is time to return once more to the territory of Catalonia, to its landscapes, fields and seasons. One feature that immediately strikes a first-time visitor to Catalonia is the emphasis placed on seasonality, and how this is ingrained into food culture. This is hardly unique to Catalonia, but seasonality goes hand-in-hand with eating produce that is local to Catalonia (or at least from a short distance outside), and eating certain products or varieties unique to Catalonia. Food, territory and identity become closely connected in this context. In this environment, food festivals centred around local specialities that are available for a short time become both a form of community promotion on the touristic level, and a source of local identity and pride. Food is the medium through which local identity is expressed at the county and regional levels, so much so that many Catalans seem to hold a culinary map of their country in their minds, associating food, people, place and season.

This culinary map is part of a system of knowledge about Catalonia, which Catalans use to demonstrate their knowledge of their nation. It has some similarities to cultural capital in its embodied state, to continue with Bourdieu's classification, 'long lasting predispositions of the mind and body' (Bourdieu, 1985: 243). In this instance, showing off this knowledge is less a marker of class hierarchies, and more a marker of belonging to a Catalan cultural group, in that acquiring this knowledge requires personal effort. In the Catalan case, the decision to acquire this knowledge represents more than just effort: it signifies an interest and enthusiasm for Catalan culture. Demonstrating this form of national knowledge (i.e. Catalan cultural capital) is a crucial element of performing national identity, and will be a continuing theme in this chapter when it comes to considering knowledge about Catalan food, regional variation and geography.

Also related to food festivals is the idea of the gastronomic calendar. This describes occasions wherein certain foods are eaten on certain days or in certain seasons, normally connected with secularised religious feast days or seasonally available produce.[1] In general, these associations are older than most food festivals, which have only sprung up in the last thirty years. Food festivals have sometimes evolved from older weekly, monthly or annual markets (a food fair is normally the centrepiece of any food festival). Such markets are important centres of county identities throughout Catalonia and provide a strong link with the past, while also helping the local to become the national. As one representative of a newly developed festival explained, 'the Catalan people like to go out into the street', thus fitting newly developed festivals into a historical behaviour from Catalonia's past. They are also locales where seasonal produce can be bought.

Through considering seasonality, one comes to see its connection with landscape, itself another central part of Catalan culinary and national identity. Indeed, it is at times difficult to talk about these concepts lineally because of the interconnectedness between these themes and a number of other strands, including markets, food fairs and tourism. For that reason, I have created a conceptual framework to show, very simply, how these concepts are related (Figure 4.1). What I wish to show with this chapter is

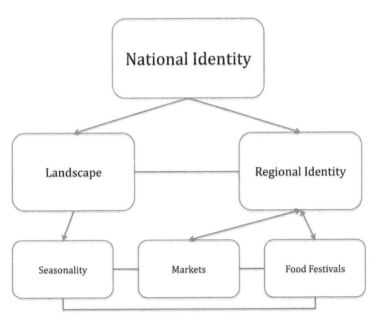

Figure 4.1 Conceptual framework of how the subjects to be discussed in this chapter relate to one another in the Catalan context. Figure created by the author.

how ideas about national identity are jointly connected with landscape and regional identity, which are themselves linked to one another. Landscape is also strongly related to seasonality, which is made manifest in markets and food festivals. These in turn are also strongly tied to regional identities.

I will begin by first discussing the gastronomic calendar and its relationship with seasonality, and will then go on to explain how this feeds into notions of regional awareness of other areas of Catalonia and the *excursionist* ideal of knowing the nation. This in turn moves into the way in which markets are centres of national identity construction, where I will compare weekly markets with recently developed food fairs/festivals. Next, I consider the attitudes to Catalan produce, and 'locavore' (local eating) movements such as Slow Food,[2] which place an emphasis on concepts such as local foods, organic produce and heritage varieties. Then, I consider how landscape is expressed in a culinary sense, concluding with a consideration of an activity particularly associated with Catalan foodscapes, the *busca-bolets,* or mushroom hunting.

The Gastronomic Calendar and Seasonality

In contemporary Catalan national culture, so central is the gastronomic, festive calendar that in 2013 Omnium was able to dedicate one of its annual calendars on Catalan themes to 'Gastronomic traditions and customs' (Figure 4.2). The images show well the concept of the yearly cycle described by many of my informants. January shows the celebration of Epiphany (Nit de Reis)

Figure 4.2 Overview of Omnium's 2013 calendar representing the gastronomic calendar. © Christian Inaraja. Published with permission.

through the *Tortell de Reis* (King's cake). The *Tortell de Reis* is a round cake in the form of a ring (seen in the centre of January's image), made from a sponge or *coca* base, covered in glazed fruits and sometimes filled with cream. The cake often comes with a decorative paper crown, and inside a figurine of a king and a bean are hidden. The person who finds the king will wear the crown for the day, whereas the finder of the bean must pay for the *Tortell*, either this year, or the next. The latter is preferred because it means the participants will have to meet again next year, so ensuring the continuance of this connection between the participants through food. This round *Tortell* is also now associated with other festive days, particularly Saint Anthony the Abbott on 17 January, though according to some of my informants this association is fairly recent.

February represents a particularly seasonal product, *calçots*, or spring onions. As I described in Chapter Two, *calçots* are generally eaten from late January to mid-March, making February the ideal month (though I was told, with disgust, that some unscrupulous restaurants had lengthened the season to late April). The point of origin for this dish is the area around the city of Valls in the south of Catalonia, and they are recognised as a Protected Geographical Indication (PGI) product. A huge, communal *calçotada* festival is celebrated in Valls during one weekend in February. I experienced several *calçotades* aside from the public one in Valls, because the practice has spread to other parts of Catalonia, and is a popular excuse for a communal dining experience during this time. It is also a uniquely Catalan food practice, perhaps contributing to its popularity in recent years (the gesture of lowering the *calçot* into the mouth is an instantly recognisable and iconic one in Catalan food culture).

The *calçot* is one of many seasonal vegetables celebrated in fairs and festivals throughout the year, based on their availability in certain areas, and sometimes related to recognised certifications such as the Protected Designation of Origin (PDO). This includes the festivals of the *fesol de Santa Pau* (Santa Pau bean) and the Garrofal peas in January, the PDO Benicarló artichoke in February, rice-harvesting festivals in September in the Ebro Delta regions (the prime rice-growing area, where it is a PDO), festivals dedicated to citrus fruits from November to March, also in the Ebro regions, the PDO *mongeta del ganxet* (*ganxet* bean) in November, and the livestock fair and food festival that celebrates both the *Pollastre del Prat* (Prat Chicken) and the Prat artichoke of the Penedès region (south of Barcelona) in December (the most suitable month for chicken, due to its association with Christmas). Olive oil festivals in the south, west and northeast of Catalonia also take place in the months of January and February, although some also take place in November and December in some areas, depending on the olive harvest.

March shows a popular figure representing Lent in Catalonia, *La Vella Quaresma*, an old woman with seven legs, each leg representing the seven weeks of Lent, holding the foods of that time: salted cod, vegetables, and a plate of *bunyols,* fried dough balls. Even non-religious households uphold these associations or make some reference to them in family meals at the weekend. In most of Catalonia *bunyols* are only eaten at Lent and Easter, whereas in Empordà (the area with which they are principally associated, and where they are called *brunyols*), they can be found all year round. In a household in Foixà, in Baix Empordà, Easter Sunday was the day when my informants made *brunyols* with another family who travelled from a neighbouring town. When I tried to ascertain how long this had been going on, I was told this was a 'family tradition', and the latest manifestation of a connection between two families. Another festival which is also strongly associated with a food is St. Joseph's Day (19 March), celebrated as Father's Day. The food for this day is the *crema catalana*, or *Crema de Sant Josep* for this association. The *bunyols* are also an example of the prevalence of sweet foods in the gastronomic calendar, and the well-developed pastry and confectionary industry in Catalonia is sometimes referred to as an identifying feature of Catalan culinary identity.

April, the usual month of Easter, represents a godparent giving an old-fashioned *mona* to his godchild (normally done on Easter Sunday or Monday). Until the twentieth century, the *mona* was a bread loaf baked with eggs, with the number of eggs representing the age of the child, their shapes becoming more elaborate as more eggs were added. In the 1930s, *mones* began to be made from chocolate, which is now the dominant medium, in the form of elaborate chocolate houses, eggs, rabbits and chickens (similar to Easter eggs in the English-speaking world – Figure 4.3). Another variation combines both, with a sponge cake base and a chocolate egg on the top, which one of my informants considered more 'traditional', because it was closer to the older style of *mona*. The *mona* has now become an art form in Catalonia, with bakers and chocolatiers vying to produce innovative and unusual signature creations every year. In Barcelona and larger cities, families generally go for a walk over Easter weekend to admire these *mones* in local shop windows (Martí Escayol, 2004).

However, whilst I was in Catalonia, interpretations of the older style of *mona* (Figure 4.4) were becoming increasingly popular. The most publicised of these old-style *mones* in the media were made by a bakery in Barcelona, which Barcelona resident Mon took me to see on a food shopping trip in spring 2014. She pointed out that this style of *mona* appeared to become more popular around the time of the rise in pro-independence sentiment. Perhaps Catalans felt a new impetus to express past cultural artefacts (like food) in light of the increased emphasis on history as the source of national

Figure 4.3 Modern chocolate *mones*, in the shapes of violins, cars, animals and football boots. Photograph by the author.

identity, a strong current at the time due to celebrations of the tercentenary of 1714.

The responsibility for providing a *mona* is taken very seriously in Catalonia. I heard of two occasions where a godparent had neglected this duty, and they were both sources of regret and disappointment. The *Tortell de Reis*, the *mona*, and the individualised case of the Empordan *brunyols* show an interesting aspect of Catalan food culture, which is the way that social ties (whether amongst distant kin or godparents) are kept up through exchanges of food.

May celebrates the month's association with Sant Ponç, patron saint of herbalists and beekeepers. According to the 2013 Omnium Calendar, 'In Catalonia, it is tradition to organise markets in the street where one can find remedial herbs, aromatic or for cooking, honey, syrup, comfitures, typical spices of the territory, caramels, sweets and preserved fruit' (Omnium Cultural, 2013). During this month and through to June, gastronomic festivals and fairs are primarily dedicated to herbs, honey and jams.

The next important festival is St. John's Eve (La Nit de Sant Joan) on 23 June, strongly associated with *Coca* (sweet flatbread), seen on the character's head in Omnium's calendar. Fire is also a symbol of the day, as it is a night of bonfires and fireworks. The bonfires are lit throughout Catalonia by the *Flama del Canigó* (Flame of Canigó), a lantern that is lit on the Canigó

Figure 4.4 An old fashioned *mona* with eggs, which a Barcelona baker recently revived. Photograph by the author.

mountain in the Pyrenees, and lights other tapers and torches that are brought to the different cities, towns and villages throughout the Principat. This feast day is also one of the three principal Catalan festivals, along with St. George's Day (23 April) and the National Day (11 September) – interestingly these two do not have a specific food associated with them, though efforts are now underway to find foods for them (as will be discussed in Chapter Five).

July celebrates seafood and in particular *sardinades* (sardine-eating celebrations), evidenced by the brazier and the sailor singing *havaneres*.[3] The month also contains the saint's day of sailors, Santa Maria del Carme, on the 16 July. August is often the month of the Festa Majors (annual village or town festival) and communal dinners. At home, these would be celebrated with 'the typical dish of the territory', emphasising also the regionality inherent in Catalonia's gastronomic landscape.

There are no associated foods for 11 September (the Diada), Catalonia's national day. In Omnium's calendar, *pa amb tomàquet* is the assigned dish for September and the Diada, proving the association of this food with national identity as discussed in Chapter Two. In common with Omnium's Catalanising agenda, the blurb emphasises the celebration of the fall of Barcelona on 11 September 1714, which is 'a good moment to pay homage to the humblest of our foods, which has also become a characteristic symbol of Catalans, the *pa amb tomàquet,* and the wine drunk in a *purró*'. The remark underscores once more *pa amb tomàquet's* role as a national food, and also the communal nature of the event through the shared drinking vessel, the *purró*. *Purrons* are present at most communal festive events and are shared by all visitors.

October is the month of mushrooms, demonstrated in Omnium's calendar by a *boletaire* (mushroom hunter) climbing a stylised wooded mountain. This is an obvious choice, because the activity of mushroom-picking is an essential component of Catalan culinary identity, and one of the most common self-identified features of its gastronomic uniqueness.

The major festival of the autumn period is *Tot Sants* (All Saints), held on 1 November. This time of year is associated with chestnuts, sweet potatoes and *panellets*, small sweetmeats of almond flour and nuts. Omnium's image represents the autumnal *castanyada* (roast-chestnut eating events), with the stereotypical old woman over her brazier, the roasted chestnuts wrapped in newspaper cones (something several informants particularly described), and a selection of *panellet* varieties along the top of the image. Finally, December presents all the associated foods for Christmas and St. Stephen's Day, including *canelons, galletes* pasta for the broth, *turró* (nougat), cava, *escudella, carn d'olla* and *neules* (curled biscuit straws).

About half of these months receive their associations with particular foods because of the seasonal availability of these foods, such as the *calçots* for February, the herbs and fruits in May and June, seafood in the summer months, mushrooms in October, chestnuts for November and so on. Heavier foods can be found in the winter months, which is considered to be a seasonal variation because of climate rather than available produce. This association between the gastronomic calendar and their associated foods begins in early life, as *panellets* are often the first foods that children make in school, as part of the autumn celebrations. So engrained is the connection between season and produce that eating certain festive foods outside their associated remit creates revulsion, such as the year-round presence of packaged *panellets* for tourists in Barcelona's airport, or the extension of the *calçotada* season into April for commercial reasons.

Seasonality is not the only factor to consider here. The gastronomic calendar is essential to claims of gastro-cultural uniqueness. Most Catalans realise that they eat, with a few exceptions, the same foods as their neighbours. This is so even for signature dishes, such as *escudella i carn d'olla*, *canelons*, and *crema catalana*. The first two are present in neighbouring cuisines (as my informants recognised), and *crema catalana* is almost identical to French *crème brûlée*. However, what marked them out as different was their application in Catalan cuisine thanks to the gastronomic calendar. As Núria, a food historian, pointed out, not only are *canelons* a popular weekend dish in Catalonia, they are also associated with St. Stephen's Day, which is not the case in Italy. Likewise, *crema catalana* has a very strong association with St. Joseph's Day (19 March), so much so that another name for the dish is *crema de Sant Josep*. This association is repeatedly enforced in cookbooks, adverts and commercial entities, for instance the Barcelona Cakemaker's Guild, which has created a day-to-day calendar with the associated foodstuff for each day. This calendar is prominent in most bakeries in Catalonia, continually reinforcing the gastronomic calendar. Llet Nostra (literally 'Our Milk'), a company specialising in Catalan-produced milk and milk-based products, will often do annual discounts and campaigns around St. Joseph's Day to promote the *crema*.

During a cooking session with Mon, in which we made her version of *crema catalana*, she used the dish to explain that the gastronomic calendar was Catalan cuisine's most salient feature. This connection that was recognised at a national level was brought home to her on a personal one by her experience of St Joseph's Day and *crema*:

> For me [St. Joseph's day] relates very much to tradition ... My father is called Josep [Joseph], and we never passed a St. Joseph's Day without doing *crema* at home ... for me, since a young age I have always understood festivals by their foods. It is something that comes together.

Her comment shows well how the festive or religious calendar is connected with the gastronomic calendar. It also shows how national food culture comes to be experienced at the individual level. Linked in with this is also the idealisation of following seasonality through the gastronomic calendar and consuming 'products of the land'. The latter was a common phrase, representing ideals such as connection with locality, landscape, history and naturalness. Such concepts are similar to ideas related to recent food movements such as Slow Food or what Pratt (2007) calls 'alternative' food movements. Yet these sentiments should not be simply classed as a sub-set of these movements. Moreover, while these foods are often inherently tied up with ideas about the seasonality of produce, they also have great significance in the eyes of Catalans as markers of a unique culinary identity by virtue of their exclusivity to the Principat. While many of these foods are not unique to Catalonia, their use on festive days has a claim to distinctiveness.

However, there is another, more pressing ideal demonstrated in the gastronomic calendar. When consuming dishes on particular days associated with the festive gastronomic calendar, there is an awareness on an individual level that throughout the rest of Catalonia, other Catalans are eating the same dishes. This was brought home to me during a Good Friday meal that I ate with an older couple, Pep and Rosa-Maria, at their *masia* farmhouse in the hills above the town of La Garriga. The main dish on the menu was a cod and egg dish *Bacallà de Divendres Sant* (Good Friday cod). The dish is topped with a *truita de trampa* ('false pancake'), an example of subsistence cuisine as it was made only with eggs, flour and water, with no added vegetables or meat. Ideally it is served with a sauce (as in this dish) to soak up the liquid. Although Pep and Rosa-Maria were not religious, they still insisted on referring to the continued sway of Lent until its end on Sunday, so as to respect the gastronomic calendar. The dish itself respects seasonality

Figure 4.5 *Bacallà de divendres sant*: Good Friday cod prepared by Pep. Photograph by the author.

in its other ingredients, such as spinach and beans, and the large quantity of eggs (both boiled and in a pancake) – spring is considered the egg 'season' thanks to higher quantities of eggs. Pep was also keen to point out the dish used a *sofregit*, proof of its identification as a Catalan dish. As we prepared the *Bacallà*, Pep explained that he had gathered variations of this recipe from several households across Catalonia. He had further popularised this version (from a local La Garriga household) on his television show.

In describing what this dish meant to him, he summed up the real importance, the central feature of the gastronomic calendar in Catalan gastronationalism: 'There is a connection at the level of all Catalonia, you feel linked to a culture, we're all doing the same this Good Friday'. By eating the same things that others throughout Catalonia are eating, an individual Catalan can feel a connection with other Catalans. Much like language, or the collective celebration of national days, following the gastronomic calendar creates a connection between the individual and the greater Catalan nation through the shared consumption of the same foods. In this sense, an imagined community of the nation is created not by reading the same texts (or in B. Anderson's case, newspapers), but by eating the foods, at the same moment. Jane Fajans (2012) has come to a similar conclusion in her consideration of traditional Brazilian cuisine, for instance with the *feijoada*, which is commonly consumed on Saturday lunch, and in restaurants on a Wednesday.

Undoubtedly, Fajans' conclusions also apply to those of Catalonia, yet I take this concept further. Pep's words expressed a sentiment that is present throughout Catalonia, and that I saw expressed through the consumption of the yearly cycle of foods in the gastronomic calendar. The Catalan imagined community-through-food has a unique development (and difference) in the form of this gastronomic calendar. It is not simply knowing that foods are shared in a general sense (though this is present too), it is knowing that other Catalans are consuming these shared foods *at the same moment in time throughout the year*.

Regional Awareness

Related to the notion of collective national awareness through eating the same foods at the same times, collective awareness can also be expressed through knowledge of the different foods that are eaten in other parts of Catalonia. The strong sense of regionality and regional identity in Catalonia plays a role in this awareness. One aspect that informants continually emphasised was how each county, and even individual towns and villages, had their own particular dishes. These dishes themselves made up the greater whole of Catalan cuisine, just as the counties and their particular identities made up the ideal of a plural Catalonia. Their origins are recognised and emphasised, even if they have spread to other parts of Catalonia. My fieldsite of Vic, for instance, is famed for the products of its *llonganissa de Vic* cured sausage. The consumption of *calçots* (spring onions) began in Valls (a town south of Barcelona), but has moved into other parts of Catalonia in the last two decades. Lleida, one of Catalonia's most important cities, is associated with snails, thanks to a large-scale festival celebrating snail eating since 1980 (the *Aplec del Caragol*). In all these instances, these foods are prepared and consumed elsewhere, but have still retained their association with place.

These are just a few examples of how Catalans characterise other counties and towns by their foods. If I mentioned that I was visiting a particular locale, my informants would start listing products associated with that place. Oriol, a designer based in Barcelona, explained it thus:

> Gastronomic understanding here is very rich … Like you go to Osona, and you have to return with a *llonganissa* or *pans de pessic*. And in Lleida you have to eat snails. And you go to the south, and maybe you'll do a *calçotada*. People have great awareness of all the gastronomy and the diversity: the oil from Garrigues, wine from Priorat … I think [this knowledge] identifies us culturally, as an area.

This final sentence from Oriol's quote refers to a way in which Catalans use the national knowledge of Catalonia to demonstrate their personal cultural capital as good Catalans. Later in our conversation, Oriol mentioned the *trinxat* (boiled cabbage with bacon) and its association with Cerdanya, and the areas of the *xató* in the Penedès counties south of Barcelona, where a 'Xató route' has been developed. The *xató* is a winter salad, consisting of lettuce, anchovies and other fish, and characterised by the *xató* sauce, a *romesco*-like sauce made of nuts, vinegar, oil, breadcrumbs and the *nyora* pepper. This kind of knowledge appeared frequently in photo-elicitation sessions. Other foods included dried fruits and rices for the areas around Tarragona and the Ebro Delta, artichokes for the town of Hospitalet de Llobregat, immediately south of Barcelona and olive oil using the *arbequina* olive variety. This latter type is now a PDO, associated with the town of Arbeca in the Garrigues olive oil county. So characteristic is this aspect of Catalan culinary identity, that the third iteration of *Cuina* magazine's 'Catalan's Favourite Dish' contest in 2018 focused on local dishes to give a platform to regional dishes from towns and villages in the Principat. These attitudes amongst my informants parallel a remark by journalist Xavier Domingo in an edited volume by one of Catalonia's most important gastronomic writers, Nèstor Luján. In describing the prevalence of sweet cuisine in the context of twentieth century national Catalan cuisine, he described how 'everyone is an expert in sweet things and knows, in each village and city, who does the best *cabell d'àngel*[4] or jams' (Domingo, 1989). Examples of this expertise can be seen in the regional cakes, promoted at a Catalonia-wide level as representatives of other parts of Catalonia, for instance *xuixos* (cream stuffed dough rolls) from Girona or the *pans de pessic* (small, muffin-like sponge cakes) from Vic that Oriol mentioned.

What is important to emphasise, however, is the strong awareness of these characteristics amongst Catalans. By showing this knowledge of the diverse and varied characteristics of Catalonia, individuals express affiliation with the Catalan nation. Gastronomic awareness is tantamount to national awareness. This extends to an acceptance of variations of national staples, in the '*receptari comarcal*' (county recipe selection), and even variation between individual homes. This (sometimes very large) variation is attributed to the 'richness' of Catalan cuisine.

Memory also plays a role here, as for example in chef Carme Ruscalleda's recollections of childhood visits to her paternal grandparents. She remembered vividly how the rice and *escudella* made at her parents' and maternal grandparents' homes on the coast were different from that of her paternal grandparents forty miles inland. Cuisine was sometimes described as a language, highly relevant in the Catalan case wherein language is the founding component of a separate Catalan identity. Food historian Núria explained dialectical and culinary variations throughout the Catalan-speaking countries in this way:

> You have a way of speaking, and every part of Catalonia has a different accent … There are singularities and many dialects of Catalan, the oriental, the occidental. So, with the dishes one does the same. The same rice in Cadaqués, one goes down the map and touching Valencia it already uses saffron. And in Cadaqués one never includes saffron. It is like an accent, it changes at every piece of land, the dish and the language keeps changing.

In this way, there is a universally accepted dish and language, which has small, minute variations associated with a particular place. Food is a metaphor for the Catalan language, the bedrock of Catalan identity.

This regional awareness is strongly connected with the *excursionist* ideal of intimately knowing the Catalan territory, land and characteristics. Such knowledge is acquired by travel, visiting other areas of Catalonia as internal tourists.[5] Sat and her mother expressed their Catalanism principally in this way, by making a conscious effort to 'know the country'. In her family, they aimed to do an outing every week, normally on Sundays after mass. In this way, they got to know Catalonia, and gained a comfortable familiarity with their nation's territory. It is this familiarity that leads to 'gastronomic understanding', because of how strongly foods are tied up with this experience.

They may be taken away as a reminder of the visit (e.g. *llonganissa* or *pans de pessic*) or may even be the motivation for the visit (such as visiting a market, food festival or for a food-related experience). The remainder of this chapter will discuss such experiences, which must be viewed through the lens of the importance of national knowledge to national identity. In fact, my process of integration in the eyes of Catalans I knew was greatly helped by travelling around Catalonia for data collection. By familiarising myself with different parts of Catalonia in the flesh, I was learning more about their nation, and in doing so gaining national knowledge as a Catalan would.

Trubek (2008) and others have described how the development of the Michelin Guide came about as part of a strategy to encourage French citizens to get to know regional identities via their respective *cuisine régionale* in the late nineteenth and early twentieth centuries.[6] Caldwell (2011) also illustrated how the Soviet government made a concerted effort to encourage their citizens to become aware of the diverse ethnic identities in the Soviet Republics. Through cookbooks, cultural food exhibitions and travel, the diverse territorial identities were accepted through their sublimation into a greater Soviet national identity (an approach the Franco government also attempted with a united Spanish identity). Today, the European Union has sought to undermine state power by emphasising regional identities within Europe, to create a supranational identity of a 'Europe of the regions' (Shore, 1993; Karolewski, 2010).

Thus the emphasis on regionality as part of the greater whole is not unique to Catalan gastronationalism. Indeed, it is a useful means of explaining away contradictions in culinary terms to the unified high culture so essential to nationalism (especially a cultural nationalism like that of Catalonia). What are particular here, however, are the motivations behind these sentiments today, as Catalans feel a new sense of urgency to practice what it means to be Catalan due to the sense of a threatened identity from the policies of the Spanish state. In such situations, regional identity within Catalonia, as part of Catalan identity, is also under threat from the Spanish state. Through these actions, the conversion of the regional into the national is an essential part of ensuring solidarity through troubled times.

One could also question whether the discussions of food and their associated produce are examples of regionalism more than of national identity. It is undoubtedly true that regional identity plays a strong role in Catalan identity formation. But this is because Catalan identity is recognised as being composed of these smaller building blocks. It is also through *excursionisme* in the contemporary form of internal tourism by Catalans within Catalonia that this becomes reality. At a regional level, the representatives of food identity are local and seasonal products (occasionally PDOs and PGIs) and town-, village- or county-specific foods. At the national level, there are the dishes that are recognised throughout Catalonia, e.g. *pa amb tomàquet*, and the desserts and dishes associated with the gastronomic calendar. Through tourism/*excursionisme*, and the development of awareness of other parts of Catalonia, regional and national (food) identities become interlinked.

Market as National Space

This ideal of knowing Catalan territory is evident in the privileged place given to markets in Catalan gastronationalism. A demonstration of their importance can be seen in a tourist brochure, *Catalonia is Gastronomy* (Massanés, 2010). It is written in both Catalan and Spanish, showing that it is aimed at internal tourism within Catalan-speaking areas, as well as the Spanish tourist market. The first chapter presents an image of a contemporary woman with an old-fashioned wicker basket in the square of Vic, picking out colourful mushrooms and fresh vegetables from a stall. On the page opposite, the introductory text reads, 'Cuisine is geography, history and culture. Tasting the products and enjoying them is synonymous with passing through the customs of a country. We invite you to do gastronomic tourism in Catalonia' (Massanés, 2010: 7). For the Catalan-conscious tourist, food is the best way to experience their nation and its culture, and markets are the principal medium.

The market space acts as a nexus for past and present identities, and centres of interaction, through its role as a source of food. While foods that are not in season or from the local area can now be bought in markets, these locales are regarded as the ideal location to see seasonality in action through purchasing Catalan-specific produce and varieties, and interacting with local growers. These perceptions of the market were noted by anthropologist Michelle de la Pradelle (2006) in her ethnography of the market at Carpentras in Provence, France. In her words, 'everyone is more or less convinced that market products are different from all others ... This presumed difference ... is assuredly one of the main sources of the market's enticement and inducement power' (La Pradelle, 2006: 101), a parallel that can certainly be found in Vic, albeit for different reasons.

In both Catalan markets and that of Carpentras, attending a market has a performative, experiential aspect, more emotional and social than economic or utilitarian. Markets create a 'festive moment', that 'breaks up the daily monotony if only by rendering the city space unfamiliar' (La Pradelle, 2006: 60). In both Vic and Carpentras, markets have been essential in crafting city identity. They are an 'essential reference in self-definition and celebration of local identity ... [The market is] a way of collectively commemorating the original vocation of the place. The market is the soul of the city' (ibid.: 11–12).

There are two main types of market in Catalonia. The first is a regular weekly market, many of which have continued for over a hundred years or longer. The first recorded reference to Vic's market was in AD 889, followed by further mentions in 911 and 957 (Ponce and Ramisa, 2006). It is not surprising that such markets are often related to identity in the context of connectedness with the past, due to their long history. Like the *senyera* flag, markets have their origins in the mythic time of Catalonia's founding, situated within local (and by extension national) history (La Pradelle, 2006).

The other kind is more recent, the gastronomic market that occurs as part of a food fair, or festival. Today, most such markets will be based around a single food product, particular to the region and the season, such as the vegetable-related festivals described earlier in this chapter. Others include mushroom fairs or pig-based product fairs in the autumn and winter months, chestnut fairs for All Saints, citrus fairs (mainly in the south of Catalonia) for December, olive oil picking and pressing from October to March, and over the summer months strawberry, cherry, honey and herbs are just a few of the themes of food festivals. Other festivals celebrate specific varieties of products that are associated with the area and which play on its specific associations, such as the *calçotada* in Valls, the *bufet* potato market in Orís, near to my field site of Vic, the Sausage Fair in La Garriga etc. Whilst accurate figures on their number throughout Catalonia were not available, it seems certain there are well over 500. Some have lasted for over two decades whilst others are more ephemeral, not lasting beyond the third or fourth year. Simultaneously, organisers may also arrange restaurant-based *Jornades Gastronomiques* (gastronomic open days) that are run alongside these events.

Most of the gastronomic fairs and similar events date from after the end of the Franco period (post 1977). This is not a trend unique to Catalonia, and many such festivals have sprung up in Europe after World War II (Boissevain, 1992) to promote regional tourism, products and the economy, as well as to protect local foods and identity from the perceived threats of globalisation and urbanisation (for instance, the *lardo* festival of Colonnata, Italy, as studied by Leitch, 2010). In Catalonia, their origin can be traced to an event that occurred in 1975, when Franco was still alive, when the chef Josep Lladonosa i Giró held a 'Catalan Gastronomic Assortment'. The aim of the event was to give prominence to Catalan cuisine, which was difficult to find in restaurants of the time. The day itself not only promoted Catalan cuisine, but also provided an opportunity for other aspects of Catalan culture to be presented and celebrated, albeit in a controlled sense. The Franco government would allow an outlet for certain expressions of Catalan culture, provided these avoided controversial issues. The event demonstrated how a seemingly innocuous display of Catalan culture (in this case cuisine) was monopolised to provide a form of covert resistance, which also included *sardana* dancing and dance music, and the presence of a *senyera* in flowers on the stage at the front of the event. While the regime allowed such 'folkloric' demonstrations, for the organiser Josep and the Catalans taking part this was a covert way of flouting the regime and expressing a forbidden identity. An event celebrating food thereby became the instrument through which this could be done.

In the early years of the post-Franco era during the 1980s, there was an explosion of Catalan cultural events. Inspired by Lladonosa i Giró's event, in 1981 the Generalitat's Department of Tourism developed a yearlong, Catalan-wide Catalan Cuisine Congress, taking place in different parts of Catalonia. In the commemorative book, the councillor for commerce and tourism, Francesc Sanuy, explained that their aim was to 'to recover Catalan gastronomic identity and convert it into our cultural patrimony' (Generalitat de Catalunya, 1984: 3) and he explicitly connected such an event with the Catalans' new ability to exercise their rights. In the same book, Ramon Bagó, the Director General for tourism, stated clearly that Catalans had started connecting political freedoms with their customs and culture, and above all their roots. For this reason, it was the responsibility of tourism professionals to come up with ideas to exploit this newfound sentiment.

These concerted events acted as the inspiration and foundation for the food-centred festivals and events that developed in the years afterwards. Some annual events were even established during the Congress, such as the Valls *Calçotada* which continues today, and wine-related festivals in the Penedès and Garraf Cava regions. The background and origin of these food fairs and markets was motivated by expressions of Catalan identity in the post-Franco era.

Motivations for contemporary food fairs and festivals are often the same, thirty years on. The organiser of a recently developed sausage-based fair in La Garriga (established in 2012) agreed that this event was one of many that had appeared in recent years, but she emphasised the event's connection with and inspiration by older, weekly markets. She placed both new fairs and older markets within a 'Catalan model of commerce', claiming that the desire to go into the streets to experience fairs had been a part of Catalan social life since the Middle Ages (i.e. the national Golden Age). In making this connection, she was actively linking Catalan markets, fairs and festivals (even if recently developed) with a historic identity that is the basis of a contemporary nationalism. This view expresses La Pradelle's parallel finding, that the attendees of markets are 'laying claim to a tradition that one feels oneself to be repository of' (La Pradelle, 2006: 221). This historical connection is also related to the claims of Catalans being a mercantile, business-savvy people, in line with the national ideal of *seny*. The organiser also described Catalan markets as a 'Mediterranean model', based on sociality, community and communal eating in the market space.

The economic crisis is not a barrier to organising such events, and in reality they are a useful income generator for the local area. My contact in La Garriga pointed out that reduced incomes are an opportunity, because consumers will prefer to remain within Catalonia instead of travelling abroad. They look for points of interest or activities easily reachable by car or public transport, and these newly-developed activities are a response to such a demand.

Returning to weekly markets, municipalities also take advantage of their touristic potential, Vic in particular. Due to its busy schedule of markets and fairs throughout the year, Vic is popularly called the 'City of Markets', a name promoted in the city's tourist advertising. Historically, the city's physical location was important for the development of markets, halfway between the Pyrenees and Barcelona. Vic has a significant role in the Catalanist landscape, and the reputation of Vic as a city of markets contributes to this perception. There are two weekly markets in Vic, on Tuesdays and Saturdays. Other markets are also held throughout the year. The most important are the Mercat de Rams (Palm Market) held for the weekend of Palm Sunday, and the Mercat Medieval (Medieval Market) in December. The former is a livestock fair, which includes an extensive food market, and a market to sell Easter palm leaves ('*Rams*') after which the market is named. This fair has been referred to by name since the mid-nineteenth century, but there have been similar spring fairs in Vic since 1316 (Ponce and Ramisa, 2006).

The Mercat Medieval, on the other hand, is a more recent celebration that came into existence in 1995, as part of the post-Franco festival renaissance. The intention is to 'recreate' the Christmas fairs recorded in medieval Vic, complete with costumed stallholders, medieval-themed meals and even an area of stalls with 'medieval' items like rustic cheeses, swords, and a deliberately grotesque butcher's stall (the slabs of fly-ridden meat, offal and animal heads were not for sale). The historical connectedness and ambiance were further emphasised with reproductions of medieval coins from the local history museum, which were used as tokens to pay for goods in this precinct.

The Mercat Medieval can thus be described as an 'invention of tradition' (Hobsbawm, 1983), as my informants saw it as a descendent of past markets despite its relatively recent inception. This market (more than the others in Vic) has much in common with La Pradelle's (2006) finding that at a market one is 'perpetuating a custom, rediscovering and repracticing the gestures of a bygone time, being the repository of a heritage' (La Pradelle, 2006: 224), even if this only produces 'imitations of imitations ... to be taken in by the charm of these illusions without necessarily believing in them' (ibid.: 236). Despite the recognition of its faux-historicism, this market in particular shows how the market is a space that allows Catalans to feel connectedness with the past. Popular with internal tourists, both the Mercat Medieval and Mercat de Rams are spaces where Catalans can interact with other Catalans in a festive and convivial atmosphere.

At local markets, local produce is normally paramount. In larger annual markets this is also the case, especially in food festivals, where local producers will be given pride of place nearest to the centre of festival activities. However, many such festivals also include stalls belonging to food businesses that travel to similar events throughout Catalonia. These kinds of stalls are often given a location further away from the main acts. In fact, during fieldwork, I came to know several stall-holders well, as I saw them repeatedly at each market I visited, in different parts of Catalonia. This situation highlights the importance of travel to participants in Catalonia's fairs, both buyers and sellers, as these markets become spaces where attendees can become familiar with products, people and towns in other parts of Catalonia. In doing so, this enforces national knowledge of Catalonia, strengthening feelings of national belonging. Simultaneously, this market becomes an intersection of the personal and collective identity, where one can interact with strangers (La Pradelle, 2006), who are also members of an imagined Catalan national community.

Moreover, it is important to emphasise that Catalan markets are spaces of commensality. My experience of the annual markets of Vic demonstrated that even in festivals where food is not the main subject, food and its consumption play key roles. A feature shared by the Mercat Medieval and the Mercat del Ram is the sheer number of food-related stalls, which take over a large part of central Vic, and account for about three quarters of the stalls present. In both markets, as I engaged in participant observation with friends and informants from Vic, it became clear that a central part of the experience is buying and eating street food in each other's company, as is drinking from *purrons* left in various part of the market. Eating and drinking in the street is therefore central to the lived experience and participation of these markets.

One must also remember that these markets and fairs were a nexus of interactions between rural and urban dwellers. The importance of this location in contributing to the development of nationalist ideas should not be underestimated. The rural ideal with its connections to land, earth, homeland and, by extension, nation, could be experienced in this milieu by *excursionist* day-trippers. The primary exponent of this way of life was the '*pagès*', literally 'peasant', the tenant farmer who brought his or her produce to market. The most important Catalan writer of the twentieth century, Josep Pla (1952), dedicated a whole book (*Els pagesos*) to his interactions with '*pagesos*', most of which occurred at weekly fairs and markets. For recording and preserving Catalan culture, these individuals were seen as bastions of this idealised, rural, fast-disappearing identity that acted as the source of Catalan identity thanks to its connection with the land (Sobral, 2014 and Yotova, 2014 also note similar phenomena in Portugal and Bulgaria).

Another centre of commensality at many annual food fairs is the dining area. Most food fairs and festival organisers provide a meal, often one that allows visitors to taste the product that inspired the event. Some stalls offer small snacks, but those organised by the market itself are generally cheaper and more filling (subsidised by grants or using produce from local stallholders). Such a meal is not free, normally costing less than €5, or is included in the price of entry. In my experience, the food provided always included a large slab of white *pa de pagès* bread, with a tomato to rub into the bread to make *pa amb tomàquet*. Unless the meal is the focus of the event itself (e.g. the *calçotada*, or the *xató*), popular dishes at such events generally revolve around popular 'traditional' Catalan staples: *botifarra amb mongetes* (sausage and beans), a selection of meats and sausages for cooking on a communal barbeque that was by far the most common, variations on *escudella i carn d'olla* or *fideus*.

Such meals at food festivals and fairs normally take place at long dining tables and benches to accommodate large groups. Such meals were originally associated with the Festa Major, the annual feast day particular to each town and village, which have also been an inspiration to the more recently developed festivals. The Festa Major is idealised as another manifestation of the past (many do in fact have their origins in saint's days associated with a town). While the religious element of many of these events has been toned down, the presence of Catalan symbols such as the *senyera* and/or *estelada*, *sardana*, the *gegants* or *castells* are common. The most prominent feature of such events was usually food, so much so that there is a class of dishes called the 'Dishes of the Festa Major', which in practice have become many of the popular national dishes. Several informants emphasised how important the Festa Major was in the development of Catalan cuisine (a similar phenomenon is noted by Fajans, 2012, in Brazil).

Festivals and fairs are rarely visited alone, but often as part of a group of family or friends, who may choose to visit a particular market because of social ties in that locale. The long tables at such events are highly conducive to commensality, because they require different groups of people to sit together and interact. Conversation with strangers comes easily once seated at the long tables crowded with diners, bread, *porrons*, salad and food. I also saw how this form of communal dining was replicated at pro-independence and political gatherings, such as the public, ticketed lunches of Omnium Cultural and political parties during the Diada in September, and Festa de la Hispanitat in October. A 'traditional' form of commensality, associated with

Catalan festive events like the Festa Major, has been adopted and included in more politicised expressions of national identity, such as at the Diada.

Such environments are also a nexus of interaction with other members of the nation, between the individual who considers themselves Catalan, and others who share that identity. Through the market, food fair or communal dining, Catalans come into contact with other Catalans. Communal dining in these arenas facilitates discussion, even disputation, about any number of topics, frequently revolving around Catalan issues. The food at these events is also a popular conversation topic, further allowing the association of food with more general Catalan identity issues. The situation in these environments is not unlike La Pradelle's 'familiar stranger' concept, where a situation of 'relative anonymity' encourages greater social interaction, and a person can act independently of their personal identities and private relations (La Pradelle, 2006: 175). Conversations with strangers have fewer social ramifications than with known acquaintances. In these environments, one comes into contact with other notions of what 'Catalan identity' means (there is no single version). In discussing them, the nation is continually re-imagined and brought to mind. A similar function is also performed by discussions amongst friends, although there may be greater reticence along known fault lines. Food can, on these occasions, be a safer topic than politics.

The experience of walking through a market or fair with a Catalan is an instructive exercise in participant observation for the anthropologist, because it is through this environment that one experiences a whole gamut of associations with food in a particular location, as well as appreciating the thought process associated with the act of moving through a market from the Catalan perspective. A walk through Vic's Saturday market with Concepció, a local tour-guide, was revealing in this way, and is representative of similar, though less detailed, occurrences with other informants. On the visit, in autumn 2012, several themes became apparent. One was the way that foods in the market were tied to their role as ingredients in dishes. For example, when we saw a selection of vegetables, Concepció immediately began detailing how she would cook them in an *escalivada*,[7] a broth, on *pa amb tomàquet*, and in cod dishes.[8] This sometimes led onto her examining the ideas surrounding these foods, and their role in Catalan gastronationalism, such as the notion of *cuina d'aprofitament* (subsistence cuisine), or the 'cuisine of migrations' concept.

Seasonality and festivity also became clear during our walk, for example in the mushroom, chestnut and sweet potato stalls. She was also reminded of communal or festive foods, such as the *calçotada* via spring onions, or Christmas via the live birds sold for fattening up for this period. These foods are also national foods due to their place in gastronational identity and their use in creating signature dishes – proof again of markets as the ideal source of this produce. Concepció's remarks also showed how place and awareness of other Catalan areas were also integral to the market experience. Products like tomatoes and onions reminded her of the many varieties throughout Catalonia, and their associated locales. She listed a few varieties that she knew, describing their qualities, and the places of origin, demonstrating a kind of culinary map of the nation in her mind. She also knew that, due to the colder climate, many of these vegetables were not from Osona itself, but from warmer counties. Despite this, she still described such markets as the best place to source 'local produce'. Her attitude is in contrast to La Pradelle's (2006) findings in Carpentras, where customers presume market products can only be local.

Concepció's remarks on the *calçotada* also pointed to an awareness of other counties, due to the vegetable's association with Valls. While she noted that the *calçotada* had spread to other parts of Catalonia, one should really do an *excursió* to experience it in its place of origin. She also expressed distain for organic produce, because she believed its purveyors charged high prices for what was 'normal' food, an opinion I heard elsewhere.

Differentiating features with the rest of Spain were also something she discussed during our walk, such as the Catalan liking of mushrooms (inspired by a mushroom stall), or a more developed confectionary and pastry industry. Passing the cake shops and stalls, she also described the way that each town in Catalonia was associated with a particular cake, sweet or dish, e.g. *pans de pessic* in Vic. Any visitor who knew of this association (i.e. a Catalan) would buy a box of these in Vic, and Vic's inhabitants should generally bring one when visiting friends in other parts of Catalonia.[9] This is a form of national knowledge, knowing a place through its associated foods.

As an aside, a strong emphasis is placed on desserts, cakes and sweet foods as bearers of national identity. Some Catalan informants described themselves at times as *llaminers*, sweet-toothed. In terms of writers on Catalan gastronomy, Vázquez Montalbán (1977) is perhaps the most explicit in linking sweet cuisine to national identity. He links Catalonia's public confectionary consumption with a medieval past, claiming Barcelona as the location of Spain's first cake makers, recorded in 1382. He later adds that 'the popular pastry tradition and the more recent industrial pastry tradition have converted Catalonia into the sweetest country in Iberia' (Vázquez Montalbán, 1977: 194), and that it is no coincidence that one of Catalonia's two patron saints, the Virgin of Montserrat, is also the patroness of the cake-makers' guild.

Pro-independence groups are well aware of the potential of markets for promotion. Stalls belonging to the main Catalan cultural groups Assemblea Nacional de Catalunya (ANC) and Omnium Cultural, as well as any local pro-independence groups particular to the region or town, were found in every one of the markets I visited, whether they were weekly markets or yearly events. The use of the national flag on market food stalls is also very evident at these markets and has become a commonplace to denote that the products are Catalan and thereby guarantee their 'authenticity'. Upon talking to the stallholders who proudly displayed their wares as Catalan and alongside the Catalan flag, I learned that this label was an excellent market-ing strategy.[10] In the Seva mushroom fair in October for example,[11] the *sen-yera* was particularly prominent on stalls, and I took the opportunity to ask their owners about their motivations. They pointed to the 'sentimentalism' of the recent generation of Catalans, 'now more than ever before', and this visual symbol instantly attracted the newly sensitised Catalan consumer to Catalan-made or -grown products.

Jornades Gastronomiques – Gastronomic Open Days

Jornades Gastronomiques are an interesting phenomenon in Catalonia, one of a variety of strategies for promoting local and seasonal foods. They gener-ally occur in conjunction with food festivals and seasonal markets. Josep Sucarrats, the editor of *Cuina*, a food magazine that advertises these events, described these events as:

> A model of promotion, normally in towns or counties, and normally associ-ated with a particular product or dish. The restaurants in the town or county coordinate themselves for a few days, a month, or 15 days during a season. For example, the *Jornades Gastronomiques* of the artichoke in Sant Boi de Llobregat, or if you say *calçots* then that's the area of Valls, or in Ripollès they do *Jornades* for horsemeat. They're done throughout Catalonia. In the Terres de l'Ebre they do rice, Vic pork. It is the taking of the dishes or products associated with this territory, and the restaurants of this territory incorporate these dishes. They are local or county initiatives.

Like many other towns in Catalonia, the Hospitality Guild in Vic instituted seasonal *Jornades Gastronomiques* in 2012. One is based on 'pork and mush-room cuisine', taking place in October, and the other is focused on one of Catalonia's national dishes, *Escudella i Carn d'Olla* in February. Restaurants had a few dishes or even a tasting menu based around the theme of the *Jornades*. They were also the only *Jornades* that I was able to experience in my fieldwork. A food market took place the same weekend, and many stallholders made promotional presentations. Indeed, speaking to Francesc, one of the main organisers, he said that the most important aspect was the market, as this allowed the promotion of county products.

In Vic, the market events for the *Jornada* were held over a weekend, with the actual 'season' in restaurants continuing for two weeks more. On Sunday morning, in both instances there was a communal '*esmorzar a forquilla*', literally 'breakfast with a fork' provided for passers-by in the square. These are heavy breakfasts, more like a midday meal. Concepció had shown me something similar on our visit to the Saturday market. In both contexts, I was told that this was the type of breakfast eaten by those who came up from the countryside on market days in past eras, having walked or ridden since early morning. They are meant to be 'strong', 'filling' and high in calories. While the need for this sort of food no longer exists (attendees now come by car), the custom of restaurants providing a heavy breakfast on market days remains, another connection with the past. In the bar we visited, a large bowl of meatballs and rice rested on the counter, and Concepció remarked that the best dish was '*cap i pota*' (literally head and trotters), a dish that had fallen out of favour due to its components, but is now making a comeback.

The organisers of the *Jornades* provided a similar dish for the Sunday breakfast, 'Mushrooms with pig's snout and ear'. They called this a 'rejuvenated' dish, that had been (supposedly) rediscovered by the Guild, who described it in their promotional material as 'a very natural dish, very much of Catalonia and our land'. Originally such dishes would have been a mundane matter of making use of every morsel, but, seen in the context of the *cuina de subsistència*, these formerly 'peasant' foods have now become connected to a greater Catalan national identity. Again, a connectedness with the past becomes manifested through these foods and their consumption in the market space.

Aside from promoting historical, 'recovered' dishes, the choice of theme for the two open days is interesting, because both are foods that my informants described as typical (even stereotypical) Catalan cuisine. They are found throughout Catalonia and are not truly specific to the town of Vic. Pork and mushrooms, the theme for the November event, are foods intimately associated with Catalonia, mushrooms especially due to their connection with foraging, efficiency and the fact that they are less popular in the rest of Spain. The decision to celebrate the *escudella i carn d'olla* could be playing up to Vic's reputation as a Catalanist town. If one had to choose a particular dish to celebrate, then it could be none other than one of Catalonia's signature dishes, just as Vic is a landmark of the Catalan heartland.

Applying Seasonality in Local Produce

This discussion of markets should show how essential seasonality is to Catalan food identity. While idealising seasonality is hardly unique to Catalonia, several of my informants pointed to following seasonality as the most important concept in Catalan cuisine. When I interviewed Vic chef Magda in spring

2013, she defined her approach as '*cuina de temporada*', or seasonal cooking, describing it thus:

> To be able to use products of the season, in every season. Now, it is artichokes, therefore artichokes [on the menu] until summer. Whatever is at hand in every season. I do not want to serve cherries in January and artichokes in August. Because it is the way of eating what's good in a particular moment.

Like many of my informants, she bemoaned the loss of this approach to foods thanks to the now year-round availability of most foods. She also connected the use of seasonal produce with proximity, 'the closer the better'. Her example of black turnips, which were not grown in Vic, but were in the neighbouring county of Cerdanya at this time, shows how closely seasonality and place are connected. 'Local' in this sense meant another area of Catalonia, suggesting that 'local foods' do not always mean foods in the surrounding county.

Magda described her cuisine as '*cuina del mercat*' (market cuisine), an increasingly popular classification adopted by restaurants (not just in Catalonia), as well as '*cuina del producte*' (cuisine of the product). Chefs normally defined this with explicit reference to the availability of produce in a market, and the use of seasonal products.[12] Indeed, this was often another way of making the claim to follow a seasonal menu, and also to use local products where possible. This is not just linked to restaurants, as I also found this sentiment amongst non-food professionals, perhaps influenced by restaurants.[13] Joan, another chef in Vic, defined the phrase thus:

> It is following the seasons. What the market offers every season. Also, it is a type of cuisine, a fresh cuisine you could say. Of what you can buy every day, or every three days, and what you can prepare. It is not the cuisine of a product that was stuck in a freezer for three months.

This brings home the importance of fresh ingredients in the idea of '*cuina de mercat*', for which following the seasons is a necessity. Still, Joan admitted that there were practical problems with following seasonality entirely. Several chefs whom I interviewed, Joan included, explained that their clientele expect certain staples, even if they are out of season.

Barcelona chef Carles Gaig also called his cooking style '*Cuina de mercat*', albeit in an updated version. He sees his cuisine as the same as his mother's, although hers was more 'homemade' (he comes from a long line of restaurateurs but made the transition to a *nova cuina* style). Implicit in praising the products available at the time of the interview, he praised the variety of food available in Catalonia. Inherent in any praise of seasonality is therefore the praise of Catalonia's variety not just in landscapes but also in recipes. He expressed the general view of most of my informants, that seasonal produce meant higher quality at better prices.

While some aspects of a peasant diet might have been monotonous, seasonal variations offered some diversity.[14] Related to this is a wistfulness for certain seasons expressed in the food that would be eaten then. This has strong links to individual memories, particularly childhood memories, when for many of my informants following seasonality was less a lifestyle choice and more a necessary use of available foods. These memories have engendered nostalgia for the arrival of fresh produce at certain times of year, despite their contemporary year-round prevalence. Personal nostalgia also develops into a more general nostalgia for the past, thereby associating seasonality (once again) with an idealised past.

As an example, magazine editor Josep Sucarrats grew up in a farming family, and had many memories linked to both seasonal consumption and festive foods. He explained that due to the limited availability of foods according to the seasons, 'Catalan cuisine of the past was one of the season'. Thus in attempting to cook a 'traditional' Catalan cuisine, one should follow seasonal produce and their associated recipes to faithfully recreate its ethos, which creates, in his words, 'an illusion of the past'. Again, the emphasis on seasonality ties Catalan cuisine to visions of the past, the basis of its contemporary identity.

He also idealised the kitchen garden (*hort*) and its produce. This image was a powerful one in Catalanist imagery throughout the twentieth century, both before and after the dictatorship (DiGiacomo, 1987). Barcelona chef Fermí echoed similar sentiments, describing the *hort* as one of Catalonia's many varied landscapes ('you have mountains, sea and garden (*hort*) in very little territorial space'). The garden is the source of the basic components of the *sofregit*, the foundation of practical Catalan cuisine and the place where the most common meat-giving livestock (chicken and pork) were formerly raised.

When I asked the Barcelonan chef Carles Gaig about his attitude to using produce from Catalonia, he remarked that where possible he prefers to use it, not just for price-quality reasons, but also for 'moral' reasons to help local producers. He was also keen to stress the use of autochthonous Catalan varieties of food, taking pride in the way he was working with a farmer in the Pyrenees who cultivated a wide range of formerly endangered vegetable varieties. In his own words 'If this farmer earns a good living, and he can cultivate other things, then he can enrich our cuisine'. He added that 'In the winter, we offer beans, game, truffle, we have everything here', emphasising the richness of Catalan produce once more. Such use of Catalan products can sometimes be just a small gesture. Vic chocolatier, Ramon, noted that while he mostly uses global ingredients, he likes to use Catalan ingredients if possible, such as PDO Reus almonds.

An eagerness to inform clients about product origins shows another important element, that of '*compromís*'. A word that is difficult to translate directly into English, it can mean trust, confidence and a guarantee, and often implies all three. When buying local produce, *compromís* supposedly exists between the *pagès* who grows and sells it, and the buyer. This figure is an almost mythic character and is part of the ideal of the 'cottage and kitchen garden' ('*la castea i l'hortet*', DiGiacomo, 1987). In doing so, the character also encapsulates archetypal Catalan inheritance patterns and kinship structures. Most of the instances I have thus far described have involved chefs in professional kitchens, but I found similar ideas reiterated amongst individuals who work outside the restaurant profession. I recall several informants remarking with pride that one of their children lived '*a pagès*' (in peasant/farmer style) and grew things for them and their friends. In light of the economic crisis, which has left many with uncertain employment, growing or foraging one's own produce and selling the difference has become a viable source of income.[15]

Moreover, this activity was often seen as a way of '*fent país*', literally 'making country', a phrase used in the context of performing pro-Catalan activities. In this sense, both growing food in Catalonia and buying that food is a means of '*fent país*' by helping local producers and enjoying the fruits of the native land. As an individual with this connectedness and awareness of the land, landscapes and territory, the *pagès* is an ideal candidate to embody regional, and by extension Catalan, identity. By buying through this individual, one can vicariously claim this connection with national territory and its associated ideals. It is also in line with what Filippucci (2004: 79) describes as 'harmony, coherence, respect, original, natural, threatened, constructing the rural as a setting in which people, space and time are organically connected'.

Similarly, both consumers and producers remarked that they also liked the relationships created through foodstuffs.[16] Just like Carles, chefs often mentioned a *pagès* they knew who supplied them with various products, to prove any claims they made to seasonality or use of local products. This habit is not unique to the Catalan case (Trubek, 2008; La Pradelle, 2006), however its interpretation in a national food context is slightly different from the contemporary trend of recognising growers in restaurant cuisine. The *pagès* embodies a relationship based on trust, so that the food comes to represent people, not just land. Through using food as the principal form of exchange and basis of a relationship, connections are formulated that act as the basis for the formation of the 'imagined community' in Catalan national consciousness.

Such a philosophy was well expressed by retired freelance chef Pep, who had a philosophy of 'food with names and surnames' (*noms i cognoms*). This concept applied to the diverse regional varieties of food and vegetables, which by virtue of the place names or nicknames associated with them are assigned an identity in a particular region. Examples include chard from Santa Teresa (*bledes de Santa Teresa*), Figueres onion (*ceba de Figueres*) or Vic onion (*ceba de la Vigatana*). Because the place name comes at the end of the name in Catalan, it is seen as the 'surname', placing the product within a 'family' and giving it an origin.

One should also consider seasonality in light of the knowledge about the nation that it represents. The capacity to follow the *temporada* requires a deep understanding of what is available in a given time. This is not limited to just when food grows, but also extends to its origins and where it can be grown, because throughout Catalonia the growing times of certain fruits and vegetables varies due to local climate variations. Using this knowledge, some of my informants were even capable of guessing where fresh produce was from at a given time, and how far it had travelled. Regional identities are not the only identities under discussion, as such knowledge shows an awareness of regional variations *within* the overall structure of Catalonia.

Catalans are not against using products from outside Catalonia if the quality is better, or unavailable in Catalonia. Unlike in other food nationalisms, Catalan chefs were usually honest about using produce from outside Catalonia. Many of the restaurateurs I spoke to were willing to admit that Catalan products weren't always the best. In the English translation of his book on *paellas*, Josep Lladonosa i Giró states that 'some products that arrive from abroad can compete in quality with our own, one doesn't have to be chauvinist' (2000a: 17). A retired Empordà-based food writer, Georgina Nagàs, emphasised in our interview that local products should be protected, particularly heritage varieties, but that there should not be a 'nationalism of eating' by assuming that any product is better than any another by virtue of its origin, rather than its taste. Likewise, Barcelona chef Fermí was very much in favour of using local Catalan produce, but explained 'I'm not a Taliban' to show he was not radically against using products from outside Catalonia. He was in favour of Slow Food and claimed that most of his produce came from less than 100 km away thanks to Catalonia's variety in landscapes (which he had discussed earlier in our interview). He was also in favour of using autochthonous varieties, such as oil from Les Garrigues (PDO), the *mongeta del ganxet* (PDO), and the Prat chicken (PGI). However, he also used a French breed of chicken when in season, and grouse from Scotland.

Fermí's comments refer to several PDO and PGI food products. These appellations were developed by the European Union in 1992 to recognise and protect certain products particularly associated with an area and manner of production. The French ideology of *terroir* was the foundation for their development, that 'food and drink from a certain place are thought to possess unique tastes' (Trubek, 2008: 18) due to certain climatic and geographical qualities. This mentality has been the basis for state recognition of wines in France since the 1930s. In reality, people are essential in this process, so that this relationship is more the product of a cultural system than actual natural characteristics, as Trubek (2008) and Demossier (2011) have pointed out.

The question of the relevance of these denominations and notions of *terroir* (or better Trubek's variation, 'a taste of place') to Catalan foodscapes is an interesting one. Amongst food 'connoisseurs' in Catalonia (generally professionals involved in the food industry), questions of taste and origin are important, and perhaps are best encapsulated in the Catalan translation '*territori*'. This word often appears in advertising local produce, and the phrase '*fer país*' can also be altered to '*fer territori*'. However, in Catalonia this is not simply a borrowing of the French concept. In my interview with Pep Palau, the organiser of the Fòrum Gastronòmic, he expressed the classic definition of *terroir* in relating the concept of place and cuisine, but stressed other relationships involved in the Catalan case:

> This relationship between land and cuisine is very important, and also the place … The origin of the food is the most important. It is a vision that is not a Catalan invention, it is the French who invented this concept of *terroir*, but there has been a Catalan naturalization of this phenomenon, a Catalan application of this phenomenon that is different from the French. It is that the place, the name, the knowledge of doing it, of the tradition, the practices, these are important.

This discussion emphasises the people involved, on a par with the actual taste of place. Comparisons with attitudes in France, as discussed by Trubek (2008) are revealing in this instance. The taste of place is often emphasised in Catalonia, but not in the way that Trubek described in France. More important are the relationships formed through food, and while Trubek, and Demossier (2011), recognise they are key players in the development of notions of terroir, for the ideology of terroir itself they are merely the channel by which the qualities of the natural environment express themselves in food and drink.

Trubek also extensively discusses the idealisation of the peasant as part of *terroir*, yet this figure is still of secondary importance to the land itself. In Catalonia, on the other hand, individuals, relationships and contributing to the economic improvement of farmers are ways of '*fent país*', or '*fent territori*' on a local level. These people are recognised as important contributors to the land and landscape, and by extension a regional identity that feeds into a national one. For example, in an introduction to a booklet handed out at the Fòrum Gastronòmic in Girona, the element of human contribution was emphasised over place:

Catalonia is an authentic mosaic of landscapes that attach personality to the products that it generates, differentiating them. Landscapes that, even now, are the result of inherited wisdom and of creativity that doesn't stop. *Because it is not just nature that creates a territori.* Those who live on them and in them, who harvest the surroundings and humanise it, respect its natural character. It is this symbiosis between farmers [*pagesos*], fishermen, shepherds, producers and territory that gives us a country that's a kaleidoscope of colours, forms and living spaces. (Generalitat de Catalunya, Departament d'Agricultura, 2008; emphasis added).

Here, it is people who are recognised as the most important players in creating *territori*. In addition, the varied landscapes are connected within the overall 'mosaic' of Catalonia. Issues of the health of local and seasonal produce are also discussed in conjunction with taste, closer to Caldwell's (2011) description of Russian locavore consumption. In short, while French *terroir* ideologies place less emphasis on people, and more on a 'a *terroir* blessed by God' (Demossier, 2011: 688), the Catalan version of *territori* explicitly recognises the people and their influence on the land.

Yet there are other differences too that make Catalan ideas about the taste of place unique. As in France, ideas about territory and its influence on both cuisine and produce are embedded in Catalan culture, part of 'everyday assumptions about food' (Trubek, 2008: 9). However, these are based less on 'discerning taste' (ibid.: 12), as an explicit connection between taste and locality, and more on the symbolic value of such foods. There are indeed 'tastemakers' (ibid.: 21), chefs, food writers and gastronomes, who may be well-respected and have their work quoted when the occasion suits. However, to pay special attention to the individual nuances developed by these tastemakers is beyond the interests of most Catalans. Questions of whether a food gives pleasure and enjoyment (i.e. whether it tastes good), or has symbolic value by virtue of its origin, are more important to most Catalan consumers than the minutiae of gastronomic experiences.

In a discussion in January 2018 with Josep Sucarrats about the focus on PDO/PGI foods in his magazine's recent 'Catalan's Favourite Dish' competition in 2017, he admitted that many Catalans find the system too difficult and technical to understand. The Department of Agriculture has recognised this problem and encouraged *Cuina* to focus on foods with this designation in the campaign, to raise awareness of these products, promote their brand image and explain how to consume them. The winning dish used the PGI Prat Chicken and Capon breed, the most endangered of Catalonia's recognised foods. The intention was also to promote regional gastronomy, as chefs from the products' regions competed in initial heats to decide on the final dishes to represent each of the 20 PDO/PGIs. Chefs were encouraged to create unusual dishes with their products. According to Josep, the competition engendered strong feelings of regional identity, as chefs and participants expressed feelings of loyalty to 'their' PDO/PGI food. Another goal of the event was to 'bring the dishes to the people', hence the appearance of the two winning dishes at sponsor Ametller Origen's supermarket chain. While the event was widely regarded as a success (170,000 participated), the inspiration of the event shows a fundamental problem with local awareness and the acceptance of top-down, official categorisations and recognitions of foods under schemes such as the PDO/PGIs.

Conversations I had with Toni Massanés, the head of Fundació Alicia (a food education and research initiative), and other members of the Alicia team revealed this problem in greater detail. Toni admitted that he sometimes worried that Catalans were in danger of not knowing their foodways enough, because there is little popular support for organised movements associated with the promotion of such products. However, despite the lack of support at a popular level for these movements, Catalans still have great pride in Catalan-grown and –made products. Most Catalans might not know whether certain foods are PDO/PGIs or have a deep knowledge of autochthonous livestock breeds, just as they would not care about the intricacies of taste. Sometimes this status is completely forgotten for some products, such as the *calçots de Valls*, which was never described as a PGI by my informants, in contrast to the continued emphasis on the same status for the *llonganissa de Vic*. Yet if the product is associated with Catalonia, and moreover a specific place in Catalonia, then it can be an object of identity.

All in all, Catalans have great appreciation and affection for Catalan products, be they local produce from their county, or from further afield. That is not to say that this affection is always about Catalan *nationalism*; even informants who were strongly anti-independence or pro-Spanish still voiced affection for 'typical' Catalan foods as an expression of their regional or local identity. In a book the Generalitat published in 2003 entitled *Productes de la Terra* ('Products of the Land'), the Minister for Agriculture explained in his introduction that 'the Catalan consumer has a clear preference for food products with a name from here,[17] and more so if they are from a locale which is personally close to them' (Generalitat de Catalunya, 2003: 8), showing that this buying preference had already been noticed at an official, top down level. Note this observation makes no explicit reference to Catalan nationhood, and Catalan national identity politics in 2003 were not as polarised as they are today. However, as observed by Davidson (2007) in Catalonia, and Di Giovine and Brulotte (2014) and Ichijo and Ranta (2016) elsewhere, in recent years the Generalitat used the promotion of these foods for their own reasons: promoting Catalan identity in Europe as separate from that of Spain, promoting these foods for tourism and export to benefit the local economy, and also perhaps for the ruling party to solidify their credentials as defenders of Catalan symbols (based on Crameri, 2008).

The presence of food-focused exhibitions over the years at Generalitat-funded museums is also testament to how food and cuisine is part of this strategy of promoting Catalan cultural nationalism. This includes exhibitions at the Palau Robert such as *Eating in Catalonia: The Style of a People* in 1997 (Generalitat de Catalunya, 1997), *Cookbooks in Catalonia* in 2005–2006, and *Ferran Adrià: Risk, Liberty and Creativity* in 2013 (Generalitat de Catalunya, 2013). Similar exhibitions also played a role in the 2016 'Catalonia: European Region of Gastronomy' events, such as Palau Robert's *El Celler de Can Roca: From Earth to the Moon* (2016-2017), Barcelona Science Museum's *Sapiens: Understanding to Create* (2016–2017), and *Culinary Genius: Innovations that Mark our Cuisine* (2016) at the Catalan Museum of Archaeology. Many of these exhibitions have emphasised Catalonia's role as a centre of modern, innovative, vanguard cuisine, which works well with the image of Catalonia as a forward-looking, enlightened nation. In the *Sapiens* exhibition, the 'signature' Catalan dish *pa amb tomàquet* was the guiding theme. The *Culinary Genius* exhibition, in discussing prehistoric culinary innovations in Catalonia, implied this status as a modernising cuisine and nation existed on an almost primordial level since early human habitation of the region. Recipes and ingredients for popular Catalan dishes formed part of the exhibition, such as *escudella, coca de recapte* and the more modern 'liquid croquette', in such a way as to imply an historical continuity of the cuisine.

Returning to questions of origin, speaking with delicatessen and food-shop owners around the Plaça Major in Vic, I found that there was a general agreement that consumers were increasingly interested in Catalan food and drink issues. Some shops had even tried to source Catalan produce to cater to this demand. One of these owners explained that he saw this most in wines, as consumers now explicitly asked whether they are Catalan and were then more likely to purchase them if so. He also pointed out that this had increased noticeably since 2010, the same year of the Spanish Constitutional Court's ruling against the 2006 Catalan Statute of Autonomy, which spurred pro-independence sentiment. This connection between politicised Catalanism and the popularity of Catalan foods is unlikely to be a coincidence.

This preference for local products has also come into sharp relief since the political crisis of October 2017. During a visit in January 2018, several informants (both within the food industry and outside it) noted that there was a greater urge to buy and protect Catalan products in the face of boycotts from Spanish consumers. For example, Ada Parellada, a restaurateur who had suffered from anti-Catalan reprisals noted that there had been increased demand for Catalan wines in her restaurant. This trend was also pointed out by Marta Amrorós, the head of the Catalonia Gourmet Cluster (I discussed her reaction in the last chapter). One of the companies in the Cluster, Trias Biscuits, an iconic, well-established Catalan brand with a traditional image, has taken this even further by bringing out a range of tins called '*Identitats*' (Identities) celebrating Catalan symbols such as *castells*, the *sardana* and *gegants*. The range has been available since 2014 (a significant year in the Catalan independence movement), but they had clearly greater visibility in 2018.

Trubek (2008) does underline the centrality of nation-building in the promotion of Protected Designation of Origin in France, as a means both of protecting economic interests and developing the symbolic and essentialist connection between soil, territory and the nation. I take her argument further by suggesting that PDO/PGIs are now an essential component of Catalan culinary nationalism, a means by which the Generalitat can prove that manifestations of Catalan culture are valued outside Spain. Therefore, while there are parallels with French attitudes to *terroir* as described by Trubek, the current political situation in Catalonia has recast these in a different light.

Locavore Movements in Catalonia

The following section may seem to contradict some of the preceding statements about locality. However, the intention here is to show the flipside of the idealisation of local foods, and the multivocality inherent in discussions of regional and national foodways. One would expect an international movement that champions these ideals, such as Slow Food, to have found success in Catalonia, but this has not been the case. While one of the first conviviums (Slow Food social groupings) in Spain was established in Barcelona in 2003 (named after gastronomic writer and journalist Manuel Vázquez Montalbán), the movement failed to find real success on the popular level and remained mostly confined to Barcelona's elite diners. It is unclear precisely how many restaurants are dedicated to Slow Food in Spain or Catalonia, but of the 31 Spanish convivia and communities listed on the Slow Food Website (as of 2019), eight of them were in Catalonia. In line with the rest of the movement in Spain, Catalan Slow Food is primarily focused on the concept of 'Km 0', that is reduced food miles in favour of local produce and heritage varieties.

Despite popular recognition of the virtues of seasonality and locality, some of my informants were dismissive of the modern-day focus on these themes. Eating food according to the season and location was rarely a self-conscious choice for most Catalans until the twentieth century, but more a decision enforced by necessity. It may be for this reason that 'Km 0' or organic food is not regarded as special, as it promotes a pre-existing behaviour. The campaigns may have made it trendier, and the Slow Food 'Km 0' label is a useful one for attracting business. 'Km 0' is now a term in everyday discourse, used outside the remit of Slow Food as an organisation, to signify local foodism, often in conjunction with concepts such as 'autochthonous/ heritage varieties', 'organic produce' etc. From the lay perspective of most of my informants, these concepts tend to be elided into one homogenous group, even though in practice they are not always the same. Celebrity chef Joan Roca expressed many of these sentiments in his attitudes to 'Km 0' in our interview:

> When one speaks of 'Km 0', which I respect, it seems like a wonderful thing, that my mum did all her life, for practical reasons. There was the garden, the *masia* (farmhouse), and grandma did it too. I don't want to make something fashionable when it has always been here! There are some who want to be fundamentalist about it, but for me not.

According to my main informant on Slow Food, Lola, the idea for the 'Km 0' began in the mid 2000s at Slow Food's annual Terra Madre festival. Slow Food in Spain is based mainly in restaurants, and also produce markets organised by individual conviviums. Lola had a Slow Food restaurant and hotel in Empordà in the north-east of Catalonia. In Catalonia (including Rosselló in France), most restaurants are scattered around Barcelona, noticeably thinning out further from the city.

Lola was emphatic that there was no connection between Catalan identity and the Convivium Catalunya. For her, the Slow Food movement was global, protecting the planet and general well-being, unrelated to local-level politics (in contrast to the findings of Leitch, 2003, on Slow Food in Colonnata, Italy). The movement is also regional, rather than national, following the ideal of the European Union. Although she was critical of the behaviour of the Spanish government to Catalonia, this in no way affected her relationship with the Spanish Slow Food movement. This may have been the reason why Slow Food was less valued amongst some of my informants. By comparison, the recognition of establishments as belonging to the FICCG was more widespread, as it was more closely connected to Catalan identity.

Lola also claimed that Slow Food in Catalonia had been instrumental in saving some of the regional and autochthonous varieties of foods (contra allegedly lacklustre perceptions by Catalans themselves), such as the *Patata del Bufet*, and the *Ovella Ripollesa*. This claim was also made on the Slow Food Catalunya website, where the list of such products gives the impression that Slow Food is central to their preservation. However, most of these initiatives were separate from Slow Food. The movement identified these species as worth preserving as local foods, affiliating with them at a later stage. Take the *Ovella Ripollesa* (Ripoll sheep), whose conservation efforts began in 1987, before Slow Food became an international organisation. While the promotion of these species may have increased their usage in the restaurants that seek to affiliate with Slow Food, one should not overstate Slow Food's influence on the perpetuation of these foods. When these products are discussed in general terms in Catalonia, be it by my informants or in general media, Slow Food is not mentioned in these discussions.

My first experience of the term 'Km 0' in fieldwork was in a sarcastic context. Osona hotel owner Roger, and his father Pere, joked that all the foods served in the hotel had low food miles, being from the county or the surrounding areas … including whatever foods were delivered to a cargo airport nearby! Despite being strong Catalanists and very proud of their country's produce, they accepted the reality that Catalan land could not supply all their food needs. Other informants were cynical of Slow Food, or felt it was irrelevant to them. They pointed out that seasons are often extended, and even then, customers can be fooled into thinking a product is local because it is seasonal. *Cuina de proximitat* ('proximity cuisine', another word for local cuisine) is a buzz-phrase popular with chefs and customers alike, but it is easy to substitute one product found in the local area for one from further afield, and the customer knows no better.

Barcelona-based food historian Núria also expressed scepticism when it came to organic and Slow Food 'Km 0' ideologies. She attended a few Slow Food meetings, and while she enjoyed the ethos, she became dissatisfied with the refusal to recognise pollution and soil contamination as a barrier to local or organic foods. Moreover, she complained that the collectives focused on protecting producers, and were geared towards restaurateurs, not individuals. Finally, she became disillusioned with the strict application of 'Km 0', because there are many integral ingredients in Catalan cuisine that have to be imported, such as cod, and spices like ginger and cinnamon. Such foods cannot be 'Km 0', yet have been essential for Catalan cuisine for over a hundred years.

She believed that Slow Food was not a popular movement in Catalonia, and while there has been some attempt to apply these ideals, they are limited at a popular level. This did not prevent her from agreeing strongly with the promotion of Catalan produce, for example referring to a campaign by the Catalan supermarket chain Bonpreu to advocate the consumption of Catalan-produced food. As evinced by the advert in Figure 4.6, which advocates PDO Reus hazelnuts, the 'Km 0' phrase is applied outside of the context of Slow Food, to promote Catalan produce (the tagline is 'products from here, only from here').

Figure 4.6 A magazine advertisement from Bonpreu's campaign to promote Catalan-grown foods in their supermarkets, here PDO hazelnuts from Reus. © Bonpreu. Published with permission.

Núria's comments show how the concepts and ideologies of Slow Food are often supported, but that these sentiments do not mean support for the organisation. Discussing Slow Food with the Fundació Alicia team, they were likewise in favour of it in principle, but believed it had not worked in Catalonia. Like Núria, they saw Slow Food as movement based almost on fanaticism, a rigid adherence to a set of ideas. One of the team, Jaume, referred to the ideas of Catalan philosopher, Josep Ferrater i Mora (2012), whose work I discussed in Chapter Two. According to his theory of the Catalan character, one feature, *ironia* (irony), ensures that Catalans should not take anything too seriously. That is not to say that Catalans cannot take themselves seriously, but they also have a sense of humour and a practical approach where the perceived fanaticism of Slow Food does not fit. Slow Food is therefore antithetical to Catalan gastronationalism.

In line with Caldwell (2008), then, I suggest that, while the sentiments expressed by movements such as Slow Food or ideologies of *terroir* may be similar to those expressed in Catalonia, they should not be classed as the same phenomena. Slow Food can draw parallels with Catalan food practices and ideologies of territorial food. While the proliferations of collectives promoting Catalan produce suggests some uniformity throughout Catalonia, the reality is that there is not a single unified group to promote a universal ideology which resonates with the majority of Catalans. Some Catalans will be keen to invest in 'local' producers, and involve themselves with the revival of autochthonous, heritage varieties and PDO-recognised products by praising them, seeking them out in markets, sampling them in restaurants etc. This behaviour does not indicate an organised movement.

What is more, as I explained in Chapter Two, at the heart of all these discussions is the actual process of cooking that undoubtedly connects produce, cuisine and identity. While food grown in Catalonia is praised, food can certainly be brought from outside for use in Catalan cuisine. It is the cooking process that 'Catalanises' these products and makes them part of national cuisine.

Landscape in a Pot

A country's cuisine is its landscape in a pot.

—Attributed to Josep Pla

This quote is attributed to the Catalan writer Josep Pla, though it does not appear in any of his works. However, this saying is a very popular one in Catalonia and was regularly cited in the context of Catalonia's food identity. The attribution is also unsurprising considering the emphasis placed on landscape as a source of Catalan identity in his works. As Anna Agulló, the manager of the Josep Pla Foundation in Palafrugell explained, most of his work is a vindication of landscape, such as in the travel guides to Catalonia he wrote towards the end of his life, and musings on cuisine such as *El que hem menjat* ('What We Have Eaten', 1972) or *Alguns gran cuiners de l'Empordà* ('Empordà's great chefs', 1984). Valuing both landscape and its associated food in Catalonia was part of a project of preserving and recording these remnants of Catalan identity before their impending disappearance following the Civil War, the Franco era and mass tourism. Today, one of the Pla Foundation's main activities are walks and restaurant outings through the north-eastern Empordà region on the theme of 'Cuisine and Landscape' and 'Pla at the table'. According to Anna, these restaurants must prove that the menu follows the season according to what is available in Empordà at the moment, as well as providing 'traditional' Empordan cuisine.

In the academic literature there has been some consideration of the relationship between nationalism and ideas of landscape, locality or territory. It has been claimed that 'landscape' and 'space' are things external to human interpretation, which are turned into 'places' and 'localities' through their multivocal internalisation as part of memory and culture, at both the group and the individual levels as symbols of belonging (Lovell, 1998). While I agree that 'place' and 'locality' well describe those spaces that contribute to a sense of belonging and identity (and that is how I will use them here), 'landscape' should be considered as space imbued with meaning. While place and locality describe single sites spread over a small area, landscapes denote both larger areas and a visual phenomenon, an artefact in itself with contestable meanings attached to it (ibid.). 'Land' means both metaphoric native lands and physical soil. Following this logic, 'territory' is likewise a cultural construct, which in this context means an area of land acculturated as a bounded entity to delineate the 'locality', and by extension belonging, of a shared group identity.

Converting Regional Landscapes into Cuisine

I was curious to delve into the attitudes surrounding Pla's attributed phrase, so, where possible, I raised it with my informants and even included it in photo-elicitation. The reactions were almost uniformly positive, some discussing how Pla was an influential thinker for contemporary Catalan culture, while others referred to regionality and specific associated products, e.g. *llonganissa* sausage and Vic. One activist, Santi, explicitly drew a connection with markets, explaining how, 'When you visit a country, the nicest thing is to go see a market. It tells you a lot about a country'. Hence the connection between markets, seasonality and landscape.

Some of my informants drew particular comparisons between this quote and the worldview of Joan Roca, a celebrated *nova cuina* chef who became something of a national hero when his restaurant was voted best in the world in 2013 by the magazine *Restaurant*. Joan Roca does indeed see both landscape and product as one of the key tenets of his philosophy, and he himself refers to Pla's attributed saying. Roca's application of landscape to his cuisine will be discussed presently, but in his work on his culinary approach, *El Celler de Can Roca*, he explains clearly how landscape has influenced him:

> In the kitchen, we are seduced by the idea of 'eating a landscape', a landscape that has given character and essence to our people and that, in a natural way, is present on our burners and our tables. Traditional cuisine incorporates the landscape from local history, roots … We have many things in common, such as the essence of our landscape and the memories created by looking at the sea we share.
>
> Landscapes are key to our cuisine. The revisiting of the products of seasonal changes, the lasting but expected feeling of the ephemeral product. (Roca, 2013: 183)

This quote well expresses many of the ways in which landscape is connected to memory, seasonality and identity in Catalonia. His words parallel nationalist literature by relating the development of a people to its landscape, a fundamental and even primal connection, which he applies in a culinary sense. Memory (another part of his culinary ideology) unites people through shared experiences of landscape and the fruits of these landscapes in the form of seasonal produce.

One of the characteristics of Catalonia according to many informants was the great regional variety in geographies and their associated cuisines, a kind of unity in diversity when it came to visualising the uniform whole of Catalan cuisine. This acceptance of variety is an ideal of Catalan identity, which applies in a culinary sense. Knowledge of this variety also demonstrates self-awareness of Catalonia and the cultures of its constituent parts, essential for a cultural nationalism like Catalanism.

This connection between land, place and cuisine is applied in several ways to Catalan culinary culture. Firstly, each place is associated with particular foods. This may be a dish (or several dishes), or a series of products that have come into being from the climate, topography and situation of that particular region. Basic knowledge of these characteristics is a means of expressing national knowledge about one's own country, and also of experiencing the different parts of the native land. These different products can encapsulate the taste of those places (Trubek, 2008). Finally, these landscapes can even be replicated in the construction of foods and dishes themselves, which physically encapsulate the places associated with them.

In my fieldsite of Vic, and other Catalan regions that I visited, there is a widespread recognition of the associated products of that particular region. For Vic, these are mushrooms, truffles and potatoes. Vic chef Isidre explained his conception of place, landscape and its associated food as 'identifying the landscape with the dish. The landscape gives you a lot, and finally the dish. Each landscape equals a cuisine'. His remark also referred to the idea attributed to Pla of putting a landscape in a pot through cooking. Regarding varieties and microclimates, Joan Roca provides some interesting views on the importance of geographical variety in his descriptions of the fundamental points of Catalan cuisine at the start of his first book, *La Cuina de la Meva Mare* ('My Mother's Cuisine'):

> What we must have clearly in mind is that Catalan cuisine is not just one regional cuisine (*cuina de regió*) but also a collection of cuisines from varied corners with great typological characteristics between them and that become very particular microclimates. In a few kilometres we can find a great diversity of cultivation, at the seashore, in the interior, and in the mountains. Each area has its own stamp of identity. There is not just one *sofregit* or one *picada*, but a group of *sofregits* or a group of *picades*, depending on the cook who is making them at a particular time. (Roca, 2004: 11)

He then goes on to praise the particular locations of Catalonia that are especially known for their produce, for example turnips from Capmany in Empordà and Cerdanya; potatoes in Solsona, Camprodon, Olot or those of the *bufet* in Osona. Awareness of locality and origins within Catalonia is central to his understanding of Catalan cuisine, as it is made up of many cuisines.

Other landscape-related regional variations have historically influenced localised cuisines. A good example is the local tree variety and resulting firewood, which has influenced the development of regional cooking tools and receptacles. In the area of the south coast (i.e. south of Barcelona), the main tree is pine, which produces a lively, vigorous flame. In the interior, by contrast, fire is made with oak. Instead of a flame, it produces a *xup-xup* (simmering). The result is that, for instance, a *romesco de peix* (a local name for a fish stew) from Tarragona was made over a flame, but a *suquet de peix* (another local fish stew) from Empordà was historically prepared with a cooking style called *caliu* (slow burning heat). These styles remain today, even though in modern kitchens cooking is rarely done over a flame. In terms of cooking implements, the area of the *romesco* (i.e. south of Barcelona), uses a metal pan to produce strong, direct heat. In Empordà, the equivalent is a *cassola*, a ceramic pan that slowly distributes heat. Each is adapted to the heat source based on the wood. The ingredients might be similar or even the same, but the cooking styles, implements and resulting dishes are different.

This also had its effect on sauces, such as the *sofregit*, which are universal throughout Catalonia, but which themselves had regional variations in recipe and importance thanks to the effect of wood. For example, the classic *sofregit* added at the start of a meal is ideal over a slow-burning heat associated with oak in the north and centre of Catalonia. But with the strong, pine-based flame, a *sofregit* cooked in this way will be overdone. This is the reason for adding the *romesco,* to cool the food later in the cooking process.

These differences bring out the sharp contrast between the northern and southern regions of Catalonia (Barcelona and the Llobregat river being the geographic divide). I found this difference was often explained in the context of Old Catalonia (north) and New Catalonia (south). In popular discourse the presumed difference is due to the history of the Moorish occupation of the Iberian Peninsula, when in fact the geographic concept is based on different social structures between the areas to the north and south of the Llobregat in the ninth to thirteenth centuries.[18]

Other features that vary depending on landscape include the taste of meat thanks to the grass eaten by animals, i.e. the 'taste of place' (Trubek, 2008). But more than that, regional cooking styles could be affected by the landscape itself. Not just wood, but also climate could affect styles of cooking, and even food preservation. This is significant because, while such a 'taste of place' or *'terroir'* has generally focused on how landscape affects food itself as it grows (for example, sunlight, nutrients, drainage, soil type etc.), there has been less consideration of how landscape and location affect cooking styles. In both popular contexts beyond Catalonia and in academic literature an emphasis is placed on the *products* of the land in the cuisine, not what is done with them afterwards.

All these factors underline the essentialness of regional diversity to Catalan culinary culture, and by extension Catalan gastronationalism. To Catalans, Catalonia represents an ideal of how an area with regional differences can accept and respect those differences to become a unified, greater whole. This apparent harmony is a subtle rebuke, from the perspective of Catalan politics, to the centralising forces of the Spanish state. According to this logic, Spain is also made up of many different regions, cultures and nations (as recognised in its constitution), and should follow the Catalan example of accepting this variety, as opposed to asserting cultural hegemony over its constituent regions.

The role of specific climates and 'natural' features, such as local flora and fauna, also play a part in gastronationalism. These features are manifestations of the native land, in all its associated emotive concepts. This land represents a territory, one of the fundamental requirements of a nation (Smith, 1986). Catalan landscapes represent difference, distinct from surrounding regions (in practice, the borders of Catalonia share some geological and climatic characteristics with these regions). They are sources of emotion and memory, spaces where the individual memory may be combined with collective, national memory (Sutton, 2001). They are a form of cultural capital, as Catalans represent national knowledge by describing them, discussing them, visiting them and recreating them in the mind. Taking this notion further, acquiring this capital can be a form of integration, as I found when I gained this knowledge through travel, and subsequently demonstrated it in conversations with Catalans.

Landscape on the Plate

Thus far, the discussion has centred on how to experience landscape or place by selecting foods from that region, and cooking in particular regional styles. Mon, a professional cooking instructor, described this cuisine as 'cuisine of products of the land'. It is a cuisine that uses products from the area in which it is produced. Presentation is less important than taste, as the dish represents the products that can only be found in a Catalan landscape. In this instance, place of origin is most important for the dish.

Mon also conceptualised a second, different strand of using landscape in Catalan culinary culture, which she called 'cuisine that imitates landscape'. Mon's differentiation was the most useful emic conceptualisation of the 'landscape on a plate' I found amongst my informants. In this section, the focus is on the latter kind, (which I also call 'landscaped cuisine'). It is a cuisine that tries to manifest the actual physical landscape through cuisine, and its recreation on a plate. It frequently occurs in confectionary, in what Mon called the '*pastissseria de paisatge*' (landscape confectionary). She particularly referred to the work of Albert Adrià (Ferran Adrià's brother), who created a line of desserts on this theme. For example, in one of his creations called *La Terra* (the land), he tries to recreate the colour of the soil in different sections of Catalonia; red, edible 'soil' in the central areas, brown for the north. In another of these desserts, he placed a black truffle in the middle, so that, as Mon explained, one can truly taste the land.

The truffle-inspired dessert appears to have spread across the network of Catalonia's restauranteurs (chefs share ideas and recipes across the region – Bernardo et al, 2016). Osona's best-known *nova cuina* chef, Nandu Jubany, presented a similar dessert at a workshop at the 2013 Fòrum Gastronòmic in Girona. The Fòrum's theme that year was 'Land', which inspired his decision to showcase this dessert. His idea was also based on truffles as the produce of the land, which Jubany connected more explicitly in his interpretation with Osona's regional landscapes. He introduced the dish by explaining that 'at home, we go searching for truffles. We are in a territory where there are truffles, and we like to get things that are real'. The truffle is a particularly emotive product where landscape is concerned, because

Figure 4.7 Nandu Jubany's truffle dish, presented at the Forúm Gastronòmic Girona, the 'forest floor' bowl and truffle hunter's knife, the 'harvested' truffle with 'moss' and chocolate 'twigs'. Photograph by the author.

it is so closely tied to localised conditions. It is well-suited to represent a 'real', 'unadulterated' and 'natural' product of the 'territory' (mushrooms are similar in this regard). In the words of Michèle de La Pradelle, reflecting on the truffle market in Carpentras, truffles are 'a nugget of raw nature ... the truffle's rustic appearance evokes the wilderness', which makes it 'the "natural product" par excellence' (La Pradelle, 2006: 140–141).

In Jubany's dessert, he recreated the forested terrain where truffle-hunting occurred. The dish was interactive, as the diner had to search through a 'forest floor' to find the truffles in their bowl, with the aid of an implement that imitated a truffle-hunting knife. The 'earth' as Nandu described it was made using crushed biscuits in different flavours and shades of brown, green moss from pistachio, cocoa-flavoured sponge cake that used Estrella Damm (a Catalan brand of beer), as a base, chocolate twigs and leaves. Jubany explicitly drew parallels between the composition of the dish and the truffle landscape, such as the leaves representing the holm oak under which truffles are found. The dessert was presented in large bowls, passed around the rows of spectators. With no cutlery aside from the truffle 'knife', diners had to get their hands dirty while looking for the truffles in their food, a parallel of the truffle-hunting experience. In this way, landscape was literally transposed onto the plate. By performing such landscape-based activities, the diners were encouraged to vicariously enter and experience these landscapes.

Nandu Jubany was one of those chefs who believed that, while Catalan origins of food are ideal in some circumstances, they are not essential. So, while using truffles from Osona would be ideal, to taste Catalonia's land-scape, this ideal could also be flexibly adapted to ideals of an open Catalan identity and practical realities. Food from outside Catalonia can be trans-formed into being Catalan by being converted into a Catalan landscape. During an interview later, he explained that truffles had experienced a bad year in 2012–2013, and his local truffle hunter and supplier needed to import them from France and Italy in 2013.

This imitation of the landscape was one of several strategies used by *nova cuina* chefs to root themselves in Catalan culinary heritage. Nandu Jubany refined this strategy in his personal discourse, as did several other such chefs. Carme Ruscalleda, for example, has focused heavily on the seasonality of produce from local environments as the foundation of her culinary ideology, environments which also act as an inspiration for her cuisine. Like other informants, she emphasised Catalonia's good fortune in having 'garden, sea and mountain', and the fact that each territory had its own particular produce. Ruscalleda's work is based on finding inspiration through territory in this sense; the 'cuisine of the products of the land' to follow Mon's model.

Further examples of the 'cuisine that imitates landscape' can be found in the work of the chef Joan Roca. Landscape is one of the principal compo-nents of his particular cooking approach.[19] Like Adrià and Jubany, he had his own variations of a truffle dessert (complete with freeze-dried moss) suggest-ing perhaps a culinary standard or expectation amongst chefs to include this product. During our interview, he explained that he understood landscape in cuisine as 'reproducing something that we observe in the landscape': for example, a dish that represents the colours of the Mediterranean through taste and scent using five sauces, each representing a particular aspect of the landscape, such as pine nuts for the pine trees, olive for the olive trees, and bergamot for lemon tree.

In his book *El Celler de Can Roca* (2013), Joan and his brothers Josep and Jordi provide other examples of foods inspired by landscape, such as 'Sea Snails in Fennel', an example of *mar i muntanya* cuisine that imitates snails crawling through either a marine or agricultural landscape, and 'St George's Mushroom Bonbon', similar to his truffle dessert, wherein the diner has to pick 'the mushrooms' out of freeze-dried moss.

In the book Roca also described his attempts to literally distil soil into edible form through new technologies, and how he and his brothers have attempted to bring the Girona landscape outside into the restaurant by the inclusion of a triangular tree grove in the centre of the restaurant. He later explained in our interview how landscape inspired him:

> An abstract ideal, playing with colours that represent the Mediterranean. It is landscape to do a dish from a walk in the month of April, you see in the same place some *coriolus* (a type of mushroom), snails, that just came out following an afternoon shower, rosemary, thyme in flower. With this I will do a herb soup with *coriolus* and snails. Here we're cleverly observing the landscape.

This example demonstrates the thinking and connectivity between landscape and foods, and its use in *nova cuina* settings. These ideas were not isolated to the 'culinary elite', as vanguard chefs are not the only ones to imitate the landscape in their own designs. Their ideas inspire and influence many chefs and restaurant owners across Catalonia. I spoke to several county restaurant co-operatives during my fieldwork, and most of their self-promotion centred around making the landscape manifest in their menus. For example, the collective *Cuina del Vallés* focused on promoting regional PDOs and local products. Another collective, *Noguera Cuina*, developed *Jornades Gastronomiques* specialising not on regional foods, but on regional landscapes that inspired a set tasting menu. Dishes here were both 'landscaped cuisine' and 'cuisine of products of the land'. The enduring popularity of this idea amongst customers is further proof of its significance in the Catalan restaurant scene, and its culinary culture.

While on the subject of Catalonia's restaurant scene, it is beneficial here to briefly consider Catalonia's immense success in modern, global, restaurant cuisine. As of 2019 Catalonia had 66 Michelin stars spread over 54 establishments, and the region's global renown was important to its 2016 role as European Region of Gastronomy. A study of the phenomenon by the Universities of Barcelona and Girona suggested a number of different reasons for this (Bernardo et al, 2016). The creative influence of Ferran Adrià has undoubtedly played a role, not just in putting Catalonia on the map, but also through inspiring future generations of chefs. Partly thanks to his influence, there is an excellent concentration of training schools, meaning that young chefs can remain in the region, and continue to be influenced by Catalan cuisine in either family restaurants or high-end Michelin-starred establishments. Returning to the theme of this chapter, Catalonia's geographic advantages also play a role. This includes the territory itself, its products and elements of Catalan social life. As the report states, Catalonia has a territory capable of providing a great diversity of products, 'just as from the sea as from the mountain' (ibid.: 127) which favours gastronomic experimentation. The report also emphasises the region's historic role as a 'territory that receives cultures throughout its history' and its proximity to other countries, such as France. Strategies to ensure the continued presence of

Catalonia in global vanguard cuisine was also a theme of the Third Congress of Catalan Cuisine in 2018–2019.

Landscaped Cuisine outside Restaurants

The application of landscape in food is not limited to restaurants. The strong regionality of confectionary and baked goods has already received mention, with each town or county having its own associated product. Confectionary is the most popular medium, due to the combination of portability, creative potential and durability. Some of these mimic the physical landscape.

Anna, a woman in her late twenties, explained a particularly good example of a regional food that imitates the landscape from her home village. She and her family had lived in Vic since her childhood, but their original home village was in the Terra Alta mountains in the extreme southwest of Catalonia. At the local bakery, one could find a small, sweetened loaf, shaped in the form of the surrounding mountains (Figure 4.8). Anna recalled fondly how they would buy one to take back to Vic after family visits. Eating the bread when they arrived in Vic was a way of concluding their visit and remembering their home through consuming a symbol of the landscape.

Figure 4.8 Bread representing the landscape of the Terra Alta mountains. Photograph by the author.

During a visit to Anna's home village, we visited this baker. Aside from this distinctive bread, the owner was proud to produce *coques* from cherries and hazelnuts that grew in the surrounding orchards, which formed a major part of the landscape surrounding the village. She was proud to point this connection out to me, stressing not just the antiquity of her cakes as 'traditional' to the area, but also the way in which they represented the area itself – 'cuisine of products of the land' in this instance. Through preparing these foods, she and the villagers were literally eating the surrounding landscape. The pride of using products from an identificatory landscape is not limited to new cuisine.

One can also compare this situating of the landscape on food with the feast day of one of Catalonia's two leading saints, Saint Mary of Montserrat, a strong national symbol even in secular Catalanism. According to Vázquez Montalbán, (1977) sponge cakes with decoration that imitates the mountains of Montserrat are the associated food in the gastronomic religious calendar. These cakes make explicit the connection between national symbols (in this case the Virgin of Montserrat), and the landscape of their place of residence (here the Montserrat mountains), a significant symbolic location and very visible feature of the landscape in both Catalonia's physical geography and contemporary culture (Figure 4.9).

Unlike some of the better-established foods associated with place, such as the *brunyols* of Empordà, or the *pans de pessic* in Vic, more recent initiatives have developed in the last few years to create place-associated food souvenirs. One is a 2011 initiative by a young baker, Gerard Fresquet, in the Ebro Delta to create the 'Deltakuki', a biscuit to make manifest the area in edible form. Located in the extreme south of Catalonia on the border with Valencia, the county is known for its rice fields, wetlands and seafood industry. The area was only settled in the nineteenth century following the reclamation of this land from the sea, mostly by immigrants from other parts of Spain.[20] It still remains poorer than the rest of Catalonia, though the council is keen to utilise the area's touristic potential. In terms of gastronomy, it has a reputation throughout Catalonia for the quality of its rice dishes, and in Vic several of my informants made yearly visits to the area for an '*arrosada*' (rice eating event), and to buy local rice.

Rice as the Delta's prime product was key the baker Fresquet's inspiration for the biscuits, 'basing them', as he explained, 'in the culture of the territory'. These biscuits have a map outline of the Ebro Delta stamped on them. The biscuit also has a white upper and a brown lower section, representing the landscape of the region in two seasons: the brown rice fields before planting, and the white of the ripening rice plants. Connectivity with the Delta is therefore stressed in multiple ways, including through the use of a 'floating' map image, a local and emblematic product (rice), and the landscape that

Figure 4.9 *Pastís de Montserrat*, advertised in a shop window. Note the mountains imitated in the decoration, also mentioned in the text of the poster. Photograph by the author.

the cultivation of this product engenders. The Deltakuki is therefore an example of both Mon's 'cuisine of products of the land' and also landscaped cuisine.

Deltakuki's inventor admitted that they are more popular with tourists than with locals due to their expense (although a reputation for innovation is favourable in the eyes of local customers). As of 2019, they are still in existence, though not yet a distinctive and emblematic product of the county for outsiders. Time will tell if it develops into a more widespread and renowned product, or eventually disappears.

Busca bolets – Mushroom Finding

An important feature of Catalan culinary *excursionisme* is the *busca-bolets*, literally 'mushroom finding'. Another phrase that is sometimes used is *caça-bolets* (mushroom hunting), however the latter seems to have fallen out of fashion, being associated with Barcelonan weekend tourists who do not take the activity seriously. The mushroom season runs from October to April, though knowledgeable enthusiasts search out the less common spring and summer varieties. The official season is from October to Christmas, when the weather should be wet and cool enough to encourage mushroom growth, before the hardest frosts. In the peak season, there is a veritable mushroom mania throughout Catalonia. Stalls selling all the various mushroom varieties spring up on market squares, and they are the subject of dedicated food fairs and festivals, in particular in the northern and central regions that provide the best climate and landscape.

Mushrooms are an obligatory presence on menus at this time, especially if the restaurant is participating in mushroom-related *Jornades Gastronomiques*. There are other ways that the 'mushroom mania' will appear in public life. Food classes and courses are organised to disseminate mushroom recipes and recognise different varieties, mushrooms become the subject of newspaper and magazine articles, and didactic mushroom exhibitions appear in town halls. The yearly showing of '*Caçadors dels Bolets*' ('Mushroom hunters'), one of Catalonia's most beloved television series, also runs during this time.

Through the actual experience of the *busca-bolets,* the connection between identity, food and territory becomes apparent. I was unlucky that my 2012–2013 fieldwork coincided with one of the worst years for mushroom hunting in Catalonia, because the summer and autumn of 2012 were the hottest and driest for several years. Still I managed to go on three mushroom hunting expeditions, one in the peak season in late October 2012, another in January 2013 and a spring *múrgola*-finding (morels) in April 2013. I also experienced another mushroom hunt in September 2014, when the wet summer had been more conducive to early mushroom hunts.

During mushroom-hunting season, groups of *boletaires* ('mushroom finders') take to the countryside to search out mushrooms in particular spots. These spots are closely-guarded secrets due to the nature of mushroom growth. The early riser has the advantage, especially if others know their particular sites. There is a pointed rivalry with other *boletaires*. Ahead of the publication of this book, I had to promise never to reveal any of the locations in print.

Sometimes this knowledge might be so closely guarded that it remains a secret even within families, or between parents and children. Knowledge is transmitted via kin, but it might skip a generation. Most of my *boletaire* informants seemed to have learnt how to recognise species and some locations from a grandparent, uncle or aunt, supplemented by their own knowledge and exploration. It is a sign of close friendship and trust to go mushroom hunting with friends. Even then, there is a nagging sense of competitiveness that pervades the meetings.

The *busca-bolets* is also an activity strongly associated with Catalans, and several of my informants throughout fieldwork remarked that other regions of Spain do not share this obsession. In the words of one of my companions during one outing, *busca-bolets* was 'very much from here, a very Catalan activity, and very much our own'. His wife noted that in the rest of Spain it is much less common, though it has become more popular in other places, such as Andalucía and the Basque country (note how she separated up Spain into different areas, as opposed to considering Spain as a unified whole). In this respect, Catalans see their passion for mushroom hunting as a culinary '*fet diferencial*' (differentiating feature). During the same meeting, some of the group agreed that, while mushroom hunting also happens in other areas of Spain, it does not have the social significance it holds in Catalonia, nor the range of recipes. Through various sources I also heard that in recent years the *busca-bolets* had become a more popular activity in Catalonia itself, which may be part of a trend of increased performance of Catalan activities, to get in touch with national identity in a time of perceived threat.

Just as walking through a market alongside a Catalan is a useful experience for the field researcher, so is the embodied experience of a *busca-bolet* excursion. Driving through Catalonia's landscapes to specific locales, then searching through these areas on foot really brings home the connectedness engendered by this activity with land (both the physical soil and metaphorically), their landscapes and the territory. Trying to find mushrooms in unfamiliar and at times impenetrable woods, I realised how well successful *boletaires* need to know their country. It really hit home to me how *boletaires* must have a mental map of all the locations where they can find mushrooms. These locations might not be in the same county, but can be locales in different counties throughout a large area of Catalonia, 20–30 kilometres apart.

Knowing the location allows Catalans to refamiliarise themselves with a landscape that might not be seen for the rest of the year, reinforcing links with diverse areas of Catalonia. Through this activity, *boletaires* are literally '*fent país*', constructing their country and national identity by experiencing it first-hand. The *bolets* become national objects, taken from their territory of Catalonia, grown naturally in the soil. It was also through participating that I recognised that we were doing *excursionisme*, a central part of Catalan identity since the nineteenth century. During the actual search for mushrooms, one needs to get deep into the undergrowth and close to the soil, which makes clear the physicality of the connection between *bolets* and the Catalan land. Getting in touch with the land and its produce as a national duty in Catalonia is also strikingly similar to the findings of Raviv in Israel, who also found that 'Food was an instrument for reconnecting with the land and with nature … Putting down roots through acquiring an intimate knowledge of the land was an ideal' (Raviv, 2015: 6).

Related to this perception of landscapes is also the way they have been socialised as places of human habitation. In two of the mushroom hunts I attended, as we drove from place to place for different mushrooms my informants would point out large *masies*, the sturdy farmhouses and manors associated with Catalan rural areas. Everyone in the car remarked on the resident family name, local name of the house and stories from the family, scandals, sometimes recipes. Again, just as with mushroom hunting, this activity shows that Catalans have something like a mental map of their landscapes, one that is intimately tied up with both food and the people to be found there. I also noticed this trait while driving with Catalans in other contexts. On another trip, my informants pointed out that their hunts normally took place near a town that is considered the geographical centre of the Principat. In this sense, it was significant for them to perform a uniquely Catalan activity (the *busca-bolets*) at the centre of Catalan territory, and by extension the area where this identity would be strongest.

The importance of landscape as a source of memory outside food also appeared when I was driving with Pere and Adelina to their holiday house in the Pyrenees. They pointed out castles and fortified towns built after 1714, to strengthen Bourbon control of Catalonia. They saw them as a continued reminder of their mistreatment by Spain, and after three hundred years these places remained forceful mementoes of the fraught Catalan–Spanish relationship (the anniversary of 1714 had inflamed these sentiments). By travelling through Catalonia in this instance, 'landscape itself becomes historicised … nature becomes part of the dynamic processes which allow for movement through the very remembrance of settlement and belonging' (Lovell, 1998: 11).

As in the market walk with Concepció, during mushroom hunting trips *boletaires* often discussed recipes related to the kinds of mushrooms we might find, or other local produce we came across, such as wild herbs. As in the market, mushrooms or other gatherable foods became aide-memoires for various recipes. For example, in my second mushroom hunting trip with Concepció and her friend Catalina, upon finding the yellow *camagrocs* ('yellow foot') mushrooms, they instantly launched into discussions of how they could use them, such as in a *truita de patates* (potato omelette), pump-kin soup, or freezing them for later use. When we saw some wild thyme, Concepció was reminded of a fish dish particular to her husband's family, which was the first she learned from her mother-in-law on her arrival in the marital home.

This requires a collection of recipes, and knowledge about the best way to cook them. This then is why recipes are often explained in relation to foods: it is through cooking that national Catalan foods (national objects), with their associated inherent meanings, are ingested and embodied within Catalans themselves. At the same time, on a more visible level, the act of cooking and eating these foods together in a sociable context means that they are a catalyst for group identity development, when ideas about the Catalan nation, culture and politics can be discussed. On each of my trips, the preparation and consumption of mushrooms is an essential element to conclude a proper *busca-bolets*, as were regular food stops along the trip to eat *pa amb tomàquet* with *llonganissa*, ham and other cured sausages, ideally in the wood or a farmhouse tavern (these are also part of my informants' mental landscape maps).

Consuming Landscape, Consuming Catalonia

This chapter has provided an overview of the intersections of landscape, food and territory as the foundations of national identity. In the case of mushroom hunting, the act of picking them is a national activity, further Catalanised by cooking them in Catalan dishes. Other dishes reproduce landscape in foods. Landscape is itself a symbol of Catalonia as a nation, hence it is possible to both consume the landscape through the produce of this landscape, and also through a symbolic, physical manifestation of this landscape. The variety of regional cuisines, landscapes, microclimates and different products may imply regional fragmentation. In reality however, this is accepted as part of the discourse on the diversity of Catalonia, where difference and variety are idealised.

Through the market, food fair or communal dining tables, one interacts with other members of the imagined community. As B. Anderson (1983) pointed out, one can never come into contact with all members of the nation, hence the need for it to be imagined, with help from material culture like print media, monuments and so forth. In the same way, no individual Catalan can ever meet every other Catalan. Yet, I suggest that through an individual's interaction with a few other members in these communal spaces, microcosms of the Catalan nation emerge which facilitate the creation of an imagined community.

It is also in these contexts that ideas about the nation, what it means, and what form it takes are discussed. This very discussion has a dual role: it is both a performative aspect of identity, which also brings the nation into being. Demonstrating national knowledge, the Catalan cultural capital, such as by discussing the culinary map and its seasonal produce, or listing regional food varieties or dishes, or knowing enough about mushroom lore and having such familiarity with the territory to be a successful *boletaire*, are all markers of in-group identity. This showing-off is also a performance, that reasserts and demonstrates to onlookers a sense of being Catalan. I myself participated in this performance, when I was able to talk with authority about different regional cuisines, and my own experiences of travel across Catalonia. The act of journeying across Catalonia, experiencing the territories and regional intricacies of the nation first hand, is likewise a significant performance of national identity. That this activity is called *fent país*, that one 'makes the country' by visiting it, is testament to the role of this activity in both national identity creation and performance.

Such discussion can also, on occasion, manifest more specific identities, such as whether the individual is inclined to be pro/anti-independence. There is no universal agreement on what makes the Catalan nation. Indeed, discussions about the minutiae of Catalan cuisine parallel discussions about the finer points of politics and issues like independence, and both can become heated. Yet through this disagreement, and the associated exchange, consideration and disputation of ideas, the nation is continually re-formed and re-envisaged by discussants.

Notes

1. I discuss this relationship in more detail in Johannes (2018b).
2. Slow Food is a non-profit organisation that encourages the tasting and protection of local, ancient or heritage varieties of food through promoting small-scale

agriculture, and 'slowness' through thought in preparation and conviviality in food consumption, versus mass-produced, standardised products, and fast foods. The movement was begun in 1986 by founder Carlo Petrini, a leftist intellectual and journalist, as part of a resistance campaign to the opening of McDonalds near the Spanish Steps in Rome. Its structure is focused on 'convivia' or local societies, based on pre-existing food and drink societies. The movement's heartland has been the Piedmont region of Northern Italy, where its headquarters are still based, so Italians have been a driving force. It became an international non-profit organisation in 1989 with the development of the Slow Food Manifesto in Paris and is now present in 150 countries worldwide.

3. A singing style that originated amongst sailors and fishermen on the north-east coast of Catalonia, inspired by trips to Cuba (hence the reference to Havana).

4. A stringy, semi-transparent jam made with pumpkin pulp, served either on its own, or, more commonly, as a pastry filling.

5. The activity is a product of the social changes brought about by modernisation and industrialisation in nineteenth century Catalonia, as a consequence of both the rise of romantic Catalan nationalism, and improved methods of transportation (railways and automobiles) that reduced travel times considerably and opened up previously remote areas to visitors.

6. Parallels can also be drawn between the contemporary Catalan idealisations of subsistence cuisine and the regional cuisine that 'subsumed traditional peasant fare … elevating the traditional notion of "making do with what was on hand" to a uniquely important way to cook, one that represents the best of France as an agrarian nation' (Trubek, 2008: 33). However, Trubek does not go as far to connect such ideals to national identity as in the Catalan case.

7. A popular dish of roasted summer vegetables, normally peppers, onions or aubergine.

8. I also found a similar pattern during mushroom-hunting.

9. Oddly, native Vigatans do not eat *pans de pessic* themselves.

10. This refers to experiences from 2012–2013. The situation may have changed post-2017.

11. One of the principal mushroom fairs in central Catalonia, and a short distance from Vic.

12. Part of this may have been due to the influence of French *nouvelle cuisine*, though my informants did not mention this connection.

13. As Amy Trubek points out, restaurants are increasingly important in food-related decisions, and ideas about food are 'more likely to be passed from chef to customer than from mother to daughter' (Trubek, 2008:161).

14. Although I cannot rule out some idealisation of the past on the part of my informants.

15. La Pradelle (2006: 240) recognised a similar phenomenon in Carpentras, that stall holding and selling at markets increases after a recession, 'stallholder markets wherever they are function as a refuge for persons who have not been able to find a place for themselves in the labour force since the late 1980s recession'.

16. Parallels can be drawn with Caldwell's (2007) ethnography of Russian natural foods, where the inherent sociality of handpicked food and its associations with people gave it a privileged place in the minds of her informants.
17. Written as '*el consumidor de casa nostra*', a popular phrase which literally means 'of our house', but which is also used to describe the Catalan people. Such a phrase is often used in the context of shared identity in Catalonia, suggesting that house equals nation.
18. After the Christian reconquest of Old Catalonia in the ninth century, feudalism dominated these areas from the tenth until the thirteenth century. This was in contrast to New Catalonia to the south, which was reconquered later in the twelfth century, and which had a different set of laws that encouraged repopulation and discouraged bondage to the land.
19. The others include notions such as Tradition, Memory, Academicism, Product, Wine, Innovation, and Sense of Humour.
20. This background and the Ebro Delta's location have often been the reason why the county is seen as more Spanish and less Catalan than the rest of Catalonia.

Chapter 5
FLAGS AND FLAVOURS
NATIONAL DAYS AND THEIR FOODS

This chapter continues the focus on the gastronomic calendar, this time with a focus on Catalonia's three national celebrations (*diades*): the Diada de Sant Jordi (St. George's Day) on the 23 April, La Nit de Sant Joan (St. John's Eve) on the 23 June, and the Diada (Catalonia's national day) on 11 September. Despite the emphasis on the gastronomic calendar as a source of Catalonia's unique culinary identity, only one of these *diades* has an established food associated with it: the *Coca de Sant Joan* for St. John's Eve, a sweet flatbread topped by sugared fruit and nuts. This apparent anomaly has led to attempts to associate all these days with a particular food, generally baked goods such as the *Pastís de la Diada* (Diada cake) or *Pa de Sant Jordi* (St. George's Bread). Commercial interests play a part in these attempts, and the Barcelonan Guild of Cake-makers has been a particular driving force. Most Catalans are aware of this contradiction, yet still have mixed reactions to these new foods. The intention of this chapter is therefore to consider the appearance of these new foods, to understand the development of gastronational foodways going forward.

To briefly introduce these three festive days, St George's Day celebrates Catalonia's patron saint. Over the last century this has become a Catalan Valentine's Day-come-literary celebration, 'the day of the book and the rose', to celebrate Catalan literature. St. John's Eve on the 23 June, is a celebration that Catalonia shares with the rest of Spain, but which has evolved to become a celebration of Catalan identity through the *'Flama del Canigó'*. Finally, there is Catalonia's national day on 11 September, simply called the 'Diada' (the Festival). This day provides the focus for most militant Catalanism, and in recent years has become part festive day, part political protest.

The Diada is an example of what Quiroga (2007: 148) describes as the 'sacralization of national symbols [that] takes place in patriotic ceremonies where the nation is endowed with holy qualities and patriotic liturgies acquire a religious character previously reserved for the deity'. While one should be cautious in drawing too many parallels between national identity and religious experience (à la Durkheim, 2001, or Connerton, 1989), the Diada is a day consecrated to the unmitigated celebration of Catalanism. The day has been celebrated since the *Renaixença*, allowing participants to feel some connectedness with past performances as a 'collective autobiography' (Connerton, 1989:70), and in doing so, strengthen group identity.

There has been a greater recognition in recent years of the role of national days in nationalism. David McCrone and Gayle McPherson (2009), in the introduction to their edited volume on national days, make clear that such days are indispensable for reinforcing national identities. Despite conflicting discourses surrounding such days, they are essential to understand 'how national identities are made, unmade and remade' (McCrone and McPherson, 2009: 8). There has however been little focus on the foods associated with national days. Palmer (1998: 189) briefly mentions Thanksgiving and Christmas as celebrations of 'annual re-assertion of a national sense of belonging', and Avieli (2018) has considered the intersections of roasting meat, masculinity and managing space in Israel's national day, but these are notable exceptions.

St. George's Day and La Diada are the most obviously Catalan celebrations. St. George's Day celebrates Catalonia's patron saint, and the Diada is a day with unique significance to Catalonia. Llobera (2004) compares the differing atmospheres of these two festivals, recalling how they appeal to different expressions of Catalanism. St. George's Day is described as 'popular' 'universalist' (through its integration of immigrants), 'profane, present-orientated, civic' and involved with the 'culture of leisure'. The Diada, on the other hand, is more serious, 'official, particularist, past-orientated, heroic, sacred' and demonstrates a 'culture of resistance and love and grievance' (Llobera, 2004: 124). Llobera also stresses the ubiquitous presence of the national flag and red roses (St. George's flower) on St. George's Day, as it is these symbols that visibly mark the Catalanist nature of the day.

St. John's Eve is more problematic, being celebrated throughout the Iberian peninsula, so it could indeed have become a focus of Spanish unity rather than Catalan difference; St. John is a patron saint of Spain, not just Catalonia. However, its association with Catalanism was assured thanks to anti-Francoist activities centred on the day during the dictatorship, in the form of the *Flama del Canigó*, youth group activism and *excursionisme*.

Each of these festivals has developed to represent and appeal to different aspects of Catalan identity, and they provide strong foci of identity in Catalonia, an assertion that corroborates Llobera's findings. There are other festivities that are almost universally celebrated throughout Catalonia (Easter, Christmas, All Saints' Day and so forth), but these are placed in a different category to the Catalan-specific days, celebrated throughout the rest of Europe. They are still celebrated in a Catalan way (for instance through food and the gastronomic calendar) but are not unique enough to become a focus of difference.

It must also be stressed that the national days are not primarily family celebrations. Some families may meet for a meal together, to eat a *Pastís de la Diada* or *Pans de Sant Jordi* for dessert if the family has accepted these newer foods, but this is not the norm. These are primarily public festivities that take place outside the home and in the public sphere. As such, the food associated with these days is closer to street food, especially the *Coca de Sant Joan* and the *Pa de Sant Jordi*. This is interesting from the perspective of nation-building, as these national days provide a focus of group identity in the context of Catalan nationalism in different ways. Related to the importance of the gastronomic calendar in constructing identical behaviours across the nation, I argue that, as in food festivals, public commensality becomes a means for creating Catalan community identity.

One of the main intentions of this chapter is to tease out the relationship between food and one of the most obvious symbols of nationalism: the national flags. In Catalonia, I have found these to be enduring and emotive symbols, and their presence is the clearest visual delineation of Catalanist sentiments. In the case of the *estelada*, this is also a demonstration of support for independence, and the number of these flags in public places became noticeably greater during my stay (a fact commented upon both by my informants and the news media). During two of Catalonia's national days, St George's Day and the Diada, foods emblazoned with the *senyera* have become common, suggesting obvious nationalist associations. One can find similar examples of this behaviour worldwide. In wartime Japan, the so-called 'Rising sun' *bento* lunchboxes imitated the Japanese flag by placing a red pickled plum in the centre of a rectangle of white rice, or rice in a cone to represent Mount Fiji, complete with a Japanese flag. These are both examples of overt means of attaching national symbols to foods, most obviously the national flag, but also landscape in the latter case (Ohnuki-Tierney, 1993).

However, the relationship between food and the national flag is not always simply one of positive associations. For example, in Dominican cuisine a dish called '*La bandera*' (literally 'the flag'), became symbol of the country's poverty due to the expense of the ingredients (Marte, 2013). Hence the need to examine cases of flags appearing in food according to their individual contexts. In Catalonia, this can lead to some surprising findings. I was also curious to see whether adding a *senyera* (or *estelada*) 'Catalanises' a food, particularly if it is from outside the area (in practice I found this not to be the case).

The first half of the chapter will discuss the roles of food in Catalonia's three national days, followed by a more in-depth discussion of the foods associated with these days. This will be followed by a description of the role of food (specifically sausages) in Catalonia's 'anti-festival', Dia de la Hispanitat. I then return to focus on the Diada as it was celebrated in 2014, the Tercentenary year of the original defeat of Barcelona. The chapter concludes with a sweet 'dessert' with a discussion of the role of chocolate in Catalan gastronationalism.

St. George's Day, 23 April

St. George's Day is perhaps the most cherished festive day in Catalonia. The main individual expression of the day is for men to give women a rose, while women give men a book, as a token of love. Not only has it developed romantic associations, it has also become a celebration of literature, books and by extension the Catalan language. By being a day of literature, it is the day on which the Catalan language is celebrated in the most overt way in the whole year. As the Catalan language is the most significant manifestation of Catalonia's separate identity, the importance of this day for national affirmation should be apparent.

Commemoration began in the 1930s, due to the day's literary associations, as the birthday and date of death of Shakespeare, and also the date of Miguel Cervantes' deaths. No reference at all is made to the religious nature of the day (unlike the Diada de Montserrat, Catalonia's other patron saint, five days later), indicating a secularisation of this former Christian saint's day. On the day itself, in towns and cities throughout Catalonia, booksellers, charities, Catalan cultural organisations and political groups set up their own stalls selling books and/or roses. Government institutions and buildings also open to the public. Such governmental open-days on *diades* mark Catalonia's government institutions as symbols of a separate identity and foci of loyalty.

Until recently, St. George's Day has not been intrinsically associated with a particular food in the gastronomic calendar, such as *crema catalana* with St. Joseph's Day, *panellets* with All Saints' Day and so forth. In the words of the writers of a cookbook dedicated to festival foods:

> This day has remained more marked by cultural and patriotic symbols than by gastronomy. The thing that one cannot miss about today is the rose and the book and the street shared with fellow citizens. In contrast, the menu does not have any obligatory or complimentary attachment. (Sano and Clotet, 2012: 84)

Figure 5.1 *Pans de Sant Jordi* and a *Pastís de Sant Jordi* in a Barcelona bakery. Photograph by the author.

Here again the emphasis is on the public nature of the festival. In recent years, a food specifically developed for the festival has been the *Pa de Sant Jordi* (St. George's bread – Figure 5.1). This is a fairly recent invention, created in 1988 by a Barcelona baker Eduardo Crespo, at his Fleca de Balmes (Balmes Bakery). This made 2013 the 25th anniversary – a fact celebrated in packaging from that year at this particular bakery. This is a flat savoury bread, containing nuts, cheese and *sobrassada* (a spicy Mallorcan sausage that is eaten like mincemeat).[1] Their most obvious characteristic are the four bars of the *senyera* flag emblazoned on the bread, the colouring from the *sobrassada* creating the red colour, and the cheese lending a yellow tinge to the other bars in the centre. This bread has spread from its original bakery and can now be found in most Barcelonan bakeries for the festival, and also in Vic.

This promotion of *Pa de Sant Jordi* was often to be found in newspapers and magazines. According to an online article for the magazine *Cuina* (Cuina.cat, 2013):

> To each celebration, a food. The Catalan calendar is full of festivities that are celebrated with acts, traditions and something to content the palate and the stomach. St. George *could not be an exception* … A roundel decorated with the four bars of the *senyera*, it [*pa de Sant Jordi*] has become a classic of the Diada. (Emphasis added)

The attachment of food to festivals in the gastronomic calendar is seen as a central element in the celebration of the principal feast days in Catalonia. Any possibility that there is now *not* a food associated with a festive day is denied, in order to make the festival into a total sensory experience of national identity. Another 2013 article on the foods associated with the day took a similar line, claiming that 'there is no festival without gastronomy and in this sense St. George's Day is not an exception', considering the *Pa de Sant Jordi* and also the use of rose petals in food are the 'protagonists' of the day (Carlas, 2013). *Pa de Sant Jordi* was also described as 'typical of the day', and a recipe to use with the bread was included.

In Barcelona in 2012, 2013 and 2014, *Pa de Sant Jordi* was being sold in most bakeries, as well as at stalls in the main thoroughfares in the city centre where the bookstalls are located, or outside bakeries, along with small tasters to appeal to passers-by. The *Pans* are not ubiquitous, nor are they the only foodstuffs on display, though they are the most frequently occurring. Also present were cakes in the shape of books (advertised as 'edible books' by the Barcelona cake-makers' guild), another form of the *Pastís de Sant Jordi*. Sometimes these did not have the shape of books but were instead simple cream and sponge cakes like those found the rest of the year, decorated with *senyeres*. In recent years, gourmet food producers have used the day as an inspiration to create other foods related to the day, such as sausages flavoured with rose- petals, rose-petal bread, biscuits shaped like roses or books, rose-flavoured chocolates, to name but a few such food products.

There is no definite context for eating *Pans de Sant Jordi*, as no Catalan acquaintances talked about buying them. In Barcelona, they were eaten as street food straight from the bag, though it is difficult to know if it was tourists or Catalans who were doing so in this context. It is impossible to know their precise level of popularity, though on questioning some of the bakers they remarked that they managed to sell most of them, and the fact that they are continually prepared every year suggests there is a market (if not, they would cease selling them).

As an experiment to elucidate the context for their consumption, I bought two loaves of this bread from original Fleca de Balmes in 2013. In Vic, I gave them to two middle-aged informants, Concepció and one of her friends. The result was bemusement. Concepció's friend had never seen them before, possibly because she hailed from Girona. Concepció had seen them but remarked 'Those are from Barcelona. You will not find them here' (which I later found to be inaccurate, as Vic bakers did sell them). They were considered very new, too new to be deemed traditional for the day at the present time. Both women remarked on how they were probably a good moneymaking scheme for bakers, and that this was always happening with feast days now. They seemed to consider *Pans de Sant Jordi* an example of the perceived over-commercialisation of festivals, rather than a recognised, long-standing symbol of the day. Nonetheless, they were happy to accept them and thought them to be a nice idea, even if they were a gimmick.

There are also cakes that are prepared for the festival, the *Pastissos de Sant Jordi*. Their origins are not as clear as the *Pans de Sant Jordi*, though they are certainly older. Due to their recentness, neither the *Pans de Sant Jordi* nor the similar *Pastís de la Diada* (Diada cakes) are described in any of the principal books on Catalan cuisine. However, Vázquez Montalbán does make reference to a *Pastís de Sant Jordi*, as 'a rectangular cake, on a thin sponge cake base with butter filling. Topped with crushed sugar, a glaze, or cocoa covering, bearing in the middle a mould of the glorious silhouette of the saint, and red roses' (Vázquez Montalbán, 1977: 206). This book, *L'Art del Menjar a Catalunya* ('The Art of Eating in Catalonia'), was published in 1977, suggesting that these cakes existed at the end of the Franco period (almost forty years ago), and in a form that has changed little until today. I also found reference to a cake recipe for a '*Sant Jordi*' in Josep Rondissoni's list of recipes for the Barcelona Women's School, for the class of 5 June 1928 (Rondissoni, 1927). From its ingredients and recipe, it appeared to have many of the characteristics of today's *Pastissos de Sant Jordi*, including nuts and a biscuit base, as well as red strawberry and yellow apricot jam as a topping. Although not stated in the instructions, the combination of red and yellow (the colours of the *senyera*) suggest that the decoration could have mimicked the Catalan flag. The June timing is odd however, as it could not be made for St. George's Day in April.

Even without the associated foodstuffs, whether considered authentic or not by Catalans, food may come into other celebrations of Catalanism that are central to this day's commemoration. For example, Carmen, a widow, fondly recalled how she and her late-husband always celebrated this day through food by dining in a Catalan restaurant, where they would exchange their book and rose, and eat something typical from Catalan cuisine. Like Christmas, this Catalan festive day is an occasion to eat 'traditional' Catalan food.

St. John's Eve, 24 June

The celebration of St. John's Eve is not an event unique to Catalonia, and its observance can be found throughout Europe. As in similar celebrations outside Catalonia, Catalan celebrations of this date centre around fire. Bonfires, fireworks and fire displays from groups of *diables* (participants dressed up as devils carrying torches) are the principal focus of the festivities. In the Franco era this event became another celebration of Catalan identity, with the creation of the *Flama del Canigó* (Flame of Canigó) in 1966. Canigó mountain is a site of huge importance in the Catalanist landscape as the highest mountain in the *Països Catalans*, and national poet Jacint Verdaguer named his first book of poetry after the mountain. The event began when a group of youth activists lit torches and lanterns at a symbolic bonfire on the mountain and carried them in secret to Francoist Spain as a symbol of hope and solidarity to other Catalans across the border.

The Catalan government has now institutionalised the *Flama del Canigó* as a mass celebration and public holiday throughout the autonomous community. After a trek to the top of the Canigó mountain, a bonfire is lit the day before St. John's Eve. From this bonfire, a flame is taken and carried, relay style, across the *Països Catalans*, lighting bonfires throughout the territories. In Barcelona, the torch arrives first in the Plaça de Sant Jaume (St James's Square), the governmental centre of Barcelona and Catalonia, where government representatives and Barcelona's *gegants* symbolically welcome the arrival of the flame. The torch is placed in a brazier, and representatives of Barcelona's districts (often cultural or sports groups) light a torch to take to their district. In Vic, the main fire is in the Plaça Major, which provides a torch for smaller bonfires in other quarters of the city.

Of the three principal Catalan festivals, La Nit de Sant Joan has a much longer association with a particular food than the other two, the *Coca de Sant Joan*. The *coca* is a kind of sweet flatbread, popular in Catalonia throughout the year. The most common type is a simple flatbread, perhaps a brioche, often flavoured with the *anís* alcoholic drink, and with sugar sprinkled over the top before baking. Vázquez Montálban describes them thus:

> Incontrovertibly typical for this night are the '*Coques de Sant Joan*' in diverse classes – of brioche, puff pastry, lardons – with their different stuffings and decorations: cream, angel's hair (a stringy pumpkin flavoured sweet), sugared fruit, pine nuts etc. (Vázquez Montálban, 1977: 207)

Other decorations can be chocolate, pine nuts, or candied fruits, the latter two of which are the most associated with La Nit de Sant Joan. The Catalan folklorist Joan Amades (1950–1951) records the existence of *Coca* eaten for Sant Joan in his *Costumari Català*, a guarantee for many Catalans of its entrenched associations with the holiday. *Coca* is a highly commensal food in other contexts in Catalonia, for example, as a street food at fairs and markets, or a simple and economical dessert in public meals at festivals. The festival itself is based outdoors, and my informants strongly associated this food with outdoor street parties, a festive atmosphere, and for younger informants, the end of the school year. It is expected that the *coca* will be bought from a bakery, cake shop or supermarket, as it is complicated and time-consuming to make at home (this is true of many, though not all, sweet dishes in Catalonia). That said, the recipe for the *Coca de Sant Joan* was one of the most viewed on *Cuina* magazine's website, even though I heard it said (including by *Cuina's* editor) that any attempt to make it at home always failed. Underlining its status as a well-established festival food, I heard my informants describe it as '*de tota la vida*' (of all one's life), a description given to something that had been present throughout the speaker's life, and a common marker of something legitimated by tradition and implied antiquity.

I experienced the festival twice, once in Barcelona (2012) and once in Vic (2013). *Coca* in its various incarnations (with toppings of fruit, pine nuts, cream or lardons) were described in the Barcelona festival publicity as 'essential'. A sign of the importance of food to the event is that, in conjunction with the Baker's Guild, the city council organised a distribution of pieces of *coca* to the public in the Plaça Sant Jaume before the arrival of the Flama. The city council were also handing out rosemary plants, as these are another seasonal product associated with this time in the gastronomic calendar. It is the handing out of pieces of *coca* that is especially significant, as the shared space of commensality centred upon Plaça de Sant Jaume becomes a place of national identity affiliation, and personal interaction through the consumption of *coca* provided by one of Catalonia's public institutions.

Figure 5.2 The handing out of coca and rosemary plants by Barcelona City Hall on St. John's Eve. Photograph by the author.

In Barcelona, the usual way to celebrate the event is to participate in one of the many street parties around a bonfire of the particular district. In Vic, the primary focus is the bonfire in the Plaça Major. Many families take the opportunity to leave the city for a short vacation, and it is also common for younger Catalans to celebrate the evening on a beach in a group of friends. Others who remain may hold small celebrations, preferably outside, to set off firecrackers and fireworks. I attended such an event in Vic, a supper gathering to eat *paella* (a *paellada*) and *coca*.

Upon arrival, the host Ignasi and a group of seven friends (all younger than 30) were setting up the *paella* dish on a gas burner. Throughout the next hour or so, they added various ingredients, crushed tomato and calamari first, followed by prawns, chicken, pork, rice and clams. The *paella* was therefore the focal point of the entire evening, and the source of conversation. In line with the male associations of the *paella* (Duhart and Medina, 2006), the men in the group were in charge of making it. As we made the *paella*, my companions admitted that this was more Valencian than Catalan, but considering this was the night of the *Flama del Canigó* they could do a dish from the *Països Catalans*. The style of the dish itself was more like the Catalan style of *paella*, remaining moist with the *caldo* (liquid) still present. Their discussion of the dish demonstrates how ideas about the relationship between the *Països Catalans*, national identity and lived reality are played out and expressed at a quotidian level. National holidays such as Sant Joan become occasions when these associations are considered and expressed.

The Diada de Catalunya, 11 September

In line with Llobera's (2004) observations, my experience was that while St. George's Day is the context for less confrontational expressions of Catalan national identity, Catalonia's National Day on 11 September is an assertive celebration of Catalan pride, and has become the focus of national protest. St. George's Day and the Diada in September are two sides of the same coin: they express the same sentiments, the same sense of identity, but St. George's Day is more subdued, a working day and more intimate. The Diada, on the other hand, has the character of a political protest, a very public celebration in the street, and a 'national' holiday for the Catalan Autonomy Community. The Diada marks the defeat of Habsburg forces by the Bourbon army in 1714, who entered the city on the 11 September, following the protracted fourteen-month siege of Barcelona.[2] The irony that this day celebrates a defeat has also not gone unnoticed by Catalans, but in doing so commemorates Catalan resistance, determination and the loss of freedoms from before 1714 (Crameri, 2008). Considering the rise in independentist sentiment over the preceding years, in the tercentenary year of 2014 the Diada became heavy with historical significance.

Like St. George's Day, the Diada has no strong links with particular foods, but food as part of Catalonia's cultural arsenal is used in multitudinous ways to prove Catalonia's different identity throughout the day. In the words of one post on a Catalanist Facebook group (Catalunya, T'Estimo) page on 11 September 2012, food is placed in the context of symbols of Catalan popular culture, such as architecture, *the gegants* and the s*ardana*:

> I was born ... where one eats *mongetes amb botifarra, allioli*, snails, *pa amb tomà-quet*, where one drinks Cava, Vichy Catalan, water from Montseny[3] ... where there are great buildings and the *gegants* pass to the sound of music.

In Omnium's 2013 calendar on Catalan food traditions, the chosen food is the *pa amb tomàquet* and *purrons*. The close association between Catalan identity and *pa amb tomàquet* has already been discussed at length, and the choice of this food for September underlines how the Diada is a particular day to celebrate and consume Catalan dishes (not unlike St Geroge's Day). More recently, *Cuina* ran an article in September 2015 entitled 'A Finger-licking Diada', stating that 'on the Catalan Diada it is not just the assertion, festival and politics that are at the forefront; gastronomy is also very present during such a special day for all Catalans'. The article lists establishments where one can find the foods associated with the day, and restaurants that are running special set menus for the day.

The Diada became a focus of celebration with the rise of political Catalanism in the nineteenth century. The first Diada in its current, pro-test-orientated form occurred in 1977, in Barcelona, to assert continued Catalan existence. Since that time, Barcelona has remained the focus and location of major events until 2012. In 2013 the day was celebrated with the Via Catalana, or Catalan Way, a 400 km human chain stretching along Catalonia's coastline. The aim was to emphasise the whole of Catalonia, from north to south. This may have been due to a discreet realisation of the irony of a focus on Barcelona, because it is here that there is the least support for independence. Those who lived in close proximity to the route of the Via generally joined it there, but many (especially those in Vic) travelled to other parts of Catalonia to take part. The 2013 Diada therefore became an opportunity for Catalans to participate in *excursionisme*, and the icon of the map and the Via upon it become a key image of the protest (cf. Urla, 1993).

In Barcelona, the principal act of the morning of the Diada is the offering of floral tributes at the statue of Rafael Casanovas, the leader of the city's defence at the siege of Barcelona. Offerings are given by Barcelonan and Catalan-wide cultural groups (*geganters*, choral societies and excursionists are exceptionally well represented), sports associations, and political parties. In 2013 and 2014 there was also an element of historical re-enactment, as recomposed regiments from 1714 left tributes and provided gun salutes at the statue. Historical re-enactments compose the principal regional celebrations of the Diada that take place in the days leading up to it, such as Vic's Marxa dels Vigatans on the 10 September. For this event, reconstituted eighteenth-century regiments from the county march to Vic for a ritual burning of the *Decreto de Nueva Planta* ('Nueva Planta Decrees'), the document drawn up by Philip v in 1715 that dismantled Catalonia's *Generalitat*.

The 2014 Diada in Barcelona was heavy with historical significance, due to the tercentenary and political background. Historical re-enactments, reconstructions, conferences and exhibitions occurred in the city throughout the year, all focused on remembering 1714. A new national museum was opened, the Born Cultural Centre, showcasing excavations carried out on the ruins of seventeenth-century houses destroyed in the siege as a place of national memory.[4]

Like the Via Catalana of 2013, the protest in 2014 consisted of volunteers arranged in the form of a 'V' across Barcelona. Participants wore either a red or a yellow T-shirt, to create the effect of a massive human mosaic representing the *senyera*. The 'V' symbolised both 'Victory' (a contradiction of the 1714 defeat which it commemorates) and 'Votar', as this was the last Diada before the planned referendum on the 9 November 2014. As in 2013, regionality was once again emphasised. Rather than requiring travel to other parts of Catalonia, this time different counties were assigned different sections of the 'V', creating a microcosm of Catalonia within Barcelona itself.

As on St. George's Day, there is no specific festival food for the Diada. Recently, there have been attempts to promote a cake for Catalonia's national day, the *Pastís de la Diada*. These cakes are almost identical to many *Pastissos de Sant Jordi*, a sponge cake with cream and jam filling, except the decoration only includes the *senyera* or *estelada*. The first recorded instance of a *Pastís de la Diada* was on 8 September 1977, when a group of members of the Barcelona Cakemaker's Guild presented a cake decorated with a *senyera* to Josep Tarradellas, President in exile of the Generalitat (Cuina. cat, 2015). The cake was designed by a cakemaker in Badalona (a town near Barcelona) Miquel Comas i Figueras, who ensured that the cake appeared in pastry shops during that Diada that year (at a time when the *senyera* was still technically illegal). This was a significant year, because it saw the first Diada celebration for four decades, and the return of Josep Taradellas to Catalan soil in October.

Despite their roots in noteworthy moments of Catalonia's recent history, these *Pastissos de la Diada* have met with some friction, more so than for the *Pastissos de Sant Jordi*. This may be because large cakes of this type are

Setembre
11
dimecres
Diada N. de Catalunya

L'Onze de Setembre, fes país amb un pastís

Figure 5.3 *Pastís de la Diada* in the cake-makers guild's calendar. Note the exhortation to *fer país* (make country) with the cake. © Gremi de Pastisseria de Barcelona. Published with permission.

associated with family gatherings that take place within the home, whereas the Diada is a celebration that takes place in the street. This is compounded by the view that the *Pastís de la Diada* is promoted for commercial interests in order to take advantage of Catalanist sentiment. Moreover, even though they have been present for over forty years, they are still considered a recent invention.

The *Pastís* has little significance for the festivities in Barcelona, or indeed the rest of Catalonia. Some bakeries remained closed, as this was the end of the holiday season. Others made no reference to the day aside from showing *senyeres* in their windows, and perhaps the calendar from the Barcelona cake-maker's guild showing the *Pastís de la Diada* (Figure 5.3). Others may adapt their current cakes by decorating them with a *senyera*. There are still a substantial number though that will sell a variation on the *Pastís de la Diada*. Attitudes in bakeries themselves are mixed: some I spoke with fell into the latter category, and were proud to contain Catalanist products, while others considered it 'something fun' not an expression of die-hard Catalanism.

In the 2014 *Diada*, I noticed that *Pastíssos de la Diada* were more prevalent in areas around the central festivities (near the Market for Independence, discussed below) and the protest march. Their strong presence in the city may support another assertion I heard from my informants in Vic, that these cakes were from Barcelona. This is significant because Barcelona was perceived as a place with a less concentrated Catalan identity, that does not support independence, and a source of new inventions as opposed to older 'traditions'. In 2014 there were noticeably more cakes with the pro-independence *estelada* flag. According to bakers I spoke with in that year, this was a reaction to the demands of an increasingly pro-independence market. Again, a less charitable reaction to this development is to see it as the commodification of pro-independence sentiment, as savvy business owners take advantage of the cultural and political movement.

A focus of the 2012, 2013 and 2014 Diada was the Arc de Triomph district of Barcelona, next to the Ciutadella Park. During the day itself, a market was held in this open space called the Mercat per la Independència (Market for Independence). The area contained a large market area selling principally Catalan memorabilia, an arena for Omnium cultural, a radio studio, a concert stage, and marquees for talks and presentations on Catalan themes.

This market deserves some discussion. In 2012, the area contained about a hundred stalls, selling a variety of Catalan memorabilia; clothing, badges, and novelty items such as fake passports and ID cards for a future Catalan state. Bookstalls too were popular, small specialist bookstores or stalls of larger chain stalls. Food stalls also held a strong place, and indeed approximately a third of the stalls were food-related; open bars for buying local Catalan beers as refreshments, or products with their own stalls. In short, the set-up was almost identical to popular food festivals. As at similar fairs, many of those attending were not from Barcelona, but had travelled from around Catalonia.

In 2013, the number of stalls was noticeably greater, and took up a larger area than the year before. The most interesting development this year was the creation of a food market in the central area of the Arc de Triomph area, with about ten stalls dedicated to Catalan produce. The official name for this was a 'Demonstration of Professions and Artisanal Products'. The market was organised by an entity called Mercats d'Abans (Markets of yesteryear), a collective of stallholders and businesses that coordinates historically-themed markets throughout Catalonia. In 2013 the entity created a new market, named '1714 History and life of a people', a reference to the significance of 1714 and another example of a historical re-enactment. In the 2013 market, each stall showed examples of different products of the Catalan countries, with large cartoon boards next to some of the stalls showing how the product was made and examples of the implements used. 2014's Mercat de la Independència also kept the same format of a large food market in the centre, this time with some stalls showing 'traditional' crafts such as wood turning, and a *barretina* stall.

As at popular food fairs throughout Catalonia, families bought food from the stalls and ate it as they walked through the market and park. Once again, national spaces became spaces of commensality through the consumption of street food. The day was also an occasion for outdoor meals (*dinars populars*) organised by various cultural and political associations to promote commensality amongst participants, as at other festivals throughout the year. I attended one hosted by Omnium Cultural in 2012, which had been running since 1999. This consisted mainly of family groups, and was filled to capacity, so was evidently a popular event. The main food was a *Fideuà*, a seafood dish from Valencia and the Ebro Delta in the south, now popular throughout Catalonia. The principal ingredients are the *fideus* (small short pieces of pasta), flavoured with calamari and prawns, served with *allioli*.

Fellow diners commented that this was a typically Catalan dish, especially for the season and an area near the sea like Barcelona, and ideal for large groups. The inclusion of *allioli*, one of the principal sauces of Catalonia, was also ideal due to its origin in the Catalan areas, combining perfectly with the theme of the event to create a rich nexus of Catalan associations.

The dessert was the common festival food of *coca* with a bar of chocolate. The meal was punctuated by the boisterous shouting of nationalist slogans, for example the '*Visca Terra Lliure*' (Long live the free land) and the Omnium slogan for that year '*I ... Inde ... Independència*'. Also provided on the tables were salad, *pa de pagès* and wine from Empordà. The selection of the latter two are particularly significant. '*Pa de pagès*' ('Peasant's bread') is a Protected Geographical Indication food. As DeSoucey (2010), West (2013) and Ichijo and Ranta (2016) have pointed out, the protection of produce through official recognition is regularly part of nationalist promotional agendas. This round white bread (much like a French *boule*) is the staple bread for both everyday and festive situations. Concerning the wine, Empordà in the north-east of Catalonia is an area with a strong Catalan identity, and is the point of origin for *mar i muntanya* cuisine. The combination of wine from this area and the use of a bread heavy with Catalan associations, alongside the other foods, creates a combination of symbols that continually enforce and flag (Billig, 1995) the identity of the event.

Reactions to the Invention of National Foods

I would like to consider here some of the reactions to the *Pastissos de Sant Jordi* and *de la Diada*, as they reveal interesting insights into the development of national foods, and the potential for cultural change. Many of the new-fangled cakes made for the Diada and Sant Jordi are similar in decoration, though the flag decorations for the Diada are more prominent, and they both fulfil a similar gap in the gastronomic calendar. *Pans de Sant Jordi* are sometimes sold for the Diada, because it also has the flag emblazoned upon it. The reaction of many informants to these types of cake was mixed, with some appreciating the use of the *senyera* while others criticised the apparent consumerist inspiration of the foods. Some informants were also dismissive of these foods, saying they were not 'traditional'.

For instance, Berta, a language teacher in her 30s in Vic, called the newly-developed foods 'very consumerist' and 'a recent invention'. When asked if she liked the *Pastissos de la Diada*, she said, 'I really like everything around the Diada, but this is an exaggeration. I would not buy it. It is a business thing'. She expressed similar sentiments about the *Pastís de Sant Jordi*, 'I really like St. George's Day, and I really like Catalonia, but these things are an excuse to sell things'. Irene, a Barcelona-based informant in her 20s, remarked 'I've seen that thing with the four bars for a few years [*Pans de Sant Jordi*], but it is not very well known'. In another conversation with her and her family in Vic, her mother agreed 'this is new ... something that the cake-makers do to make money now. It is all marketing, invented. Cake-makers and bakers want to sell, so they do this. It is not traditional'.

These new foods are also compared unfavourably with better established foods in the gastronomic calendar. I received an almost identical reaction from a group interview with Catalan activists (part of the Assemblea cultural group). These were all older than Berta and Irene, but their attitudes were notably similar. One remarked 'You might want to eat a cake like this one day, but it has no tradition at all', and others contrasted it with better-established foods in the gastronomic calendar, such as Lent *bunyols*. Amongst another group, this time of young sardana dancers in their teens and twenties, one remarked 'You see these very little, they're very modern'. That these attitudes are so entrenched across age ranges demonstrates the difficulty in creating 'traditional' foods for national days, as younger individuals are possibly influenced by statements from their elders about a food's 'newness'.

Another activist, Marta (late 50s) also made a comparison to the Easter *mona* (which she characterised as 'traditional') with *Pastís de la Diada*, which she characterised as 'total marketing' and 'invented'. This is ironic considering the *mona's* history, because the chocolate egg *mones* only came into widespread popularity in the 1930s and superseded a much older version of the *mona*. Eighty years on, this style of *mona* has now been naturalised as 'traditional'. This contrast with 'traditional' and 'invented' was regularly used when discussing these new national foods. Although my informants were presumably unaware of Hobsbawm's (1983) theory of 'invented traditions', these *Pastissos*, and the new style of *mona*, can perhaps be considered as culinary invented traditions. On that note, Marta remarked she had also seen an 'independence cake' advertised, and added 'Once we are independent, then we'll have to have a cake, to celebrate'. The implication is that such a momentous event would be incomplete without an associated food.

As with the *Pans de Sant Jordi*, the mixed reactions to the *Pastís de la Diada* does not mean it is not consumed. If Catalans did not buy it, cakemakers and bakers would not sell it. When I searched Barcelona's bakeries for these cakes at the end of the *Diada* in 2013 and 2014, I found that most had been sold already. Likewise, there were very few of the *Pastissos* and *Pans de Sant Jordi* left in bakeries on 24 April. I was able to find only one instance of a *Pastís de la Diada* being bought and consumed, with Eloi, a Barcelona-based student in his twenties. He admitted that he liked the idea of the cake, 'it makes me really happy, all the *senyeres*, it is nice'. His father, on the other hand, dislikes *Pastissos de la Diada*, because he considers them too new and untraditional. Eloi took care to point out his father is very pro-independence and takes the upholding of Catalan traditions very seriously, especially because they are originally from Empordà, so feel they have greater responsibilities to uphold Catalan values. Despite his father's disapproval, Eloi's mother will always try to buy a *Pastís de la Diada* for the day itself as a nod to the national day, which his father will grudgingly eat. Eloi's experience may sum up well the general context in which *Pastissos de la Diada* are bought.

However, one sees a difference when claiming that clever marketing might also be used for foods with more longstanding associations with festivals. For example, in response to Marta's claim that *coca* was very Catalan and had strong associations with La Nit de Sant Joan, I suggested that perhaps this association was also 'marketing'. This she forcefully denied, claiming that the festival and its food even had ancient links to the Roman period. It seemed that by doubting the antiquity of the festive food, I was seen to doubt the grounding of the festival itself (consider parallels with DeSoucey, 2010).

While there is proof that some of these foods (*Pans de Sant Jordi*, *Pastís de la Diada* etc.) have been in Catalonia for a generation or more, it seemed that they have not yet entered popular consciousness as a 'tradition', possibly because some of the population could remember a time without them. It was interesting that these attitudes were present amongst all age groups. Even younger Catalans who had grown up with them are possibly influenced by elders who viewed them as something new. It is not '*de tota la vida*'.

However, the increased Catalan awareness of recent years has engendered a demand for Catalanist products and memorabilia, and these foods are an answer to that demand. While they might once have been a side point to the national holidays, the days themselves have also taken on greater significance as a focus of Catalan identity expression. Therefore, items associated with these days have likewise come under much greater scrutiny, hence the apparent 'newness' of these products, as bakeries and cake-makers have seen an opportunity to promote them following the rise of pro-independence Catalanism. As of writing, the *Pans and Pastissos de Sant Jordi*, and *the Pastissos de la Diada* continue to be bought. There is nothing to suggest they will disappear in the future.

The *Senyera* on Food

The power of the flag as a symbol of national identity is undeniable. Emblazoned on foods, it gives them a certain appeal. Just as better-known Catalan foodstuffs for export or tourism include a *senyera* to show their origin and allow them to become national objects, so these *Pastissos de la Diada/de Sant Jordi* and *Pans de Sant Jordi* are connected to Catalan identity in a less subtle manner. In a way, it may be this that allows the survival of these foods insofar as Catalans will still buy them to acknowledge the national day because they bear the national symbol, just as they would *coca* on La Nit de Sant Joan, *Tortell de Reis* for Epiphany, or *bunyols* for Lent. Yet even with the flag, these 'new' foods still have some way to go before they take their place as a 'traditional' food. Their almost jingoistic Catalanism makes them off-putting, even though they are still consumed, albeit grudgingly.

Before finishing on this topic, however, one should not totally dismiss the use of the national flag in foods. In more home-based, individualised creations, the application of a *senyera* to food is encouraged, even praised. David, one of the *sardana* dancers, posted a photo to the shared group Whatsapp, of an Easter *mona* sponge cake he had made himself, decorated with an *estelada* in yellow and red, with the words 'CAT' (for Catalonia) written at the bottom (Figure 5.4). Judging by the admiring comments in the group chat, this was considered an acceptable application of the national flag to food.

In other instances, more everyday foods can be arranged to look like the *senyera*. For example, the *escalivada* (grilled vegetables) is sometimes

Figure 5.4 David's homemade *mona* decorated with a yellow and red *estelada*.
© David Martos. Published with permission.

arranged so that the red peppers form four bars and the onion or yellow peppers form the yellow background. Marina, a Catalan living in Oxford, also recalled how it had become popular to decorate the summer dish *braç de gitano de patates* (a mashed potato roll mixed with tuna) with red peppers to form the *senyera*. This dish is often made at schools, to encourage children to partake of their identity by familiarising them with the flag. However, when I asked whether this would in some way Catalanise a foreign food, she was confused. Either a food was part of the culinary repertoire, or it was not. A flag emblazoned upon it might be a nice gesture but did not make it Catalan. This view also applied in Catalonia itself, to 'foreign' foods, such as cupcakes or iced biscuits, which are more associated with the Anglosphere. The presence of these kinds of foods decorated with the *senyera* or *estelada* is common in food festivals, or in bakeries during the national festivals. Despite their ubiquity, they are still considered 'American' (or sometimes 'English'), not 'Catalan', and therefore not truly associated with the day.

Fent la botifarra al Dia de la Hispanitat: Catalonia's Anti-festival and Sausages

The three principal national holidays of Catalonia are clear celebrations of Catalan identity. However, there is another 'festive' day that deserves attention, which Catalans 'celebrate', but in such a way as to undermine its nature as a holiday. This is Spain's National Day on 12 October, which celebrates the anniversary of Christopher Columbus's arrival in the Americas. Because this day is a celebration of Spanish identity, amongst Catalanists it has been transformed into a day on which anti-Spanish sentiment is focused.

One of the most visible ways that Catalanists mark this event, a national holiday in Spain, is by insisting on working during that day. In 2012, both the Assemblea and Omnium Cultural made well-publicised announcements that their offices would remain open, just as they would on normal weekdays, to show the irrelevance of Spanish festivals to Catalonia. Around Vic, shops were open as usual for the morning and most remained open for the afternoon. Many of the shop windows remained decked out in the Catalan flags and displays from the Diada from the month before.

Despite the refusal to recognise the day as a holiday, the day is marked throughout Catalonia by pro-Catalan events, generally of a political and pro-independence nature. And like the other national days, food as an identifiable symbol of Catalan identity has been brought into play. As of 2012, 12 October had become the day of the *botifarrada*, or *botiflerada*, one of Catalonia's many '*-ades*' (dining events focused on one particular food), in this case for the communal eating of sausages.

The consumption and association of sausages with this day is heavy with significance. Aside from their privileged position as a food particularly associated with Catalonia, to *fer la botifarra* also has vulgar connotations as an insult. The design company Catalunyam, which specialises in Catalan food-themed T-shirts, created a design inspired by the gesture, that of placing the left hand on the crook of the elbow, and then bending it up, so that the forearm and fist stand vertically.

The common name for this is the *botifarra de pagès* ('peasant sausage', due to the resemblance between the vertical arm and the sausage), but this name can also be applied to certain varieties of sausage. Catalunyam's owner, Oriol, admitted that his design was part of a more practical Catalanism that expressed its identity, and was not explicitly anti-Spanish (he had received orders for the T-shirt from Spain, where the gesture is also used).

Botifarradepagès : catalu**nyam!**

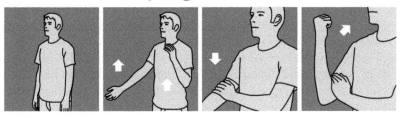

Figure 5.5 Catalunyam's image of a *botifarra de pagès*. © Catalunyam. Published with permission.

However, his designs have become one of the many militant T-shirts worn on the Diada. As he said himself, part of their intention was to say 'listen Spain' through the medium of gastronomy. Yet by its name, the *botifarra de pagès* image is not just a confrontation, it is also profoundly associated with the countryside, the *casa de pagès*, (peasant house) and the food produced there, each powerful images in the Catalan discourse of national identity (though hardly unique to Catalonia – cf. Smith, 1986; DiGiacomo, 2001 and Llobera, 2004). As Oriol said of the image, 'It is like the *botifarra* itself. It says it is a *botifarra de pagès*, rather like a peasant house'.

On the Diada in 2012, food-based protests were strongly in evidence. On one of the most prominent thoroughfares of the march was a huge sign of a sausage with the words '*A Catalunya fem botifarra*' ('In Catalonia, we make sausage'). Like Catalunyam's T-shirt, through the medium of a popular saying about food, such a phrase acts not only to express a cultural fact that can be mobilised as a source of pride and difference for insiders, it can also be turned to a blatant insult for Catalonia's opponents.

In the same protest, I also saw one protester carrying a placard with the word '*Prou*' ('Enough') across the top, with cured sausages (chorizos) hanging down. This is a reference to the expression '*chorizar*' (Castilian) or '*xoriçar*' (Catalan), a colloquialism that describes corrupt theft and cheating. In Vic, the verb was regularly used to describe the fiscal relationship between Catalonia and Spain, hence its use here to express 'enough'. Once again, food metaphors act as expressions of dissent through their multiple meanings and word-play.

Returning to the Dia de la Hispanitat, eating *botifarres* on Spain's National Day, and publicising this fact, has become a means of expressing Catalan identity on a day when Spanish identity should be celebrated. The 2012 '*Botiflerada*' in La Garriga, organised by Omnium Cultural, was a typical event from this day. The day began with a talk on the future of Catalonia as a state, followed by lunch: a salad and *mongetes del ganxet amb botifarra de la Garriga* (one of Catalonia's national dishes, sausage and beans). Both these foods (a type of haricot beans and sausage) are varieties or products particular to the area of La Garriga in Vallès, and the *mongetes del ganxet* has Protected Designation of Origin status. In this context, the emphasis on the local nature of the foodstuffs placed in a Catalanist festival shows well how such foodstuffs can be used as bearers of national identity in commensal, national settings, much like at Omnium's Diada lunch. They were also called *productes de la terra* ('products of the land') in the event publicity, and at the event itself. This is a popular phrase in Catalonia in these contexts (the Mercat per la Independència, for example, uses similar phraseology) that emphasises the connection between foods, land, rurality and by extension, nation.

The discussions over the *botiflerada* lunch were the typical themes that appeared regularly in Catalan culinary identities. The *botifarra amb mongetes* was described as 'a poor dish', 'a folkloric act' and 'a Catalan dish' by fellow diners. One remarked, indeed emphasised, that it was the sort of thing he ate at home regularly. The dish's Mediterranean nature was also emphasised, as was the importance of diversity to Catalan cuisine, and how it combined with other foods endowed with Catalanist associations such as mushrooms and snails.

These attitudes highlighted the, at times contradictory, attitude implicit in the idealisation of 'poor dishes' as subsistence cuisine, while claiming that Catalan cuisine is 'richer' than that of Spain. These claims to gastronomic richness parallel in many ways the frequent statements of Catalonia's wealth in comparison with the rest of Spain (the main source of current discontent), providing an interesting parallel between gastronomic culture and economic realities.

The Tercentenary Diada: A Celebration of 1714 in Food

Due to the tercentenary, 2014 saw a remembering of 1714 in all manner of popular acts, for example the creation of historic guided tours, the opening of a Barcelona museum showing houses destroyed in the siege, nationalistic merchandise and memorabilia. Food has also entered into these remembrances. In the new museum (the Born Cultural Centre) one wing was taken up by a restaurant run by Moritz (Barcelona's largest brewer, and another pro-Catalan brand), called 'The 300 of the Born', a reference to the tercentenary. Moritz also designed a specific beer called 'Born 1714', produced imitating techniques from the era. The space was marketed as an area where 'gastronomy converges with history thanks to an extensive menu based on historical cuisine'.

The menu itself showed a thorough attempt to associate the Catalan food of today with the siege of three hundred years ago. The food served was popular Catalan fare, such as *Escudella* and *Coques de recapta*. *Xuixos*, filled pastry cylinders originally from Girona, are called 'Cannons ... to remember the cannons that were the protagonists of the confrontation. Sweet and savoury, ideal to resist a siege'. Other entries include 'Historical breakfasts', '*Miquelet*[5] sandwiches';'The mounted cavalry: eighteenth century *tapas*'; '*Escabetxats*[6] ... which do well to maintain food in a good state during the lengthy periods of the siege'; '*Bombardejats*', to describe *bombes* (bombs), a type of stuffed croquette associated with the Barceloneta district, 'so as not to forget that Barcelona has been bombed many times'; 'A land of *Escudella*. Catalunya is a land of *escudelles*, and we serve them with the utensil that gave them their name'. The bread offered included 'White bread of the French aristocracy' or the 'Catalan black bread of the siege'. Many of these subsections included dishes that have been named after historical figures, places or events by the restaurant, such as '*Bombes del Comte-duc d'Olivares*', '*Platillo d'en Rafael Casanova*' or '*Coca de recapte tradicional de Cardona*'.[7] More information and background to these figures, events and their social context could be found on the back of the menu, allowing diners to inform themselves about national Catalan history.

The theme of September 2014's *Cuina* also centred on 1714. Its contents included a 'Menu from 1714: with recipes from three centuries ago', with recipes and an in-depth discussion of the historical cuisine, food culture and cookbooks, and a spread advertising the Born 1714 beer. The magazine also organised a series of talks (*Cicle Cuina 1714*) on food in Barcelona in the eighteenth century.

The FICCG developed a food route called '*Gastronomia 1714*' (Gastronomy 1714), and published an associated guidebook, *La Cuina del 1714* ('Cuisine of 1714', Cases et al, 2014), subtitled as 'a gastronomic route through our history'. The book begins with a prologue by the Catalan president praising 'traditional' Catalan cuisine of the era, followed by overviews of the cuisine of the eighteenth century, the route itself and information about the selection of the recipes and recipe books entitled 'A table that traverses time' – a title suggesting historical continuity through food between the eighteenth century and today. Finally, another section ('Returning to the essences') considers the similarities and differences of present-day recipes to those that have been 'revived' for the gastronomic route. In common with other gastronomic books, this section also contains praise for the richness and variety of eighteenth-century cuisine, the importance of gastronomy in Catalan culture and the joys of cooking the recipes in a convivial atmosphere to 'travel to the past to understand how our ancestors ate and lived' (Cases et al, 2014: 31).

Once again, a return to the past to recreate national memory is evident. This continues in the principal part of the book, entitled 'Monuments, Landscapes', which details eleven places involved in the war of 1714 and the events that happened there, beginning with the Born Cultural Centre. Each place is associated with a particular dish or dishes, intimately connecting food with important locations in the 1714 conflict. The associated website (which effectively contains the same information) also contained a list of the restaurants where one can find these foods, and there are details of the main tourist information points in the book itself.

The book is only available in Catalan, suggesting it is aimed at Catalan tourists, who will ideally use this book to travel through Catalonia, visiting significant locations in the history of the war, and in doing so relive their national past through food. The theme of travel in promoting national knowledge and creating national identity has been a recurring one throughout this ethnography, but the ideal of visiting sites of national memory can also be found in other media surrounding the tercentenary. For example, *Descrobrir*, the Catalan-language travel magazine under the same ownership as *Cuina*, dedicated their June 2014 magazine to 'Catalonia 1714', with the subheading 'We travel through the key scenes of the War of the Spanish Succession'. What is interesting for this research, however, is that in the *Gastronomia 1714* route places are associated with tastes.

The latter half of the book is a recipe collection of the dishes associated with each place on the route, first the 'old recipe' from a historical cookbook, then the modern-day recipe. Of the twenty-two recipes in the book, all but five are recipes based on older recipes from *La Cuynera Catalana* of 1853. Seven of the recipes are identical to those provided by the FICCG's *Corpus*. Quite how dishes have been attached to places is unclear, though the *Escudella i carn d'olla*, a food often considered one of Catalonia's national dishes, is tied to Barcelona, as is stuffed chicken, a popular Christmas dish. The *Coca de Recapte*, whilst now found throughout Catalonia, originated in 'New Catalonia' regions such as Tarragona and Lleida. Hence this dish's association with the city of Lleida, whose Bakers' Guild provided the recipe. This also applies to two other dishes, provided by restaurants in the locale with whom the recipe is associated.

In practice, none of these 'eighteenth-century' recipes are any different from those used today, and the meals are now easily found in restaurants throughout Catalonia (not just the locales to which foods are tied). The organisers and promoters of these tours and gastronomic remembrances would perhaps like to see this as an example of how Catalan cuisine has a sense of its continuity with the past. The reality is that dishes are cleverly selected to appeal to both contemporary tastes, and because they are seen as typically 'Catalan'. Dishes are the classic *Escudella i Carn d'olla, Coca de recapte d'escalivada* (thus including two favoured Catalan dishes, *Coca de recapte* and *Escalivada* in one), stuffed onions, several recipes for stuffed pigeon or chicken, examples of *agredolç* cuisine, *menjar blanc* and *bunyols*, to name a few. The four recipes in *Cuina's* 1714 issue likewise are familiar to today's tastes, and indeed could be placed in any other context outside of 1714. They include an example of *agredolç* cuisine, which is explicitly recalled as 'going back a long way with us [Catalans]', a white fish dish, a chocolate *crema catalana* (this recipe would have been impossible in 1714) and a rice dish.

Similarly, a Barcelona chocolatier, Enric Rovira, developed a set of chocolates for the tercentenary year, through which he sought to recreate the taste of chocolate from that time. Yet as he admits in the accompanying information, chocolate did not exist in solid form in 1714. However, he continues, he wishes consumers to imagine what solid chocolate would have been like considering the available ingredients. During 2014–2015, this chocolate was sold in gift packs (labelled as '*3 unces de xocolata*', an eighteenth-century measurement) with another chocolate bar representing the year 2014, which contained the fourteen traditional spices of Catalan cuisine (playing on the number fourteen).

However, a recent visit to the fields suggests that some of these remembrances were out of place. Concepció, a tour guide in Vic, claimed that no one has wanted to go on any of the routes or tours organised by tourist offices centred on importance places in the 1714 war. She bemoaned the wasted time and money involved in their creation. None of my informants were aware of Enric Rovira's chocolates or of the 1714 Gastronomic Route – they first heard of them from my questions. I tried to attend a class in eighteenth-century cuisine in 2013, but the class was cancelled, due to lack of interest. Food writer Jaume Fàbrega scorned the Generalitat's gastronomic routes, claiming that they were full of errors, and criticised other 1714-related activities and products (Fàbrega, 2014).

Yet whatever the success or motivations of these phenomena, it is not difficult to see the current of both historiography and historical recreation passing through these developments. The repeated element in all of these manifestations of culinary identity in the tercentenary celebrations is the creation of historical continuity through food. The 11 September 1714 has become a traumatic moment in Catalan national history. The uninhibited labelling of foods in the Born 300 to associate them with the siege of Barcelona and the attempts to recreate foods from that time and place them in a past construction of a national cuisine are all efforts encouraged by the Generalitat and associated bodies such as the FICCG to make the celebrations and recollection of this year more immediate and appealing to Catalans.

Perhaps the reason for these initiatives' lack of success is that they were created as 'top-down' strategies (to use Ichijo and Ranta's 2016 categorisation), by official organisations funded by the Generalitat or local council, and which were unable to appeal to the 'bottom-up' experience of food nationalism. Despite this, these food-focused remembrances are in line with similar nationalist remembrances of 1714, e.g. the creation of a national museum, historic re-enactments, touristic routes of national memory, or plays and concerts recalling the era. Moreover, the many products that private companies (more 'bottom-up' initiatives perhaps) created for or affiliated with the tercentenary demonstrates that these products were popular. As Jamue Fàbrega admitted, while calling these kinds of products 'opportunistic marketing', there is a demand for them (Fàbrega, 2014).

The celebration of this tercentenary year culminated in the Consultation for Catalan independence in November 2014. The aim of the culturally-focused tercentenary celebrations was to sensitise the Catalan population to this vote. One of the means of doing so with the commemoration was to remind Catalans of conflictual moments in their relationship with Spain. Aside from the fortunate coincidence of the tercentenary, 1714 is also no longer in living memory, so was less open to contestation. It may be for this reason that the War of the Spanish Succession became a better focus of grievance against Spain than, say, the Franco period or the Civil War.

Catalanist Chocolates

Enric Rovira's efforts were part of a series of chocolate-based expressions of Catalan culinary identity. The use of chocolate as heritage is not unique. For example, a similar situation occurred in France, with the campaign to recognise French cuisine as a UNESCO intangible cultural heritage, where chocolate has been 'newly reinvested with gourmet cachet and cultural authenticity' (Terrio, 2014: 178). In the article on 1714 cuisine in *Cuina*, chocolate is mentioned as an important drink from the era (indeed, it is one of the recipes). The use of chocolate as part of the *picada*, to add substance to a stew, is also something some informants considered peculiar to Catalan cuisine. The aforementioned 2015 article, 'A Finger-licking Diada', also described a list of sweetmakers, chocolatiers and brewers who had made products especially for this day (Cuina.cat, 2015). They are just a few of the many such examples of chocolates, sweets and other food products to be found associated with the day.

Chocolate has a privileged position in Catalan food identity. The first industrial chocolate factory in the world was founded in Barcelona in 1777, a source of pride to many Catalans. This fact was brought to my attention by more expert culinary informants in the field, such as food historian Núria Baguena, and food writer Jaume Fàbrega, to demonstrate chocolate's importance in Catalan food culture. Maria Martí Escayol, in her 2004 book on chocolate in Catalonia (*El plaer de la xocolata*, 'The Pleasure of Chocolate'), sees this factory as proof of the essential place of chocolate in Catalan culinary heritage. Ramon, a chocolatier based in Vic, began our interview by emphasising this fact, expressing frustration that this pioneering role was often forgotten in the global history of chocolate. Catalonia's particular association with sweet foods has been essential for this development. In Ramon's words:

> The tradition of cake-making, the sweet world, has always been very active in Catalonia ... to sell more, because it has always been an entrepreneurial [business], the majority of festive days are very strongly tied to this. *Crema de Sant Josep*, *Coca de Sant Joan*, Lent *bunyols* etc. There are many specialities, and though the festive days are the same as the rest of Spain (like All Saints, that's everywhere), there are concrete products that are associated with here.

His views expressed once again the role of the gastronomic calendar and its contents as something that defines and differentiates Catalonia from Spain. Yet he also drew attention to an entrepreneurial spirit in promoting these foods and their associated days. The foods he mentioned were well-loved and 'traditional' foods in the calendar. Yet here Ramon was suggesting that they too are still examples of clever marketing on the part of their purveyors. His remarks are compelling as an expert within the industry itself and suggest that national foods that are considered 'traditional' may themselves have been the product of a series of efforts to make them so. These efforts may even be on-going, both for the better-established festive foods and the newer foods such as *Pastissos de la Diada*.

He also took the view that the Catalan chocolate industry is distinguished by its creativity, linking it with the *nova cuina* movements first expounded by Ferran Adrià (Ramon and Adrià are close colleagues, and Ramon used to provide chocolate classes for El Bulli's training staff). His ideas were inspired by the ideal of a tradition of modernity in Catalan new cuisine. He suggested this was thanks partially to the Catalan ideal of openness to new influences, the closeness to other European countries (particularly France), and an inherent 'curiosity' on the part of Catalans.

Many contemporary Catalan chocolatiers have developed a reputation for their pro-Catalanist leanings. One of Ramon's English colleagues recalled that these views had sometimes led to heated arguments between the Catalan and Spanish chocolatiers in international events. Catalan chocolatiers have, on occasion, sometimes had to hide their attitudes from the Spanish-wide public. Enric Rovira, on the other hand, has no such qualms, choosing to base his market squarely in Catalonia, with other product ranges such as bars with packaging showing the *senyera* or Barça colours – inspired by the *Pastissos de la Diada* in his parent's bakery. In his own words, 'It [his Catalan identity] is pretty important … The link is evident and is manifested in the design of our products, the nomenclature, the concepts, the flavours. We try to hang onto the cultural Unique Selling Point'.

When asked about potential problems, he admitted that in Spain it was difficult to sell his products, because he shared a surname with a former leader of the Esquerra Republicana, who was known for his inflammatory, pro-independence remarks. Rovira, however, was willing to accept the consequences for the Catalanist associations. Still, when I left the field, he was having problems with his supply chains and had been forced to close his shop. Perhaps following a Catalanist marketing policy had not been beneficial in his case.

The culmination of chocolate-based creativity in Catalonia is the *mona*, the chocolate tableaux and figurines given at Easter. This art form has frequently been put to use as a form of political protest. In line with the history of chocolate in Catalonia, the *mona* was originally the domain of bakers. Even before these were made in chocolate, the folklorist Joan Amades (1950–1951) records that one of the earliest tableau representations of a *mona* in bread from 1875 was intended as a political statement. It represented a scene from medieval Catalan history, where a councillor of the Generalitat swore fealty to the city before his oath of allegiance to the Castilian kings. This had become an important moment in nationalist history, showing the Catalan governmental ideal of *pactisme* as best for ruling Catalonia.[8] The first weeks of 1875 had seen the restoration of the Bourbon dynasty in Spain, and the design of this *mona* was a subtle hint that the new monarch should rule Spain and Catalonia in a constitutionally correct way. In the same year one could also find *mones* representing contemporary Spanish politicians.

In the Franco period, a Vic chocolatier called Quim Capdevila (also a communist activist) created a *mona* on which he wrote the four ideals of the exiled Assemblea de Catalunya: liberty, friendship, statute of autonomy and coordination. The act earned him a prison sentence (Martí Escayol, 2004). Today, one can find chocolate *mones* bearing the *estelada* or *senyera*, and the Assemblea cultural organisation encouraged buying a '*Mona d'Independència*' in 2013. In this instance, these *mones* are similar to Marina's *senyera*-covered *braç de gitano*, a way of both socialising children into a national identity and providing one further way for adults to assert and express political and national belonging.

Figure 5.6 Advert from the Assemblea encouraging supporters to request a pro-independence *mona* from their cake maker. © ANC Berga. Published with permission.

National Flags, Foods and Flavours

In this chapter, I have attempted to consider the at times messy association between food and national celebrations, in order to provide an insight into how nationalist movements are lived at an everyday level. One feature that has come out is the inherent multivocality in these observations of gastronational identity: some receive a favourable reaction, others less so. One way of interpreting these reactions is to use Ichijo and Ranta's (2016) conception of top-down and bottom-up applications of gastronationalism, specifically their focus on the construction of national identities in the food industry. They consider this latter role to be an example of bottom-up or unofficial state expression of nationalism through food, however the Catalan case demonstrates that this does not necessarily imply that it will be accepted as such and will still be perceived as a top-down, imposed strategy. In practice, it may also be difficult to draw the boundaries between top-down and bottom-up, in particular where the regional government has promoted (either directly or indirectly) gastronational foods produced by private initiative, such as those for the Tercentenary Diada celebrations in 2014. Despite the mixed reactions to these food-based remembrances, it is noteworthy that Catalans continue to use food to recreate what has become a significant moment in nationalist history, and of reliving the national past through their senses (Barthes, 1961).

Creating national foods is a difficult and complex process. The addition of flags and the association of other national symbols does not automatically make a food worthy of carrying any significance greater than the sum of its ingredients. Yet what is it that *does* create national foods? The answer lies in a combination of factors. Firstly, 'traditional' foods have a feeling of timelessness in the minds of informants, brought about by their existence over a long period of time, such as the *Coca de Sant Joan* or the *mones*, in comparison with the *Pastissos de la Diada* or *de Sant Jordi*. All informants had grown up knowing of the formers' existence at a time when such foods had been ubiquitous, widely available and easily consumed. The *Pastissos* might not be very new, but they were not widely available, throughout Catalonia, until recently. Thus it may seem that they are not *de tota la vida*. The distinctiveness of these foods may also play a part, because the base of the *Pastissos* is no different from sponge-cakes found outside of Catalonia. *Coca* on the other hand has some claim to Catalan particularity (however, so can *Pans de Sant Jordi*).

Finally, these *Pastissos* are perhaps too blatantly commercialised, designed to take advantage of a time when consumers are more sensitive to symbols such as the *senyera*. These 'new' foods may also have become more visible, due to the increased focus on the day as a centre of national celebration and protest, creating an impression that they have only developed as the pro-independence movement gained support. That is not to say that more 'traditional' foods are not also commercialised in this environment, but they at least have the advantage of a wellspring of memories and stories to associate them with a more distant past. The *Pastissos de la Diada*, for example, could achieve this if they became associated with an Independence Day in the future. The non-commercial, private and individualised examples of the addition of a national flag to a food were considered more acceptable and were better received than the more commercial examples of the same phenomenon, because they are individual expressions of national affiliation that make up the greater project of Catalan nationalism.

Notes

1. While they are from the *Països Catalans*, this aspect is not mentioned in any of the discussions surrounding this food.
2. A similar day exists in Valencia on 25 April, which also commemorates the defeat of Habsburg forces, and is also a celebration of Valencian identity with popular and some political support – though with much less force than in Catalonia (Castelló and Castelló, 2009).
3. These latter two are bottled water brands. Catalan landscapes play an important part in their advertising, and these brands are national symbols in their own right.
4. Pierre Nora (1986–1992, in Llobera, 2004: 43) in his *Les Lieux de Mémoire* ('Realms of Memory') considers this issue in further detail in France. While the application of his principles to Catalonia would be interesting, to do so would go beyond the scope of this work.
5. Catalan infantry regiments.
6. A dish that includes a variety of pickled ingredients.
7. A flatbread with toppings, sometimes called the 'Catalan pizza'.
8. A type of political covenant that existed in Catalonia from the twelfth to the fourteenth centuries, to protect the interests of the nobility by controlling the power of the monarch (Llobera, 2004).

Conclusion
Cuisine as National Identity

For the anthropologist, leaving a place after a year's fieldwork can be almost as traumatic as arriving. Aside from the emotional rollercoaster of separating from the familiar faces, foods and routines of the fieldsite, I realised I had amassed a mountain of fieldnotes, interview recordings, photographs, recipes, cookbooks, newspaper clippings, magazines, assorted ephemera of sundry origin, knick-knacks, food packaging, posters, cooking implements and (mostly) non-perishable foodstuffs. How to sift through this *escudella i carn d'olla* of material to create a coherent argument, neatly divided into chapters (or courses), separating the *sopa* and *galletes* from the *carn d'olla*? If anything, the difficulty of separating the many diverse strands of Catalan gastronationalism was proof of the rich nexus of associations bound up with food and national identity in Catalonia. The reader will be able to judge if I have done so satisfactorily. What is certain is that in focusing on the lived realities, an in-depth study into a quotidian object such as food is an excellent means of penetrating discourses surrounding national identity. In the first half of this chapter, I will give a summary of the main conclusions from the Catalan case that I have presented throughout the work. In the second half, I will consider how these findings can be of use to future researchers into food and national identity, with some methodological considerations and suggestions to take beyond Catalonia.

Findings from Catalonia

It is notable how gastronationalist discourses mirror those of general nationalist ideals. The most obvious way is in the repetitive emphasis on historicism; that the national cuisine has a long history stretching deep into the past. In the case of Catalonia, the medieval golden age was also a golden age for cuisine. The cookbooks I described in Chapter One are relics of that glorified past, national symbols in their own right. They provide a proof of the historic nature of Catalan cuisine, which is essential for its contemporary legitimacy as part of national heritage. Time and again, the present is seen as a continuation of that past. Through consuming national foods, Catalans can indeed claim to be consuming some timeless aspect of their national past, one of the essential foundations of Catalonia's claims to difference. Food is also a means of experiencing traumatic moments in the national past, such as 1714. Other elements of cuisine which can claim linkages to the past include the idealisation of subsistence cuisine and seasonality (once a past necessity).

Claims to uniqueness also play a central role. Just as Catalonia's separate language and claim to a separate culture are the primary arguments for its separate national identity, so establishing a separate food culture is essential for its gastronationalism. This is essential to the discourse surrounding the *sofregit* and the *picada* as qualities that make Catalan cuisine quantifiably different during the cooking process, as well as *mar i muntanya* and *pa amb tomàquet*.

Claims to uniqueness are especially pertinent in instances where certain foods are shared with Catalonia's neighbours. It is here that the gastronomic calendar plays a part, because it is one way of claiming that foods are unique, not in their constituent parts, but through their treatment within Catalan culinary culture. The gastronomic calendar is also significant because it creates a unity in national consumption across space and time. Catalans are thereby aware that they are eating the same things at the same time, a culinary form of the 'imagined community' (B. Anderson, 1983).

Also present in the historicising discourse is the theme of Catalonia as a land of migrations. This is believed to have contributed to the great variety of cuisines in Catalonia, as well as a modern, open outlook. This is different from many (although not all) nationalisms in Spain and elsewhere, which claim at least some 'purity' of race, or a looking inwards, in contrast to Catalan nationalism. The claims to a unity in diversity, particularly in a culinary sense, however, are not unique to Catalonia (Heinzelmann, 2014 in Germany, and Fajans, 2012 report similar phenomena).

What is interesting is that in Catalonia this claim acts as a contrast to the perceived homogeneity of Spain. A central feature of Catalan gastronomic identity has been the variety of regional food identities within the area's borders. Despite this seemingly fragmented identity, these regionalities are grouped within the general arc of Catalan cuisine. Regional variation and expressing one's knowledge of this variation, are key markers of Catalan identity. Taking this further, travel is another essential element of Catalan culinary nationalism. Travelling to experience regional food is a way to familiarise oneself with other parts of Catalonia, other Catalans and the products and cuisine of those other areas, whether it is through daytrips to places of interest, specific restaurants, food festivals or markets. This activity in turn contributes to the creation of national consciousness, as practitioners become intimately aware of foods, landscapes and sites that are national symbols. This also allows the 'imagined community' to become more real through physical interactions with other members of the Catalan nation. It is also a means of '*fer pais*', making the nation through pro-Catalan action, knowing the nation and helping Catalonia and fellow Catalans.

National and festive days are essential to the practice of nationalisms, though their significance has only recently been considered (McCrone and McPherson, 2009; Avieli, 2018). In Catalonia, national days are moments when Catalan sentiment is concentrated in public displays, and public commensality, another instance of the gastronomic calendar and the imagined-community-through-food at work. Formerly festive days, celebrated only via the gastronomic calendar, have become a focus of 'traditional' Catalan culture, a bastion of precious cultural difference that has become newly relevant with the rise of pro-independence politics. These communal events are also moments where national identities can be discussed and formulated with other Catalans, in a private, familial or public setting. Discussions of national issues often slip into discussions about food and back again. It is important to recognise that even where there is disagreement, the fact that there can be discussion demonstrates that there exists a concept of Catalan cuisine as a worthy subject of discussion. When an aspect of Catalan cuisine or identity is continually debated then it means that these same elements are constantly reformulated, re-envisaged and re-evaluated, and in so doing, perpetuated. The approach taken by this book has been to see national identity as inherently performative and contested, suitable to a dynamic cultural object like food. Food, food consumption and food-related discussion provides the context for the continual development and regeneration of contemporary Catalan identity.

The context of Spain and the areas outside Catalonia must always be considered, because this is the principal 'other' against which Catalan identity has been formed. It is interesting that comparisons with Spain often stress difference, and even that Spain is not recognised as a unified entity but instead divided up into autonomous communities or cultural areas (e.g. the Basque Country, Galicia, Balearic Isles, Andalucía, Valencia and so forth). However, similarities or differences can be emphasised or denied depending on the context. For example, similarities between Catalan cuisine and that of the Catalan-speaking areas are emphasised when stressing the ideal of the *Països Catalans*.

The pro-independence movement has undoubtedly caused a deep re-evaluation of cultural symbols and personal identities in Catalonia, even amongst those who are not in favour of independence. This has correspondingly had an influence on gastronationalism. In Catalonia food has increasingly been appreciated as another Catalan cultural symbol. It is mobilised both to engender national pride within Catalonia and to promote that identity beyond Catalan borders. The pro-independence movement has therefore contributed, directly or indirectly, to a growing awareness of, and affection for, Catalan cuisine amongst Catalans themselves. To discuss, research, consume and prepare it is a legitimate means of national identity expression. Promoting it in touristic, UNESCO or European Union-wide initiatives has also been a form of top-down gastronationalism and soft power (Ichijo and Ranta, 2016) by the Catalan government, to assert their existence in opposition to that of Spain.

Still unclear, however, is the relationship between Catalan cuisine and produce from Catalonia, or from outside of Catalonia. The situation appears contradictory. While there is a clear preference for Catalan goods, to insist entirely on this ideal would be impossible. At the same time, there is definite pride in Catalan-produced foods, especially if they have some 'official' recognition, for example, under the PDO/PGI schemes. Catalans feel an emotional attachment to these products both as examples of national heritage and as national objects. The uncertainties that result from the political situation and economic recession have engendered an urge to protect those things that make up Catalan culture.

However, returning to the origin of products, a Catalan origin is not considered the most important element for ingredients of Catalan cuisine, even if it may be the ideal. What really makes them Catalan is the integration of such foods into the cuisine through cooking, or some kind of process that makes them into Catalan foodstuffs (e.g. sausage-making). In this way, non-Catalan foods can be Catalanised and made part of Catalonia's gastronationalism. Even dishes that are brought by immigrant communities can be adapted and become part of Catalan culinary culture.

This also applies to attitudes to the individual as a Catalan person. Early in in fieldwork, I was curious whether consuming Catalan food would in some way make me a Catalan. In contrast to the experiences of other anthropologists, such as Noyes (2003) in her Catalan fieldsite, my consumption of Catalan food was not regarded as making me in some sense more Catalan. This may be a result of mass tourism in the region. Tourists consume Catalan food, but that does not mean they automatically self-identify as Catalan or are considered Catalan. However, the educated consumption of cuisine, which implies an awareness of Catalan culture, does contribute to one's being perceived as Catalan. This includes an awareness of the nature of

Catalan cuisine, its history, gastronomic calendar, regional variation, seasonality and even travelling through Catalonia and experiencing these aspects. Discussions and debates about food signify to other Catalans that an individual has this knowledge. Food helps integration in this sense, not through its physical substance, but as a form of Catalan cultural capital.

This situation is strongly tied to the ideal of Catalan nationalism as an open one, and Catalonia as a 'land of migrations'. Key to this idea is the individual self-identification as Catalan by behaviour, above all learning the language, expressing solidarity with other Catalans, and knowing and practising Catalan culture. One is not Catalan by virtue of birth but must continually express and perform this identity. Being born into a Catalan family is beneficial, just as foods grown or produced on Catalan soil are in a position to be favoured. However, Catalan cuisine is not just about origins, but is equally about how territorial produce is used, transformed and interpreted. In the same way, Catalan identity is not just about origins or birthplace, but about self-identification, personal agency and the performance of Catalan identity.

Methodological Considerations: Moving beyond Catalonia

The broad intention of this work has been to contribute to the literature on the lived realities of nationalism, a response to Llobera's call for 'in-depth studies' of nationalist movements, to provide the 'building blocks' for theorising and understanding these movements. Today, as nationalist politics are rarely far from current events, the need to understand the power and attraction of these movements is greater than ever before. That attraction can only truly be understood by living within them, discussing them, and understanding how they are perpetuated at the individual level, for only then can deep conclusions be drawn about the collective. Food is an enlightening tool in the study of nationalisms from this perspective. As Raviv (2015) has pointed out in Israel, even the apparent trivialisation or marginalisation of food can reveal much about the state of the nation.

There are three interrelated areas that have not received as much attention in this book, namely power, class and gender, for the simple fact that my data did not reveal coherent conclusions about these topics. However, the gastronational researcher ignores these topics during fieldwork at their peril. One could argue, along the lines of Bourdieu (1984) that implicit in Catalan *nova cuina*, and its many imitators, are notions of class and taste. Likewise, one could also claim that the many conflicting, competing narratives from different official and unofficial stakeholders about Catalan cuisine could imply power structures. However, having studied the Catalan gastronational scene for the better part of a decade, in the face of rapid changes during that time, stakeholders have risen, influenced and then declined, as they have lost interest, funding, or popular support. Trying to develop a coherent description of any underlying power structures, aside from the very basic descriptions outlined so far, would be beyond the scope of this book. However, this could be a fruitful study for the tenacious researcher, whether in Catalonia or elsewhere. I would especially recommend, in this instance, a thorough consideration of the transfer of financial resources between government bodies and food-related organisations.

The creation and continuation of a culinary culture (what could be called gastronomy) can only be present if food is sufficiently abundant that it is not a source of anxiety. Within Catalonia, for those families and individuals so affected by the post-2008 economic recession that finding food was difficult, ideas about food identity would have little relevance. The rise of food bank usage was a growing concern during my fieldwork. According to Barcelona's food banks, the number of people assisted each month soared from 57,381 in 2008 to 152,489 in 2014 (Fundació Banc dels Aliments, 2017). The number has since declined, due to a reduction in unemployment, and the departure of immigrants, the primary recipients of food aid (ACN, 2018c). Vackimes (2013) has criticised the top-down approach of the Generalitat promoting Catalan food identity via vanguard celebrity chefs like Joan Roca and Ferran Adrià, when their cuisine is too expensive for most Catalans. While that may be true, the influence of celebrated chefs filters down to lesser-known, regional chefs who then convert their ideas into an inexpensive, popular, and often more edible, cuisine.

Distinctions by class and income are not a central part of Catalan social life, although they do exist. For instance, one woman from a landowning Vic family mentioned that she would not be comfortable allowing her own daughter to participate in 'rough' cultural activities like the *colles* of *castells* or *gegants*, which she associated with the working class. When I mentioned this to friends in both groups, and elsewhere in Vic, the reaction was normally laughter, and that such an attitude said far more about the speaker than widespread social reality. While there may be a popular, working class ethos in some of these groups (something also noted by Vaczi, 2016), in practice participants in Vic came from a variety of social backgrounds. The view that class is antithetical to nationalism, albeit an oversimplification (Pratt, 2003) may have some relevance to the Catalan case.

Inequality and economic wellbeing were a concern during my fieldwork as a result of the post-2008 crisis context, but this did not appear to have affected expressions of Catalan identity in a negative way. In practice, the economic crisis and resultant unemployment seem to have been of benefit to Catalan identity in all its forms. Newly unemployed individuals had more time to become involved in cultural activities, and sought inexpensive forms of entertainment, social interaction and personal motivation through national activities, like *castells* (Vaczi, 2016), sardana dancing, the *gegants*, organising festivals, or volunteering for civil society organisations like Omnium or the Assemblea. Some in the Catalan tourist industry have seen reduced incomes as an opportunity, which encourages stay-at-home tourism within Catalonia (and, indirectly, *excursionisme* and *fer país*). The crisis has also provided (perhaps unfairly) another claim of grievance against the central government, and a further source of mobilisation of the nation against the state.

There are other lines of enquiry that have borne fruit in this research. One is the need to consider relationships with neighbouring cuisines. Identity is often constructed in opposition to an 'other', and national identity is no exception. Identify who the 'other(s)' are, and how their foodways are characterised. Likewise, it is interesting to consider the language of food, especially in areas where language is central to national difference and identity politics.

As an ethnographer, it is impossible to ignore the importance of listening to the words and views of members of the nation about their food. This may seem obvious, but there were numerous occasions during fieldwork where my primary assumptions were swept aside by simply asking about particular foods. The practice of using the *senyera* on food, which I described in Chapter Five, was one such example. Had I presumed that the national flag on food was just another symbol of gastronational identity, I would have seriously misunderstood a crucial area of Catalan culinary identity.

However, there is a caveat to accepting informant discourse at face value. While it is essential to listen to what practitioners say about their foods, what they eat and how they prepare them, the researcher must be also be aware of culinary realities. Certain behaviours may be idealised (in the Catalan case, for instance, the *sofregit*'s lacking tomato), or condemned (*pa amb tomàquet* with crushed tomato), but that does not always translate into practice. The researcher should involve themselves in every aspect of food preparation and consumption, to both understand the contradictions and complexities inherent in gastro/nationalist movements, and also to thoroughly immerse themselves in the lived reality of such a movement. In doing so, they will come to realise that national identity is continually evolving, reformulating and shifting, even as it appears to remain stable, fixed and eternal.

GLOSSARY

❧

agredolç – See *dolç i salat*.

allioli – Literally 'garlic and oil', a creamy side sauce Catalonia shares with other *Països Catalans*, generally added at the end of a meal or consumed as a side with meat and fish.

allioli negat – A sauce or dip similar to *allioli*, but which has not yet reached its creamy consistency.

aprofitament – See '*cuina d'aprofitament*'.

arròs – 'Rice'.

Assemblea Nacional de Catalunya (Assemblea, ANC) – Catalan cultural organisation, with an explicitly pro-independence stance.

associacionisme – Alleged Catalan characteristic of forming social groups around a shared interest.

Barça – Barcelona football club, and a focus of Catalanist sentiment.

barretina – Red (or sometimes purple) wool or felt cap that is part of Catalan traditional costume. Was once an integral part of rural everyday wear, and strongly associated with the image of the *pagès* (peasant). *Barretines* act as a popular symbol of a Catalan.

bitxo peppers – A small, dried spicy pepper very like chili.

bledes de Santa Teresa – Saint Teresa's chard.

boletaires – 'Mushroom collectors'.

bolets – 'Mushrooms'.

bombes – A stuffed croquette associated with the Barceloneta district.

botifarra – 'Sausage'.

botifarra amb mongetes – 'Sausage and beans'. A popular dish and festival food that is often referred to as one of Catalonia's national dishes for this reason.

bunyols/brunyols – A doughnut-like pastry. Normally eaten at Easter time, but consumed all year round in the Empordà region of north-east Catalonia (where they are called *brunyols*).

busca bolets – 'Mushroom finding'. The activity of mushroom picking. Can also be called '*caça bolets*' (mushroom hunting).

calçotada – *Calçot* eating event.

calçot(s) – Spring onions, grown in a particular way to increase the length of their tails. They are a PGI product.

canelons – One of Catalonia's signature dishes. Minced meat stuffed into rolled-up sheets of pasta. Of Italian origin (cannelloni), they first appeared in Barcelona in the nineteenth century and became integrated into Catalan cuisine when ingredients to make them at home became available. Particularly associated with St Stephen's Day (26 December) where they should be made with leftover meat from the Christmas meal the day before.

cap i pota – 'Head and trotters'. A dish of pig's head (snout, ears and cheeks) and trotters, sliced into small pieces (or included whole as with the trotters). Served as a stew with other ingredients such as mushrooms, vegetables or small chunks of pork.

cargolada – Snail eating event.

cargols – 'Snails'.

casa – 'House'.

caseta – 'Cottage'.

cassola – 'Pot' or 'saucepan'.

castanyada – Chestnut eating event, generally associated with the autumnal chestnut season in October–November, and with All Saints (1 November).

castanyes – 'Chestnuts'.

castell – A human tower. An example of Catalan popular culture recognised as UNESCO intangible cultural heritage in 2010, participants create towers by standing on the shoulders of other participants grouped below.

casteller – A participant in making *castells*.

Catalanisme – 'Catalanism' or 'Catalan nationalism', the ideology of promoting Catalonia as a nation.

Ceba de Figueres/de la Vigatana – Different varieties of onions from the towns of Figueres and Vic. The former is known for its sweet taste.

coca (coca de Sant Joan) – Sweet flatbread that comes in many different varieties and flavours.

coca de recapte – A flatbread covered with toppings (sometimes nicknamed the Catalan pizza).

comarca – 'County'. The main administrative division used by the Catalan Parliament.

Convergència i Unió (CiU) – A centre-right coalition of two smaller parties, and the current ruling party in Catalonia. Followed a more conservative and Catalanist agenda than Esquerra, and recently came out as pro-independence.

convivència – 'Living together'. An ideal within Catalan society that implies a placid coexistence with other members of the society, dealing with conflict in an equitable and level-headed way. This term has been especially relevant as a basis for interactions with migrants to Catalonia, where it can be interpreted as a welcoming attitude and tolerance for other cultures and peoples (although in the context of migration there is not a definite consensus of the meaning and application of the term).

crema catalana – 'Catalan cream'. A crème brûlee-like dessert of custard and burnt sugar on the top. Also called *crema de Sant Josep* (Saint Joseph's cream).

cuina d'aprofitament – 'Subsistence cuisine', where the intention is to use up any available ingredients.

cuina de mercat – 'Market cuisine'. A description for a style of cooking generally used by restaurants to denote freshness and seasonality by buying from local markets and producers. See also *cuina de producte*.

cuina de producte – 'Produce cuisine'. A description for a style of cooking generally used by restaurants to place emphasis on selecting high quality ingredients as the basis of the cuisine. This normally also suggests following seasonality and buying local produce that is also often organic, so helping local producers and markets. See also *cuina de mercat*.

cuina de subsisténcia – 'Subsistence cuisine'. See *cuina d'aprofitament*.

cuina tradicional – 'Traditional cuisine'.

de tota la vida – A popular Catalan phrase meaning 'of all one's life', to describe and justify the perceived antiquity of cultural artefacts and practices.

Diada – Catalan national day, 11 September. The word can also refer to Catalonia's other national celebrations (it is generally used without a capital in this instance).

dolç i salat – 'Sweet and sour'. A style of cooking associated with Catalonia whereby sweet and savoury foods are mixed together in one dish.

El Bulli – A former *nova cuina* restaurant in Roses, Alt Empordà, run by chef Ferran Adrià. It is widely regarded as the birthplace of *nova cuina* and was a leader of many global trends in contemporary cuisine. It was the recipient of numerous international awards until its closure as a restaurant in 2011. It has now been converted into an educational and research foundation.

El Celler de Can Roca – *Nova cuina* restaurant in Girona run by brothers Joan, Josep and Jordi Roca. The recipient of numerous international rewards, it is now regarded as the centre of cutting-edge modern Catalan cuisine.

escabetxats – Dishes that includes a variety of pickled ingredients.

escalivada – A roasted vegetable dish, generally associated with the summer. Consists of peeled peppers, tomatoes, onions normally, though others can be used.

escudella i carn d'olla – One of Catalonia's signature dishes. Broth made from vegetables, meat and other animal products (leftovers can be used). The broth is eaten first, followed by the boiled ingredients within. A former subsistence food, cheap and eaten every day, it is now a popular festive food associated particularly with the Christmas lunch. *Escudella* also refers to the type of large pot in which this dish is normally made.

Esquerra Republicana (ERC) – One of Catalonia's major political parties, it follows a socialist, left-leaning and pro-independence agenda.

estelada – Pro-independence Catalan national flag.

estris – 'Tools'.

excursionisme – Travel or hiking to visit Catalan sights.

excursionist – Someone who undertakes *excursionisme*.

fent país – 'Making country'. Phrase that describes performing pro-Catalan activities.

festa – 'Party'.

Festa Major – 'Main Festival'. The annual festival in a town or village, often originating in the place's saint's day.

fet diferencial – A characteristic that differentiates Catalans from other Spaniards.

FICCG – Fundació Institut Català de la Cuina i de la Cultura Gastronòmica (Eng.: Foundation-Institute of Catalan Cuisine and Gastronomic Culture).

fideus – Small sticks of pasta that are boiled and used in staple dishes of Catalan cuisine (especially fish and seafood dishes).

Flama del Canigó – 'Flame of Canigó'. Part of the St John's Eve celebrations wherein torches are lit on Canigó mountain in French Catalonia, then brought to other parts of the *Països Catalans*.

Franja – 'Strip', the Catalan-speaking area of Aragon, directly next to the Catalan Autonomous Community.

fricandó – Also called a *flicancdó*. A stew of floured veal with mushrooms, and other vegetables.

galletes – Can mean both biscuits, and also a type of pasta that is generally put with the broth of the *escudella* eaten at Christmas.

gaspatxo/gazpacho – Catalan/Castilian words for a cold soup of crushed tomatoes, olive oil, vinegar and other vegetables. It is associated with southern Spain (especially Andalucía) and the summer months but became popular in Catalonia following the immigration of Southern Spaniards in the 1960s.

gegants – 'Giants'. Large wooden figurines that are carried around Catalan cities, towns and villages at local and national festivals, 'dancing' at specific locations on the route. The figurines may represent figures from local folklore or history, Catalan culture more generally, or even contemporary individuals.

geganters – Carriers of the *gegants*, who are also involved in their upkeep, culture and promotion.

Generalitat – Official name for the Catalan Autonomous Community's parliament.

gremi – 'Guild'.

havaneres – Popular song style associated with Catalan coast brought from Cuba in the nineteenth century. Now particularly associated with the north-east.

hereu-pubilla – 'Heir–heiress'. Generally used to refer to a system of impartible inheritance through either a son or daughter and their spouse.

hort/hortet – 'Garden' or 'cottage garden'.

iaia – 'Granny' or 'grandma'.

Junts per Catalunya (JuntsxCat) – Campaigning platform of Partit Demòcrata Europeu Català (PDeCAT).

La Vella Quaresma – 'Old Woman of Lent'. A character from Catalan popular culture who represents the period of Lenten fast.

Lliga Catalana – Main Catalan political party in the early twentieth century.

llonganissa – A type of cured sausage particularly associated with Vic, which can also be found in another areas.

macarrons – A pasta dish that uses Italian-style macaroni-shaped pasta. The pasta is often roasted with the sauce, rather than boiled, lending a particularly crispy texture.

Maoinesa – 'Mayonnaise'. Sauce associated with the *Països Catalans* as it allegedly comes from Mahon, in the Balearics. Sometimes included in the collection of Catalan cuisine's representative sauces.

Mancommunitat – Catalan self-governing body in the early twentieth century.

Marca Cuina Catalana – A designation for establishments who do Catalan cuisine, developed by the FICCG.

mar i muntanya – 'Sea and mountain'. A style of cooking associated with Catalonia where land meats and seafood are mixed together in one dish.

matança de porc – 'Pig killing'. Festive occasion where a pig is slaughtered, butchered and the resulting products handed out to participants. These are normally friends, family and employees on the property, who have helped with the process.

mercat – 'Market'.

Mercat de Rams – 'Palm Market'. Livestock and food market and fair in Vic that takes place at Easter-time and is named after the palm-leaves (Rams) sold at this time.

miquelet – Seventeenth century Catalan infantry regiments.

misèria – 'Time of misery'. The years directly following the Civil War (1936–1939) which were characterised by widespread hunger, repression and hardship.

mona – Easter food gift given by godparents to godchildren. Many designs are possible, from the old-fashioned style of a sweetened bread containing one or more eggs, to a sponge cake topped with a simple chocolate figurine, or a large and elaborate chocolate figurine. The latter is now the most popular, though the old-style mones have become increasingly popular in the last five years.

mongeta del ganxet – PDO variety of beans associated with the county of Vallès.

Mossos d'Esquadra – Catalan police force.

neules – Straw-like biscuits generally eaten at Christmas.

New Catalonia (*Catalunya nova*) – A geographic concept to describe the region of Catalonia south of Barcelona and the Llobregat River that was reconquered from the Moors in the twelfth century, and which has a different cuisine and climate to Old Catalonia (*Catalunya vella*).

nova cuina – 'New cuisine'. Cuisine first developed by Ferran Adrià in the 1990s, now part of Catalan culinary identity with many chefs such as Carme Ruscalleda, Joan Roca and Nandu Jubany.

nyora – Variety of small red bell peppers particular to Catalonia, dried for use in cooking.

Old Catalonia (*Catalunya vella*) – A geographic concept that refers to the area north of Barcelona and the Llobregat River. Between the tenth and thirteenth centuries, feudalism dominated the area, in contrast to the areas to the south which had been reconquered from Moorish dominion in the twelfth century ('New Catalonia'). The term also sometimes refers in popular discourse to area that was reconquered from the Moors in the ninth century. Today the region is characterised as being more 'traditional' than New Catalonia. Has a colder climate, and a different cuisine from New Catalonia.

oli – Oil.

Omnium Cultural (Omnium) – Catalan cultural organisation. The largest and most prestigious, with the greatest influence.

Ovella Ripollesa – 'Ripoll sheep'. An archaic breed of sheep which was in danger of being lost but has been recently revitalised to produce both meat and cheese.

pa amb tomàquet – 'Bread with tomato'. One of Catalonia's signature dishes. A slice of slightly hard bread, rubbed with half a tomato so that the juices soak into the slice (preferably of the 'hanging tomato', *tomàquets de penjar,* variety). Salt and olive oil complete the basic dish. Very popular snack or light meal. Can be accompanied by sausages and cold meats. Garlic is also sometimes rubbed in.

pa de pagès – 'Peasant bread'. A large, white, crusty style of bread. Allegedly the ideal kind of bread for making *pa amb tomàquet.* Acquired PGI status in 2012.

pa de pessic – 'Pinch bread'. A small, fluffy, muffin-like sponge cake that is especially associated with the town of Vic, where it is sold to visitors as a symbol of the city. Customarily sold in packs of six, it receives its name because it is often eaten by taking small 'pinches' of the cake. The name can also refer to sponge cake in more general contexts.

pa de Sant Jordi – 'Saint George's bread'. Small breads baked for St. George's Day, decorated with a *senyera* flag.

pactisme – An idealised characteristic of the Catalan character and history, a preference for compromise and discussion to reach an agreement.

paella – Rice dish commonly associated with the Valencian Autonomous Community, directly south of Catalonia, but very prevalent in Catalonia. It differs from Catalan-style rice dishes by the use of a wide metal pan that allows most liquid to evaporate, so is much dryer.

pagès – Literally 'peasant', but better translated as farmer or smallholder.

pairalisme – Allegiance to the paternal house. Developed into an ideology particular to the Catalan industrial bourgeoisie in Catalanism relating family, patrimony and undivided inheritance.

Països Catalans – Catalan-speaking areas.

panellets – Sweets based on almond flour and sugar (marzipan), which are associated with All Saints Day (1 November). They have Traditional Specialties Guaranteed status within the European Union, as a traditional food product with specific character.

Partit Demòcrata Europeu Català (PDeCAT) – a centre-right, pro-independence political party. Platforms as Junts per Catalunya (JuntsxCat, Together for

Catalonia). PDeCAT is a successor to the Democratic Convergence of Catalonia (CDC), which was renamed in 2017 due to corruption scandals involving the founder, Jordi Pujol.

Pastís de la Diada – Diada cake. Festive sponge cake cooked for the Diada (11 September). Decorated with a *senyera*, or, more recently an *estelada*.

Pastís de Sant Jordi – 'St. George's Day cake'. Festive sponge cake cooked for St. George's Day (23 April). Decorated with symbols of the day including the saint, roses, books and the *senyera*.

Patata del Bufet – 'Bufet potato', an originally French variety of potato which is now especially associated with the town of Orís in the county of Osona, where it is celebrated in a festival every year.

picada – Grainy sauce added to dishes at the end of the cooking process.

pintxos – Basque style *tapas*, so-named because of the use of a tooth pick to hold the individual portions together, which are generally grouped on a slice of bread.

platillo – A vegetable and meat stew.

pollastre – 'Chicken'.

pollastre de la iaia – 'Grandma's chicken'.

Protected Designation of Origin (PDO) – A designation created by the European Union to cover agricultural products and foodstuffs which are produced, processed and prepared in a given geographical area using recognised know-how.

Protected Geographical Indication (PGI) – A designation created by the European Union to cover agricultural products and foodstuffs closely linked to the geographical area. At least one of the stages of production, processing or preparation takes place in the area.

purró – Communal drinking vessel, that takes the form of a bulbous glass bottle with a spout at the side. This spout is used to pour the wine into the drinkers' mouths. It is considered impolite for the spout to touch the lips or the teeth.

rauxa – The propensity to seek relief from social constraints by excess and lack of control. The opposite of *seny*.

receptari – 'Recipe list'.

Renaixença – 'Rebirth', the name given to the nineteenth century literary revitalisation of Catalan which lead to the development of political Catalanism.

romesco – A spicy and versatile sauce, red-orange in colour and normally composed of *nyora*, dry bread, almonds (and other nuts), olive oil, *bitxo* peppers and garlic. Associated with the south of Catalonia (especially New Catalonia) it is often added to fish dishes at the end of cooking.

salvitxada – Sauce eaten with *calçots*. Many variations exist, but it normally consists of *nyora* pepper, breadcrumbs, oil, vinegar, hazelnuts and almonds.

samfaina – A dish of vegetables in a tomato sauce, which is almost identical to French *ratatouille*.

sardana – Catalan national dance.

sardanista – Someone who performs the *sardana*.

sardinades – Sardine eating events. Associated with summer, and also the *enterrament de la sardina* (burial of the sardine), which concludes the Carnival period and heralds the start of Lent.

seny – An idealised characteristic of the supposed Catalan personality, a sensible, rational, down to earth attitude, a business-like and hard-working approach to life.

senyera – Catalan national flag.

seques amb botifarra – See *botifarra amb mongetes*.

sobretaula – A discussion around a table, either during or directly after a meal. Often associated with intellectual contexts.

sofregit – The starting point for many Catalan dishes, that of a slightly cooked tomato, garlic and onion, that acts as a base for further cooking.

suquet – A rice dish.

tapas – A cuisine composed of small dishes, or where dishes are composed of several portions for sharing. It is strongly associated with contemporary Spanish cuisine, and many of the dishes use ingredients that are integral to Spanish cuisine as a whole.

temporada – 'Season'.

Terres de l'Ebre – The area around the Ebro Delta in the extreme south of Catalonia.

territori – 'Territory'.

tomàquets de penjar – 'Hanging tomatoes'. Normally used to make *pa amb tomàquet.*

Tortell de Reis – 'Kings cake'. A round cake eaten on Epiphany. Contains a bean and a king, the person with the bean pays for the cake next year, whereas the person with the king wears a crown.

Tortell de Sant Antoni – Round cake eaten for Saint Anthony's saint's day. Has the same form as the *Tortell de Reis*.

Tot Sants – All Saints' Day on 1 November.

trinxat – One of Catalonia's signature dishes. A former subsistence dish from the county of Cerdanya (north Catalonia on the border with France). Consists of boiled and mashed cabbage leaves, with a rasher of bacon or ham on top.

xató – A type of salad that uses a variety of the *salvitxada* sauce, associated with an area south of Barcelona and the winter months (January–March). Normally contains lettuce, endive, anchovies, tuna, salted cod and other seasonal vegetables.

xocolata – 'Chocolate'.

REFERENCES

ACN. 2016. 'L'escudella derrota el pa amb tomàquet com a "plat favorit dels catalans"'. *Ara.cat.* 24 October. Retrieved 2 April 2018 from https://www.ara.cat/estils_i_gent/Lescudella-derrota-tomaquet-favorit-catalans_0_1675032560.html.

———. 2018a. 'January Record Month for Catalan Exports'. *Catalan News Agency.* 21 March. Retrieved 8 April 2018 from http://catalannews.com/business/item/january-record-month-for-catalan-exports.

———. 2018b. 'Tourism in Catalonia Decreased by up to 20% in Last Quarter of 2017, Says WTO'. *Catalan News Agency.* 10 January. Retrieved 7 April 2018 from: http://www.catalannews.com/news/item/tourism-in-catalonia-decreased-by-up-to-20-in-last-quarter-of-2017-says-wto.

———. 2018c. 'Menys demanda d'ajuts alimentaris'. *Ara.cat.* 22 March. Retrieved 1 December 2018 from https://www.ara.cat/comarquesgironines/Menys-demanda-dajuts-alimentaris_0_1982801738.html.

Adrià, Ferran. 1993. *El Bulli: El sabor del Mediterráneo.* Barcelona: Empuries.

Agulló, Ferran. 1999/1928. *Llibre de la cuina catalana. (Presentació de Lloreç Torrado).* 9th edn. Barcelona: El Pedrís.

Alcàzar, Sergi. 2018. 'Piden el boicot contra el restaurante de Toni Albà'. *Elnacional.cat.* 2 January. Retrieved 6 April 2018 from https://www.ara.cat/estils_i_gent/Lescudella-derrota-tomaquet-favorit-catalans_0_1675032560.html.

Amades, Joan. 1950–1951. *Costumari català el curs de l'any.* Barcelona: Salvat Editores.

Anderson, Benedict. 1983. *Imagined Communities: Reflections on the Origin and Spread of Nationalism.* London, New York: Verso.

Anderson, Lara. 2013. *Cooking up the Nation: Spanish Culinary Texts and Culinary Nationalization in The Late Nineteenth and Early Twentieth Century.* Woodbridge: Tamesis.

Andrews, Colman. 1997. *Catalan Cuisine: Europe's Last Great Culinary Secret.* London: Grub Street.

————. 2017. 'Boycotts of Catalan Wine and Food Products are Affecting Other Parts of Spain'. 14 November. *Los Angeles Times*. Retrieved 7 April 2018 from http://www.latimes.com/food/sns-dailymeal-1857837-travel-boycotts-catalan-wine-and-food-products-are-affecting-other-parts-spain-20171114-story.html.

Angelats, Montse and Pep Vila (eds). 2003. *Avisos o sien reglas senzilles a un principant cuiner o cuinera, adaptades a la capacitat dels menos instruïts*. Vic: Patronat d'Estudis Osonencs.

Anonymous. 1968. *Catalunya llaminera*. Barcelona: Editorial Millà.

Anonymous. 1980, facsimile of 1851. *La Cuynera Catalana: Reglas Útils, Fácils, Seguras y Economicas per Cuynar Bé*. Barcelona: Altafulla.

Anonymous. 2009. *La cuinera catalana: Regles útils, fàcils, segures i econòmiques per cuinar bé*. Introduction by Carme Queralt. Barcelona: Cossetània edicions: Col. leció El Cullerot 52.

Appadurai, Arjun. 1988. 'How to Make a National Cuisine: Cookbooks in Contemporary India'. *Comparative Studies in Society and History* 30(1): 3–24.

Asano-Tamanoi, Mariko. 1987. 'Shame, Family and State in Catalonia and Japan'. In D.D. Gilmore (ed.), *Honor and Shame and the Unity of the Mediterranean*. Washington, DC: American Anthropological Association, 104–20.

Armengol, Cristina. 2015. 'L'escriptura de la cuina', *Vilaweb*. 31 May. Retrieved 16 March 2018 from https://www.vilaweb.cat/noticia/4229514/20150131/lescriptura-cuina.html.

Avieli, Nir. 2018. *Food and Power: A Culinary Ethnography of Israel*. Oakland, CA: University of California Press.

Ayora-Diaz, Steffan Igor. 2012. *Foodscapes, Foodfields and Identities in Yucatán*. New York, Oxford: Berghahn Books.

Badcock, James. 2017. 'Barcelona's Yellow Fountains Banned Over Link to Catalan Separatism'. *The Daily Telegraph*. 29 November. Retrieved 5 April 2018 from https://www.telegraph.co.uk/news/2017/11/29/barcelonas-yellow-fountains-banned-link-catalan-separatism/.

Balcells, Albert. 1996. *Catalan Nationalism: Past and Present*. Basingstoke: Macmillan.

————. 2008. *Llocs de memòria dels Catalans*. Barcelona: Raval Edicions.

Barthes, Roland. 1961/2013. 'Toward a Psychosociology of Contemporary Food Consumption'. In C. Counihan and P. Van Esterick (eds), *Food and Culture: A Reader*. 3rd edn. Abingdon, Oxford: Routledge. 23–30.

BBC News. 2017a. 'Spain Catalan Crisis: Six Things You Need to Know'. 10 October. Retrieved 8 April 2018 from http://www.bbc.co.uk/news/world-europe-41550652.

————. 2017b. 'What Do Spain's Many Flags Mean?' 29 Oct 2017. Retrieved 40 March 2018 from http://www.bbc.co.uk/news/av/world-europe-41765704/catalonia-what-do-spain-s-many-flags-mean.

Beardsworth, Alan and Theresa Keil. 1996. *Sociology on the Menu: An Invitation to the Study of Food and Society*. London: Routledge.

Beary, Brian. 2011. *Separatist Movements: A Global Reference*. Washington, DC: CQ Press.

Belasco, Warren. 2007. *Appetite for Change: How the Counterculture Took on the Good Industry*. Ithaca, NY: Cornell University Press.

Bell, David N., and Valentine Gill eds. (1997). *Consuming Geographies: We Are Where We Eat*. London: Routledge.

Bernardo, Mercé, Anna Arbussà and Raúl Escalante. *Cuina de Relacions: Anàlisi de la concentració geogràfica de restaurants amb estrelles Michelin a Catalunya*. Barcelona: Edicions de la Universitat de Barcelona.

Bestard, Joan. 1990. 'Marrying a Relative: Household Structures and Organization of the Matrimonial Domain'. *Critique of Anthropology* 10(2 & 3): 121–138.

Bestard-Camps, Joan, and Jesús Contreras Hernandez. 1997. 'Family, Kinship and Residence in Urban Catalonia: The Modernity of "Pairalisme"'. In M. Gullestad and M. Segalen (eds), *Family and Kinship in Europe*. London: Pinter, 61–75.

Billig, Michael. 1995. *Banal Nationalism*. London: Sage Publications.

Boissevain, Jeremy. 1992. 'Introduction: Revitalizing European Rituals'. In J. Boissevain (ed.), *Revitalizing European Rituals*. London: Routledge, 1–19.

Bosch, Sofia. 2017. 'Here's How Bad Economically a Spain-Catalonia Split Could Really Be'. *CNBC*. 29 September. Retrieved 18 July 2019 from https://www.cnbc.com/2017/09/21/heres-how-bad-economically-a-spain-catalonia-split-could-really-be.html.

Bourdieu, Pierre. 1984/2010. *Distinction: A Social Critique of the Judgement of Taste*. Translated by Richard Nice. London: Routledge.

———. 1986. 'The Forms of Capital'. In J.G. Richardson (ed.), *Handbook of Theory and Research for the Sociology of Education*. New York: Greenwood Press, 241–258.

Brandes, Stanley. 1990. 'The Sardana: Catalan Dance and Catalan National Identity'. *Journal of American Folklore* 103(407): 24–41.

Bray, Zoe. 2011. *Living Boundaries: Frontiers and Identity in The Basque Country*. 2nd edn. Reno, NV: Center for Basque Studies.

Brenan, Gerald. 1990/1943. *The Spanish Labyrinth*. Cambridge: Canto.

Caldwell, Melissa. 2011. *Dacha Idylls: Living Organically in Russia's Countryside*. Berkeley and London: University of California Press.

Carlas, Magda. 2013. 'Menú amb roses, per Sant Jordi'. 18 April. *La Vanguardia*: 10.

Cases, Adrià, Magda Gasso, et al. 2014. *La cuina del 1714*. Barcelona: Comanegra.

Castàn, Patricia. 2017. 'Las cenas de grupo reaniman sin euforia la caída de la restauración en Barcelona', *El Periódico*. 10 December. Retrieved 7 April 2018 from https://www.elperiodico.com/es/barcelona/20171210/las-cenas-de-grupo-reaniman-la-caida-de-la-restauracion-en-barcelona-pero-sin-euforia-6480782.

Castelló, Enric and Rafael Castelló. 2009. 'One Country, Three National Days: Nations, Citizenship and Media Discourses in Valencia'. In D. McCrone and

G. McPherson (eds), *National Days: Constructing and Mobilising National Identity*. London: Palgrave Macmillan, 181–196.

Castells, Manuel. 2004. *The Information Age: Economy Society & Culture. Vol. 2: The Power of Identity*. 2nd edn. Oxford: Blackwell.

Catalan News Agency (CNA). 2015. 'PP Splits Valencian Society with Its Identity Signs Law against Catalan Language and Scientific Criteria'. 10 April. Retrieved 21 March 2018 from www.catalannewsagency.com/society-science/item/pp-splits-valencian-society-with-its-identity-signs-law-against-catalan-language-and-scientific-criteria?highlight=YToxOntpOjA7czo5OiJ2YWxlbmN pYW4iO30=.

Catalunyam. 2013. 'Pa amb tomàquet'. *Catalunyam*. Retrieved 28 June 2015 from http://www.catalunyam.cat/producte_edit.php?id=15&id_col=0&id_mod=0.

Centre d'Estudis d'Opinió. 2012. 'El paper de la llengua com a signe d'identitat nacional: Una aproximació'. *Centre d'Estudis d'Opinió, Generalitat de Catalunya*. Retrieved 30 March 2018 from http://ceo.gencat.cat/web/.content/30_estudis/03_publicacions/Apunts/2012_10_Apunts_llengua.pdf.

———. 2015. 'Edat i cultura política de la societat catalana. 2007–2014'. *Centre d'Estudis d'Opinió, Generalitat de Catalunya*. Retrieved 30 March 2018 from http://ceo.gencat.cat/web/.content/30_estudis/03_publicacions/Apunts/2015_10_05_Apunts_edatculpol.pdf.

———. 2016. 'Dossiers de premsa: Barometre d'Opinió Política. 3a Onada 2016'. *Centre d'Estudis d'Opinió, Generalitat de Catalunya*. Retrieved 30 March 2018 from http://upceo.ceo.gencat.cat/wsceop/6008/Dossier%20de%20premsa%20-%20835.pdf.

———. 2018. 'Press Report: Political Context Survey 2018'. *Centre d'Estudis d'Opinió, Generalitat de Catalunya*. Retrieved 30 March 2018 from http://upceo.ceo.gencat.cat/wsceop/6508/Abstract%20in%20English%20-874.pdf.

Chaytor, H.J. 1933. *A History of Aragon and Catalonia*. London: Methuen.

Congdon, Venetia. 2015. 'Catalan Markets: Constructing National Cuisine and Space through the Market Scene'. In M. McWilliams (ed.), *Oxford Symposium on Food and Cookery: Food and Markets, 11–13 July 2014*. Oxford; London: Prospect Books, 104–113.

———. 2017. 'Regionalists and Excursionistes: Catalan 'Regions' and National Identity'. In J. Riding and M. Jones (eds), *Reanimating Regions: Culture, Politics and Performance*. Oxford: New York: Routledge, 79–94.

Connerton, Paul. 1989. *How Societies Remember*. Cambridge: Cambridge University Press.

Contreras, Jesús. 2006. 'Cuina catalana i identitat cultural'. In N. Baguena (ed.), *Cuina Catalana: Nadala 2006. Any XL*. Barcelona: Fundació Lluís Carulla.

———. 2007. 'Immigració i pràctiques alimentàries'. TECA [Associació Catalana de Ciències de l'Alimentació], 11: 26–34.

Conversi, Daniele. 1997. *The Basques, the Catalans, and Spain: Alternative Routes to Nationalist Mobilization*. London: Hurst.

Counihan, Carole and Penny Van Esterick. 2013. 'Why Food? Why Culture? Why Now? Introduction to the Third Edition'. In C. Counihan and P. Van Esterick (eds), *Food and Culture: A Reader*. 3rd edn. Abingdon, Oxon: Routledge.

Crameri, Kathryn. 2000. *Language, the Novelist and National Identity in Post-Franco Catalonia*. Originally presented as a dissertation (Ph.D.), University of Cambridge. Oxon: Legenda.

———. 2008. *Catalonia: National Identity and Cultural Policy, 1980–2003*. Cardiff: University of Wales Press.

———. 2014. *'Goodbye, Spain?': The Question of Independence for Catalonia*. Eastbourne: Sussex Academic Press.

Cuina.cat. 2013. 'Llibres i roses comestibles per Sant Jordi'. 19 April. *Cuina.cat*. Retrieved 15 April 2018 from http://www.cuina.cat/actualitat/llibres-i-roses-comestibles-per-sant-jordi_102096_102.html.

———. 2015. 'Una Diada per llepar-se els dits'. 9 September. Retrieved 17April 2018 from *http://www.cuina.cat/actualitat/una-diada-per-llepar-se-els-dits_104065_102.html*.

Cunill de Bosch, Josep. 1908. *La Cuyna Catalana: Aplech de fòrmules pera prepara tota mena de plats ab economia y facilitar, propi pera servir de guia a les mestresses de casa y a totes les cuyneres en general*. 1st edn. Barcelona: Llibreria de Francesch Puig.

Cruces Roldán, Cristina. 2014. 'El flamenco como constructo patrimonial. Representaciones sociales y aproximaciones metodológicas'. *PASOS. Revista de Turismo y Patrimonio Cultural* 12(4): 819–835.

Dalmau, Antoni. 1969. *200 Plats casolans de cuina catalana*. Barcelona: Editorial Millà.

Davidson, Robert A. 2007. 'Terroir and Catalonia'. *Journal of Catalan Studies* 1(1): 39–53.

Delamont, S. 1995. *Appetites and Identity: An Introduction to the Social Anthropology of Western Europe*. London: Routledge.

Del Arco Blanco, Miguel Ángel. 2010. 'Hunger and the Consolidation of the Francoist Regime (1939–1951)'. *European History Quarterly* 40: 458–483.

Del Carmen, M. c. 1940. *Cocina Familiar: Colección de recetas para guisar bien i con economia. Consejos para atender bien la mesa; Modo de servir et té*. Barcelona: Tipografia La Academica de Serra y Russel.

Del Río Luelmo, Jesús, and Allan Williams. 1999. 'Regionalism in Iberia'. In P. Wagstaff (ed.), *Regionalism in the European Union*. Exeter: Intellect. 167–187.

Demossier, M. 2011. 'Beyond Terroir: Territorial Construction, Hegemonic Discourses, and French Wine Culture'. *Journal of the Royal Anthropological Institute* 17: 685–705.

De Nola, Robert. 1969/1520. *Libro de Cozina*. Introduction, notes and vocabulary by Carmen Iranzo. N.p.: Taurus Edicions.

DeSoucey, Michaela. 2010. 'Gastronationalism: Food Traditions and Authenticity Politics in the European Union'. *American Sociological Review* 75(3): 432–455.

DiGiacomo, Susan M. 1987. '"La Caseta i l'hortet": Rural Imagery in Catalan Urban Politics'. *Anthropological Quarterly* 60(4): 160–166.

———. 2001. '"Catalan is Everyone's Thing": Normalizing a Nation'. In C. O'Reilly (ed.), *Language, Ethnicity & the State*. London: Palgrave.

Di Giovine, Michael A. and Ronda L. Brulotte 2014. 'Introduction: Food and Foodways as Cultural Heritage'. In R.L. Brulotte and M.A. Di Giovine (eds), *Edible Identities: Food as Cultural Heritage*. Farnham: Ashgate. 1–28.

Domènech, Ignasi c. 1924. *La Teca: La Veritable Cuina Casolana*. 10th ed. Barcelona: Quintilla i Cardona. S.L.

———. c. 1930. *Àpats: Magnífic manual de cuina pràctica catalana, adequate a tots els gustos i el més variat i seleccionat de Catalunya*. 1st edn. [Place and publisher unknown].

———. 1960. *La Teca: La Veritable Cuina Casolana de Catalunya*. 10th edn. Barcelona: Quintilla i Cardona. S.L.

———. 1979. *Àpats*. 3rd edn. Barcelona: Laia.

———. 2005. *La Teca: La Veritable Cuina Casolana*. 19th edn. (3rd Cossetània). Barcelona: Cossetània Edicions: Col.leció El Cullerot No 35.

Domingo, Xavier. 1989. 'La cuina catalana al segle XX'. In N. Luján (ed.), *Mil Anys de Gastronomia Catalana*. Barcelona: Generalitat de Catalunya. 84–107.

Duhart, Frédéric and Xavier F. Medina. 2006. 'An Ethnological Study of *Paella* in the Valencia Area of Spain and Abroad: Uses and Representations of a Mediterranean Dish'. In P. Lysaght (ed.), *Mediterranean Food: Concepts and Trends*. Zagreb: Institute of Ethnology and Folklore Research.

Durkheim, Émile. 2001. *The Elementary Forms of Religious Life*. Translated by C. Cosman. Oxford: Oxford University Press.

Edensor, Tim. 2002. *National Identity, Popular Culture and Everyday Life*. Oxford: Berg.

———. 2006. 'Reconsidering National Temporalities'. *European Journal of Social Theory* 9(4): 525–545.

Elliott, John Edwin. 1963. *The Revolt of The Catalans: A Study in the Decline of Spain (1598–1640)*. Cambridge: Cambridge University Press.

El Nacional/Efe. 2018. 'Botín pide "volver al seny" y tender puentes de diálogo en Catalunya' 16 January. *El Nacional.cat*. Retrieved 13 April 2018 from https://www.elnacional.cat/es/economia/ana-botin-seny-dialogo-catalunya_229932_102.html.

———. 2017. 'Una comida catalano-madrileña une por el "diálogo" a Carmena, Serrat y Sardà'. 15 November. El Periódico. Retrieved 7 April 2018 from https://www.elperiodico.com/es/politica/20171115/comida-catalano-madrilena-dialogo-6425187.

Erickson, Brad. 2011. 'Utopian Virtues: Muslim Neighbors, Ritual Sociality, and the Politics of *Convivència*'. *American Ethnologist* 38(1): 114–131.

European Commission. 2017. *Statement on the Events in Catalonia* [Press Release]. 2 October. Retrieved 15 June 2019 from http://europa.eu/rapid/press-release_STATEMENT-17-3626_en.htm.

Fàbrega, Jaume. 2014. 'Botifarra dolça i ratafia del referèndum' 25 July. Diari de Girona. Available 7 March 2018 from http://www.diaridegirona.cat/ opinio/2014/07/25/botifarra-dolca-ratafia-del-referendum/680140.html?fb_ action_ids=751971871534096&fb_action_types=og.recommends.

Fajans, Jane. 2012. 'Brazilian Food: Race, Class and Identity in Regional Cuisines'. London, New York: Bloomsbury.

Ferguson, Priscilla Pankhurst. 1988. 'A Cultural Field in the Making: Gastronomy in 19th-Century France'. *American Journal of Sociology* 104(3): 597–641.

Ferrater Mora, Josep. 2012. 'Les Formes de la Vida Catalana i altres assaigs'. Barcelona: Edicions 62.

FICCG. 2015a. Objectius. Retrieved 29 May 2015 from http://www. cuinacatalana.eu/ca/pag/marca-objectius/.

———. 2015b. Àmbit d'aplicació. *Objectius*. Retrieved 29 May 2015 from http://www.cuinacatalana.eu/ca/pag/marca-objectius/.

Filippucci, P. 2004. 'A French Place Without a Cheese: Problems with Heritage and Identity in Northeastern France'. *Focaal – European Journal of Anthropology* 44: 72–86.

Fischler, Claude. 1988. 'Food, Self and Identity'. *Social Science Information* 27: 275–292.

Fragner, Bert. 1994. 'Social Reality and Culinary Fiction: The Perspective of Cookbooks from Iran and Central Asia'. In S. Zubaida and R. Tapper (eds), *A Taste of Thyme: Culinary Cultures of the Middle East.* London: I.B. Tauris, 63–71.

Freedman, Paul. 2007. *Food: The History of Taste.* London: Thames and Hudson.

Fundació Banc dels Aliments. 2017. 'Banc dels Aliments Barcelona Memoria 2017 angles'. Fundació Banc dels Aliments, Barcelona. Retrieved 1 December 2018 from https://www.bancdelsaliments.org/es/gestion-transparente/.

Gade, Daniel W. 2003. 'Language, Identity, and the Scriptorial Landscape in Québec and Catalonia'. *The Geographical Review* 93: 429–448.

Garcia-Arbós, Salvador. 2005. *El llibre de l'Allioli.* Girona: Brau edicions.

Garcia-Fuentes, J.M., M. Guàrdia Bassols and J.L. Oyón Bañales. 2014. 'Reinventing Edible Identities: Catalan Cuisine and Barcelona's Market Halls'. In R.L. Brulotte and M.A. Di Giovine (eds), *Edible Identities: Food as Cultural Heritage.* Ashgate: Farnham, 159–174.

Garcia Massagué, Mònica. 2012. *501 Receptes Catalanes que has de conèixer abans de morir.* Badalona: Ara Llibres.

Gardner K. 1999. 'Location and Relocation: Home, "The Field" and Anthropological Ethnics (Sylhet, Bangladesh)'. In C.W. Watson (ed.), *Being There: Fieldwork in Anthropology.* London: Pluto. 49–73.

Garth, Hannah. 2013a. 'Introduction: Understanding Caribbean Identity through Food'. In H. Garth (ed.), *Food and Identity in the Caribbean.* London and New York: Bloomsbury, 1–15.

———. 2013b. 'Cooking Cubanidad: Food Importation and Cuban Identity in Santiago de Cuba'. In H. Garth (ed.), *Food and Identity in the Caribbean*. London and New York: Bloomsbury, 95–106.

Gellner, Ernst. 1983. *Nations and Nationalism*. Oxford: Blackwell.

Generalitat de Catalunya. 1984. *Congrès català de la cuina*. Barcelona: Generalitat de Catalunya, Department de Comerç i Turisme.

———. 1997. *Menjar a Catalunya: L'Estil d'un Poble*. Barcelona: Generalitat de Catalunya.

———. 2003. *Productes de la terra*. Barcelona: Generalitat de Catalunya: Departament d'Agricultura, Alimentació i Acció Rural.

———. 2005. *Llibres de Cuina a Catalunya: Llibre de l'exposició*, Barcelona: Palau Robert.

———. 2008. *Catalunya L'origen és Qualitat*. Barcelona: Generalitat de Catalunya: Departament d'Agricultura, Alimentació i Acció Rural.

———. 2009. 'Osona Fitxa Comarcal. Barcelona: Generalitat de Catalunya: Departament d'Agricultura, Alimentació i Acció Rural'. Retrieved 13 April 2018 from http://agricultura.gencat.cat/web/.content/de_departament/de02_estadistiques_observatoris/22_territori_ruralitat/dades_fec_2007_fitxes/fitxers_estatics/osona.pdf.

———. 2013. *Ferran Adrià and elBulli: Risk, Freedom & Creativity. Exhibition booklet*. Barcelona: Generalitat de Catalunya.

———. 2017. 'Catalan exports 2016'. Issue 31, 30 May. Catalonia in Business (Catalonia Trade and Investment). Retrieved 8 April 2018 from http://catalonia.com/newsletter_news/newsletter/issue31/exports-2016.jsp.

———. 2018. 'Sectors in Catalonia: Food and Drink. Catalonia Trade and Investment/Acció'. Retrieved 8 April 2018 from http://catalonia.com/trade-with-catalonia/food-drink.jsp.

Gibson, Gary. 2010. *Spain's Secret Conflict* (film). Birmingham: Endboard Productions Ltd.

Giner, Salvador. 1980. *The Social Structure of Catalonia*. Sheffield: Anglo–Catalan Society.

Goody, Jack. 1982. *Cooking, Cuisine and Class: A Study in Comparative Sociology*. Cambridge: Cambridge University Press.

Gore, Sarah, and John McInnes. 1998. *The Politics of Language in Catalunya*. Edinburgh: University of Edinburgh.

Grewe, Rudolf. 2009/1979. *Llibre de Totes Maneres de Potatges de Menjar*. 2nd edn. Barcelona: Editorial Barcino.

Guibernau, Montserrat. 2002. *Between Autonomy and Secession: The Accommodation of Catalonia Within the New Democratic Spain*. Brighton: Sussex European Institute.

———. 2004. *Catalan Nationalism: Francoism, Transition, and Democracy*. London: Routledge.

Guirado, Manel. 2012. *101 Plats de la Cuina Catalana que has de tastar*. Barcelona: RBA Libros.

Gvion, Liora. 2012. *Beyond Hummus and Falafel: Social and Political Aspects of Palestinian Food in Israel.* Berkeley: University of California Press.

Hall, Ben. 2019. 'Spain's Sánchez Tries to Steer Clear of Convulsions over Catalonia'. 22 April. *Financial Times.* Retrieved 15 June 2019 from https://www.ft.com/content/e2eade28-626a-11e9-b285-3acd5d43599e.

Hall, Jaqueline. 2001. *Convivencia in Catalonia: Languages Living Together.* Barcelona: Fundació Jaume Bofill.

Hansen, E.C. 1977. *Rural Catalonia under the Franco Regime: The Fate of Regional Culture Since the Spanish Civil War.* Cambridge: Cambridge University Press.

Hargreaves, John. 2000. *Freedom for Catalonia? Catalan Nationalism, Spanish Identity, and the Barcelona Olympic Games.* Cambridge. Cambridge University Press.

Harrison, Simon. 2003. 'Cultural Difference as Denied Resemblance: Reconsidering Nationalism and Ethnicity'. *Comparative Studies in Society and History* 45(2): 343–361.

Heinzelmann, Ursula. 2014. *Beyond Bratwurst: A History of Food in Germany.* London: Reaktion Books.

Helstosky, C. 2004. *Garlic and Oil: Politics and Food in Italy.* Oxford: Berg.

Hobsbawm, Eric and Terence Ranger. 1983. *The Invention of Tradition.* Cambridge: Cambridge University Press.

Hosking, Geoffrey. 2016. 'Why Has Nationalism Revived in Europe?' *Nations and Nationalism* 22(2): 210–221.

Ichijo, Atsuko, and Ronald Ranta. 2016. *Food, National Identity and Nationalism: From Everyday to Global Politics.* Basingstoke and New York: Palgrave Macmillan UK.

Idescat. 2013. 'Cens de població i habitatges: Coneixement del català'. Institut d'Estadística de Catalunya. Retrieved 30 March 2018 from https://www.idescat.cat/economia/inec?tc=3&id=da04.

Institut Català de la Cuina. 2011. *Corpus del Patrimoni Culinari Català.* Barcelona: RBA Libros.

Jenkins, Richard. 2000. 'Not Simple at All: Danish Identity and the European Union'. In I. Bellier and T.M. Wilson (eds), *An Anthropology of the European Union.* Oxford: Berg, 159–178.

Johannes, Venetia. 2018a. 'Performing National Identity in Heritage Tourism: Observations from Catalonia'. In C. Palmer and J. Tivers (eds), *Creating Heritage for Tourism.* London: Routledge, 24–38.

———. 2018b. 'El calendari gastronòmic: Culinary nationalism in Catalan festivals'. *Ethnoscripts* 20(1): 58–78.

Johnson, Enrique and Yeray Carretero. 2017. *Catalonia's Independence Crisis and Its Impact on Catalan Companies' Reputation.* Madrid: Reputation Institute. Retrieved 15 June 2019 from https://www.reputationinstitute.com/sites/default/files/pdfs/Catalonia-Independence-Study-2017.pdf.

Just, Roger. 1989. 'Triumph of the Ethnos'. In E. Tonkin (ed.), *History and Ethnicity.* London: Routledge. 71–88.

Karolewski, Ireneusz Pawel. 2010. 'Chapter 4: European Nationalism and European Identity'. In I.P. Karolewski and A.M. Suszycki (eds), *Multiplicity of Nationalism in Contemporary Europe*. Lanham and Plymouth: Lexington Books. 59–80.

Keating, Michael. 1996. *Nations Against the State: The New Politics of Nationalism in Quebec, Catalonia, and Scotland*. Basingstoke: Macmillan.

Keeley, Graham. 2014. 'Spain Goes to Court to Halt Catalan Vote'. *The Times*. September 29 2014: 31.

Keown, Dominic. 2011a. 'Introduction: Catalan Culture: Once More unto the Breach?' In D. Keown (ed.), *A Companion to Catalan Culture*. Woodbridge, Suffolk and Rochester, NY: Tamesis. 1–12.

———. 2011b. 'Contemporary Catalan Culture'. In D. Keown (ed.), *A Companion to Catalan Culture*. Woodbridge, Suffolk and Rochester, NY: Tamesis, 13–40.

Kim, Chi-Hoon. 2016. 'Kimchi Nation: Constructing *Kimjang* as an Intangible Korean Heritage'. In C. Man Kong Lum and M. de Ferrière le Vayer (eds), *Urban Foodways and Communication*. Lanham, MD and London: Rowman & Littlefield. 39–53.

Klumbyte, Neringa. 2009. 'The Geopolitics of Taste: The "Euro" and "Soviet" Sausage Industries in Lithuania'. In M.L. Caldwell (ed.), *Food and Everyday Life in the Postsocialist World*. Bloomington: Indiana University Press: 130–153.

La Pradelle, Michèle de. 2006. *Market Day in Provence*. Chicago and London: University of Chicago Press.

Laudan, Rachel. 2013. *Cuisine and Empire*. Berkeley: University of California Press.

Lavi, Liron. 2013. 'Making Time for National Identity: Theoretical Concept and Empirical Glance on the Temporal Performance of National Identity'. *Nations and Nationalism* 19(4): 696–714.

Llei 2/1993, de 5 de març, de foment i protecció de la cultura popular i tradicional i de l'associacionisme cultural. Generalitat de Catalunya, Departament de la Presidència. Retrieved 15 April 2018 from http://portaljuridic.gencat.cat/ca/pjur_ocults/pjur_resultats_fitxa?action=fitxa&documentId=73601.

L'Esquella de la Torratxa. 1923. *L'art del menjar*. 23 February. Retrieved 18 July 2019 from https://arca.bnc.cat/arcabib_pro/ca/catalogo_imagenes/grupo.do?path=1208231.

Leitch, Alison. 2003. 'Slow Food and the Politics of Pork Fat: Italian Food and European Identity', *Ethnos: Journal of Anthropology* 68(4): 437–462.

Lladonosa i Giró, Josep. 1982. *La Cuina Que Torna*. Barcelona: Laia.

———. 1996. *El Gran Llibre de la Cuina Catalana*. 2nd edn. Barcelona: Grup Editorial 62: Salsa Books.

———. 2005. *El Gran Llibre de la Cuina Catalana*. 3rd edn. Barcelona: Grup Editorial 62: Salsa Books.

———. 2000a. *The Book of Paella*. Barcelona: Editoria Empúries, S.A.

———. 2000b. *La cuina de dos grans mestres*. Barcelona: Editoria Empúries, S.A.

Llobera, Josep R. 1989. 'Catalan National Identity: the dialectics of past and present'. In E. Tonkin (ed.), *History and Ethnicity*. London: Routledge: 247–261.

———. 1996. 'The Role of Commemorations in (Ethno) Nation Building'. In C. Mar-Molinero and A. Smith (eds), *Nationalism and the Nation in the Iberian Peninsula*. Oxford and New York: Berg Publishing. 196–201.

———. 1997. 'Aspects of Catalan Kinship, Identity, and Nationalism'. *Journal of the Anthropological Society of Oxford* 28(3): 297–309.

———. 2004, *Foundations of National Identity: From Catalonia to Europe,* New York and Oxford: Berghahn Books.

Lourenço, Lina and João Rebelo. 'Cultural Heritage Policy: The Alto Douro Wine Region – World Heritage Site. Is There an Argument for Reinforcing the Role of the State?' *PASOS. Revista de Turismo y Patrimonio Cultural* 4(3): 421–428.

Lovell, Nadia. 1998. 'Introduction: Belonging in Need of Emplacement?' In N. Lovell (ed.), *Locality and Belonging*. London: Routledge: 1– 24.

Luján, Nèstor. 1989. *Mil Anys de Gastronomia Catalana*. Barcelona: Generalitat de Catalunya.

———. 1990. *Diccionari Luján de Gastronomia Catalana*. Barcelona: Edicions la Campana.

Lukes, Steven. 2005. *Power: A Radical View*. 2nd edn. London: Palgrave.

M.j.c. 2014. 'El origen no catalán del pan con tomate'. 30 June. ABC Actualidad. Retrieved 7 April 2018 from http://www.abc.es/catalunya/20140630/abci-origen-catalan-tomate-201406251404.html.

MacClancy, Jeremy. 1997. 'At Play with Identity in the Basque Arena'. In S. Macdonald (ed.), *Inside European Identities*. Oxford and New York: Berg. 84–97.

———. 2007. *Expressing Identities in the Basque Arena*. Oxford: School for Advanced Research Press.

Man Kong Lum, Casey and Marc de Ferrière le Vayer. 2016. 'At the Intersection of Urban Foodways, Communication, and Intangible Cultural Heritage: An Introduction'. In C. Man Kong Lum and M. de Ferrière le Vayer (eds), *Urban Foodways and Communication*. Lanham, MD and London: Rowman & Littlefield. 1–21.

Marte, Lidia. 2013. 'Versions of the Dominican Mangú: Intersections of Gender and Nation in Caribbean Self-making'. In H. Garth (ed), *Food and Identity in the Caribbean*. London, New York: Bloomsbury. 57–74

Martí Escayol, Maria Antonia. 2004. *El Plaer de la Xocolata: La història i la cultura de la xocolata a Catalunya*. Barcelona: Cossetània edicions.

Martí i Pérez, Josep. 1994. 'The Sardana as a Socio-Cultural Phenomenon in Contemporary Catalonia'. *Yearbook for Traditional Music* 26: 39–46.

Martorell, Eladia. 1917. *Carmencita o la buena cocinera*. Barcelona: Librería Subiriana.

Mas i Solench, Josep M. 1990. 'The Civil Law of the Catalans'. Generalitat de Catalunya: Barcelona. Retrieved 12 April 2016 from www.raco.cat/index.php/Catalonia/article/download/106433/160728.

Massanés, Antoni. 2010. *Catalunya és gastronomia*. N.p.: Generalitat de Catalunya, Agència Catalana de Turisme.

McCrone, David, and Gayle McPherson, (eds). 2009. *National Days: Constructing and Mobilising National Identity*. Basingstoke: Palgrave Macmillan.

McDonald, Maryon. 1989. *'We Are Not French!': Language, Culture and Identity in Brittany*. London: Routledge.

McDonogh, Gary W. 1986. *Good Families of Barcelona: A Social History of Power in the Industrial Era*. Princeton, NJ: Princeton University Press.

McRoberts, Kenneth. 2001. *Catalonia: A Nation without a State*. Oxford: Oxford University Press.

Medeiros, António. 2013. *Two Sides of One River*. Translated by M. Earl. Oxford and New York: Berghahn Books.

Minder, Raphael. 2017. *The Struggle for Catalonia: Rebel Politics in Spain*. London: Hurst and Co. Ltd.

Mintz, Sidney W. 1996. *Tasting Food, Tasting Freedom*. New York: Basic Books.

Mount, Ian. 2019. 'Four Catalan MPs suspended from Spanish parliament'. 24 May. *Financial Times*. Retrieved 15 June 2019 from https://www.ft.com/content/16005280-7e26-11e9-81d2-f785092ab560.

Mount, Ian and Ben Hall. 2019. 'Polarised Spain faces months of coalition talks' 26 April. *Financial Times*. Retrieved 15 June 2019 from https://www.ft.com/content/48d3ed7e-674d-11e9-9adc-98bf1d35a056.

Narayan, Uma. 1995. 'Eating Cultures: Incorporation, Identity and Indian Food'. *Social Identities: Journal for the Study of Race, Nation and Culture* 1(1): 63–86.

Nationalia. 2010. 'Spanish Constitutional Court Cuts Back Catalan Statute of Autonomy'. *Nationalia*. 29 June. Retrieved 15 June 2019 from http://www.nationalia.info/en/news/764.

———. 2013. 'Census Reveals 73% Speak Catalan in Catalonia, 95% Understand it, 56% Can Write it'. *Nationalia*. Retrieved 12 April 2015 from www.nationalia.info/en/news/1664.

Nett, Mané. 2013. 'La Unesco y su lucha por la Diversidad Cultural'. *Comunicación y Medios* 27: 178–183.

Nielsen, Nikolaj. 2013. 'EU Commission: Catalonia Must Leave EU if it Leaves Spain'. 17 September. Retrieved 23 April 2015 from https://euobserver.com/enlargement/121466.

Noyes, Dorothy. 2003. *Fire in the Plaça: Catalan Festival Politics after Franco*. Philadelphia: University of Pennsylvania Press.

———. 2011a. 'Festival and the Shaping of Catalan Community'. In D. Keown (ed.), *A Companion to Catalan Culture*. Woodbridge, Suffolk and Rochester, NY: Tamesis. 207–228.

———. 2011b. 'Traditional Culture: How Does It Work?' *Museum Anthropological Review* 5(1–2). Retrieved 15 December 2014 from http://scholarworks.iu.edu/journals/index.php/mar/article/view/1046/1120.

O'Brien, Oonagh. 1994. 'Ethnic Identity, Gender and Life Cycle in North Catalonia' In V.A. Goddard, J.R. Llobera and C. Shore (eds), *The Anthropology of Europe: Identities and Boundaries in Conflict*. Oxford: Berg, 191–207.

Ohnuki-Tierney, Emiko. 1993. *Rice as Self: Japanese Identities through Time*. Princeton, NJ: Princeton University Press.

Omnium Cultural. 2013. *Calendari de tradicions i costums – gastronomia*. Omnium Cultural. Retrieved 28 September 2015 from http://cultura.gencat.cat/web/. content/cultura_popular_nova_web/05_documents_i_recursos/01_materials_ didactics/documents/arxiu/sd_calendari2013_complet.pdf.

Organic Law 6/2006 of the 19th July, on the Reform of the Statute of Autonomy of Catalonia. *Generalitat de Catalunya: Catalan Autonomous Community*. Retrieved 18 July 2019 from https://www.parlament.cat/document/ cataleg/150259.pdf.

Palmer, Catherine. 1998. 'From Theory to Practice: Experiencing the Nation in Everyday Life'. *Journal of Material Culture* 3: 175–199.

Pericay, Gaspar. 2010. 'The Spanish Constitutional Court Shortens the Current Catalan Statute of Autonomy'. 28 June. *Catalan News Agency*. Retrieved 21 March 2018 from http://www.catalannews.com/politics/item/the-spanish-constitutional-court-shortens-the-current-catalan-statute-of-autonomy.

Pilcher, Jeffrey M. 1998. *¡Que vivan los tamales! Food and the Making of Mexican Identity*. Albuquerque: University of New Mexico Press.

Pi-Sunyer, Oriol. 1974. 'Elites and Noncorporate Groups in the European Mediterranean'. *Comparative Studies in Society and History* 16(1): 117–131.

———. 1978. 'Through Native Eyes: Tourists and Tourism in a Catalan Maritime Community'. In V.L. Smith (ed.), *Hosts and Guests: The Anthropology of Tourism*. Oxford: Basil Blackwell. 149–155.

———. 1983. *Nationalism and Societal Integration: A Focus on Catalonia*. International Area Studies Program. Amherst, MA: University of Massachusetts.

———. 1987. 'Town, Country and Nation'. *Anthropological Quarterly* 60(4): 167–173.

Pla, Josep. 1952. *Els Pagesos*. Barcelona: Editorial Selecta.

———. 1972. *El que hem menjat*. Barcelona: Edicions Destino.

———. 1984. *Alguns grans cuiners de l'Empordà*. Barcelona: Llibres a mà.

Pomés Leiz, Juliet. 2014. *Catalan Cuisine*. Barcelona: Zahorí de Ideas.

Ponce, Santi and Maties Ramisa. 2006. *El Mercat del Ram, la fira de la ciutat de Vic*. Vic: Ajuntament de Vic.

Pratt, Jeff. 2003. *Class, Nation and Identity: The Anthropology of Political Movements*, London: Pluto Press.

———. 2007. 'Food Values: The Local and the Authentic'. *Critique of Anthropology* (27)3: 285–300.

Quiroga, Alejandro. 2007. *Making Spaniards: Primo De Rivera and the Nationalization of the Masses, 1923–30*. Basingstoke: Palgrave Macmillan.

Ranachan, Emma Kate. 2008. 'Cheering for Barça: FC Barcelona and the shaping of Catalan identity'. MA Thesis, McGill University.

Raviv, Yael. 2015. *Falafel Nation: Cuisine and the Making of National Identity in Israel.* Lincoln, NE and London: University of Nebraska Press.

Redacció. 2017. '"Em nego a menjar pa amb tomàquet sense pernil," la consigna d'una jove unionista a les manifestacions de Barcelona'. 10 October. Catalunya Diari. Retrieved 7 March 2018 from https://catalunyadiari.com/societat/em-nego-menjar-pa-tomaquet-pernil-consigna-d-jove-unionista-manifestacions-barcelona.

Richards-Greaves, Gillian. 2013. 'The Intersections of "Guyanese Food" and Constructions of Gender, Race, and Nationhood'. In H. Garth (ed.), *Food and Identity in the Caribbean.* London and New York: Bloomsbury, 75–94.

Robertson, Alexander F. 2008. 'Regeneration in Rural Catalonia'. *European Journal of Sociology* 49(2): 147–172.

———. 2010. 'Conviviality in Catalonia'. *Gastronomica: The Journal of Food and Culture* 10(1): 70–78.

———. 2012. *Mieres Reborn: The Reinvention of a Catalan Community.* Tuscaloosa: University of Alabama Press.

Roca, Joan. 2004. *La cuina de la meva mare: Les receptes fonamentals d'El Celler de Can Roca.* Barcelona: La butxaca.

———. 2013. *El Celler de Can Roca.* Barcelona: Librooks.

Rodés, Andrea. 2017. 'Mass demonstration in Barcelona in Favor of Catalunya Staying in Spain'. 8 October. *Al Día.* Retrieved 7 April 2018 from http://aldianews.com/articles/politics/mass-demonstration-barcelona-favor-catalunya-staying-spain/50182.

Rondissoni, Josep. 1924. *Classes de cuina: curs 1924–1925.* Barcelona: Institut de Cultura i Biblioteca Popular de la dona.

———. 1925. *Classes de cuina: curs 1925–1926.* Barcelona: Institut de Cultura i Biblioteca Popular de la dona.

———. 1927. *Classes de cuina: curs 1927–1928.* Barcelona: Institut de Cultura i Biblioteca Popular de la dona.

———. 1930. *Classes de cuina: curs 1930–1931.* Barcelona: Institut de Cultura i Biblioteca Popular de la dona.

Roser i Puig, Montserrat. 2011. 'What's Cooking in Catalonia'. In D. Keown (ed.), *A Companion to Catalan Culture.* Woodbridge, Suffolk and Rochester, NY: Tamesis, 229–252.

Ryder, Alan F.C. 2007. *The Wreck of Catalonia: Civil War in the Fifteenth Century.* Oxford: Oxford University Press.

Salvia, Marta. 1923. *Art de Ben Menjar: llibre Català de Cuyna.* 1st edn. Barcelona: Imprempta La Renaixensa.

———. 1952. *El Arte de Bien Comer: Manual de Cocina Práctica.* 9th edn. Barcelona: Ediciones Aedos.

———. 1968. *Art de Ben Menjar: llibre Català de Cuyna.* 13th edn. Barcelona: Ediciones Aedos.

Sano, Kazuko, and Narcís Clotet. 2012. *Cuina Catalana per a festes i tradicions.* 3rd edn. Muval, Solsona: Grata Lectura.

Santamaria, Santi. 2008. *La cocina al desnudo: una visión renovadora del mundo de la gastronomía*. Madrid: Temas de Hoy.

Santanach, Joan (ed.). 2006. *Llibre de Sent Soví: Volum d'homenatge a Rudolf Grewe*. Barcelona: Biblioteca Barcino.

———. 2008. *The Book of Sent Soví: Medieval Recipes from Catalonia*. Translated by Robin Vogelzang. Barcelona: Editorial Barcino.

Schacht, Ryan N. 2013. 'Cassava and the Makushi: A Shared History of Resiliency and Transformation'. In H. Garth (ed.), *Food and Identity in the Caribbean*. London and New York: Bloomsbury. 15–30.

Scott, James C. 1990. *Domination and the Arts of Resistance*. Ann Arbor, MI: Yale University.

Shore, Cris. 1993. 'Inventing the "People's Europe": Critical Approaches to European Community "Cultural Policy"'. *Man, New Series* 28(4): 779–800.

Skey, Michael. 2011. *National Belonging and Everyday Life: The Significance of Nationhood in an Uncertain World*. Basingstoke and New York: Palgrave Macmillan.

Smith, Angel. 1996. 'Sardana, Zarzuela or Cake Walk? Nationalism and Internationalism in the Discourse, Practice and Culture of the Early Twentieth-Century Barcelona Labour Movement'. In C. Mar-Molinero and A. Smith (eds), *Nationalism and the Nation in the Iberian Peninsula*. Oxford and New York: Berg Publishing. 171–190.

Smith, Angel and Clare Mar-Molinero. 1996. 'The Myths and Realities of Nation Building in the Iberian Peninsula'. In C. Mar-Molinero and A. Smith (eds), *Nationalism and the Nation in the Iberian Peninsula*. Oxford and New York: Berg Publishing. 1–32.

Smith, Anthony D. 1986. *The Ethnic Origin of Nations*, Oxford: Blackwell.

———. 1991. *National Identity*. Reno: University of Nevada Press.

Sobral, José Manuel. 2014. 'The Country, the Nation, and the Region in Representations of Portuguese Food and Cuisine'. In N. Domingos, J.M. Sobral and H. West (eds), *Food Between the Country and the City: Ethnographies of a Changing Global Foodscape*. London and New York: Bloomsbury. 145–160.

Statista. 2019. 'Share of Electorate Voting in Parliamentary Elections in Catalonia from 2003 to 2015'. Retrieved 15 June 2019 from https://www.statista.com/statistics/467666/catalan-election-voter-turnout/.

Stothard, Michael. 2017. 'Barcelona Brand Suffers After Independence Turmoil'. 30 November. *Financial Times*. Retrieved 17 April 2018 from https://www.ft.com/content/dd1436ac-d5c6-11e7-a303-9060cb1e5f44.

———. 2018. 'Spain Offers Referendum on Greater Catalan Autonomy'. 3 September. *Financial Times*. Retrieved 3 September 2018 from https://www.ft.com/content/09d9feba-af83-11e8-8d14-6f049d06439c.

Strubell, Miquel. 2008. 'Bulls and Donkeys: National Identity and Symbols in Catalonia and Spain'. Paper presented at the Anglo Catalan Society: 9th Annual Joan Gili Memorial Lecture. Retrieved 2 July 2015 from http://www.anglo-catalan.org/downloads/joan-gili-memorial-lectures/lecture10.pdf.

Sutton, David. 2001. *Remembrance of Repasts: An Anthropology of Food and Memory*. Oxford: Berg.

Talaya Águeda, Esteban, Juan Antonio Mondéjar Jiménez et al. 2008. 'Análisis de la inversión de los programas de innovación rural en patrimonio cultural como elemento dinamizador del turismo'. *Revista de análisis turístico* 5(1): 16–29.

Tercer Congrés Català de la Cuina. 2019. 'Present i futur de la cuina catalana: Una estratègia de país de cara a l'horitzó 2025'. Retrieved 19 June 2019 from http://www.congrescataladelacuina.cat/dossier_3congres.pdf.

Terrio, Susan. 2014. 'French Chocolate as Intangible Cultural Heritage'. In R.L. Brulotte and M.A. Di Giovine (eds), *Edible Identities: Food as Cultural Heritage*. Ashgate: Farnham, 175–184.

Torrado, Llorenç. 1985. *Els Embotits a Catalunya*. Barcelona: Federació Catalana d'Indústries de la Carn.

Torras i Bages, Josep. (1982) 1966. *La Tradició Catalana*. 3rd edn. Barcelona: Biblioteca Selecta.

Tree, Matthew. 2011. *Barcelona, Catalonia: A View from The Inside*. (iBooks E-book). Barcelona: Cookwood Press.

Trubek, Amy B. 2008. *The Taste of Place: A Cultural Journey into Terroir*. Berkeley: University of California Press.

Trueta, Josep. 1946. *The Spirit of Catalonia*. Oxford: Oxford University Press.

Turespaña. 2015. 'Turísticos en fronteras'. Retrieved 7 April 2018 from http://estadisticas.tourspain.es/es-ES/estadisticas/frontur/mensuales/Nota%20de%20coyuntura%20de%20Frontur.%20Septiembre%202015.pdf.

UNESCO. 2003. 'Text of the Convention for the Safeguarding of the Intangible Cultural Heritage' presented at the General Conference of the United Nations Educational, Scientific and Cultural Organization, Paris, 29 September–17 October 2003. Retrieved 26 October 2018 from https://ich.unesco.org/en/convention#art2.

Urla, Jaqueline. 1993. 'Cultural Politics in an Age of Statistics: Numbers, Nations, and the Making of Basque Identity'. *American Ethnologist* 20(4): 818–843.

Vackimes, Sophia Carmen. 2013. 'Catalan High-End Restaurants and National "Heritage"'. *Catalan Journal of Communication & Cultural Studies* 5(2): 271–284.

Vaczi, Mariann. 2016. 'Catalonia's Human Towers: Nationalism, Associational Culture, and the Politics of Performance'. *American Ethnologist* 43(2): 353–368.

Vázquez Montalbán, Manuel. 1977. *L'art del menjar a Catalunya*. Barcelona: Edicions 62 S.A.

———. 2004. *L'art del menjar a Catalunya*. Barcelona: Salsa Books.

Vicens Vives, Jaume. 1954. *Notícia de Catalunya*. Barcelona: Àncora.

Vilaweb. 2012. 'La Plataforma per la Llengua considera 'impròpies' d'un ministre les paraules de Wert'. *Vilaweb*. 2 October. Retrieved 12 April 2015 from http://www.vilaweb.cat/noticia/4044506/20121002/plataforma-llengua-considera-impropies-ministre-paraules-wert.html.

Waldren, Jaqueline. 1996. *Insiders and Outsiders: Paradise and Reality in Mallorca*. Providence and Oxford: Berghahn Books.

Wardhaugh, Ronald. 1987. *Languages in Competition*. Oxford: Blackwell.

Watson, C.W. 1999. 'A Diminishment: A Death in the Field (Kerinci, Indonesia)'. In C.W. Watson (ed.), *Being There: Fieldwork in Anthropology*. London: Pluto, 141–163.

West, Harry G. 2013. 'Appellations and Indications of Origin, *Terroir*, and the Social Construction and Contestation of Place-Named Foods'. In A. Murcott, W. Belasco and P. Jackson (eds), *The Handbook of Food Research*. London: Bloomsbury. 209–228.

Wilk, Richard R. 1999. '"Real Belizean Food": Building Local Identity in the Transnational Caribbean'. *American Anthropologist* 101: 244–255.

Woolard, Katherine A. 1986. 'The "Crisis of the Concept of Identity" in Contemporary Catalonia, 1976–1982'. In G.W. McDonough (ed.), *Conflict in Catalonia: Images of an Urban Society*. Gainesville: University of Florida Press. 54–71.

Yotova, Maria. 2014. 'Reflecting Authenticity: "Grandmother's Yoghurt" between Bulgaria and Japan'. In N. Domingos, J.M. Sobral and H. West (eds), *Food Between the Country and the City: Ethnographies of a Changing Global Foodscape*. London and New York: Bloomsbury, 175–190.

INDEX

❦

Photographs are denoted by the use of *italic* page numbers.